ROYALTY'S STRANGEST CHARACTERS

ROYALTY'S STRANGEST CHARACTERS

Geoff Tibballs

ROBSON BOOKS

To the memory of Chester

This edition published in Great Britain in 2005 by Robson Books,
The Chrysalis Building, Bramley Road, London W10 6SP

An imprint of Chrysalis Books Group plc

British Library Cataloguing in Publication Data
A catalogue record for this title is available from the British Library

ISBN 1 86105 827 6

Typeset by SX Composing DTP, Rayleigh, Essex
Printed and bound in Great Britain by Creative Print and Design, Ebbw Vale, Wales.

Contents

INTRODUCTION

Just as the monarchy has been hereditary in many countries, so insanity has been hereditary in many monarchs. Conditions such as syphilis, porphyria and schizophrenia – not to mention megalomania, paranoia and barbarity – have been handed down through the generations of the world's royal houses along with the crown, to create a succession of mentally and physically retarded rulers. In some cases – notably among the Habsburgs, who reigned over vast areas of Europe for eight centuries – inbreeding exacerbated the situation, so that cousins married each other and uncles married nieces. The biggest problem facing guests at a Habsburg wedding was deciding on which side of the church to sit.

From the moment the Bible described the ancient Babylonian ruler Nebuchadnezzar II imagining that he was a goat, history has been rich in strange rulers. The Roman Emperor Caligula wanted to appoint his horse to the consulate; Charles VI of France was convinced that he was made of glass; and Queen Juana of Spain travelled everywhere with her late husband's coffin. Some were insanely obsessive: the Russian Tsar Peter the Great had a fixation with dwarfs, while at the opposite end of the scale Frederick William I of Prussia recruited the tallest men in Europe to form his own freakish private army. Others – like Ivan the Terrible, Christian VII of Denmark and Murad IV of Turkey – were insanely cruel. There have been tragic figures, rulers who have abused their position with bizarre excesses and extravagances, and finally the plain eccentric, a category that includes almost the entire royal house of Bavaria.

With such a wealth of larger-than-life characters from which to choose, a number failed to make the cut for this book, principally those whose little foibles were not wholly representative of their overall character. For example, the founder of modern Ethiopia, Emperor Menelik II of Abyssinia, was an outstanding leader who decided that the cure for any disease was to get his teeth into a good book . . . literally. Accordingly, whenever he felt unwell, he would eat a few pages of the Bible. Stricken with illness in 1913, he devoured the entire Book of Kings . . . and dropped dead. After staying at London's Ritz Hotel, King Amanullah of Afghanistan became so fascinated by English traditions that he tried to make the wearing of bowler hats compulsory amongst men in his native country. Philip, Prince of Calabria, the eldest son of Carlos III of Spain, had a fixation with gloves, occasionally wearing sixteen pairs at a time, while Ferdinand II of Sicily was so vain that he refused to allow his portrait on his country's postage stamps to be marred by an unsightly franking mark. To deter unwanted flies, King Pepi II of Egypt always kept a supply of naked slaves handy, their bodies smeared with honey. George II of England performed a curious nightly bedroom ritual. He used to stand outside his mistress's bedroom at precisely one minute to nine and on the stroke of nine o'clock he would enter the room, pull down his breeches and have sex, often without bothering to remove his hat. He also sold tickets to his subjects so that they could watch him and his family eating Sunday dinner. More sinisterly, Queen Ranavalona of Madagascar executed any of her subjects who appeared in her dreams, and Queen Henrietta, wife of Leopold II of the Belgians, kept a pet llama that she taught to spit in the face of anyone who stroked it. For anyone who feels strongly that the aforementioned kinky kings and quirky queens should have been included, I humbly apologise.

Time has judged some monarchs more kindly than others. George III, once mocked as a barking mad tree-hugger, is now viewed sympathetically, his bouts of manic behaviour being attributed to the hereditary blood disease porphyria, which attacks the body's nervous system. A medical expert has even found mitigating circumstances to excuse the behaviour of that most notorious of tyrants, Vlad the Impaler. Without wishing to compare him to either of the aforementioned pair, will Prince Charles be remembered with similar compassion in centuries to come? Will historians portray him as a harmless eccentric who liked to talk to his plants or as a callous adulterer who treated his young wife appallingly? In the meantime he still has a few years to claim his place among royalty's strangest characters.

As ever, I am indebted to the wisdom and enthusiasm of Jeremy Robson and to my editors at Robson Books, Clive Hebard and Rob Dimery. I would also like to thank the staff at the libraries of Nottingham, Westminster, Sheffield, Birmingham, Leicester, Hammersmith and Lincoln.

Geoff Tibballs, 2004

THE QUEST FOR IMMORTALITY

SHI HUANGDI, EMPEROR OF CHINA (259–210BC)

The first emperor of China, Shi Huangdi has gone down in history as a mighty ruler who united the country, standardised written characters and currency, and oversaw the construction of road and canal networks as well as the linking of various border walls into one Great Wall. These practical achievements were all the more remarkable given that he suffered from advanced paranoia and devoted most of his energies to staying one step ahead of the Grim Reaper. To say that he had a fixation with his own mortality would be an understatement, although after at least three attempts on his life his fears were perhaps understandable. He didn't just have a date with death, they were practically engaged.

The roots of his paranoia lay in his rise to power. At the age of thirteen he became King of Qin (pronounced Chin), a state in the northwest of modern-day China, and immediately began to see enemies around every corner. At first he ruled alongside his prime minister, Lu Buwei, who just happened to be a clandestine lover of Shi Huangdi's mother and was widely suspected of being the young king's father. When he came of age and learned of his mother's assorted infidelities, Shi Huangdi had her banished and ordered Lu Buwei to commit suicide by taking poison. With family matters resolved, Shi Huangdi set about conquering Qin's six rival states. In an effort to ensure success in battle, he introduced one of the world's first bonus systems: if his generals returned home victorious, they were allowed to keep their heads. It was quite an incentive and by 221BC, his unique blend of brutality and bribery had seen the other states annexed, whereupon he declared himself the first emperor of unified China, taking the name of the new country from his homeland.

'The Tiger of Qin', as he was known, was ruthlessly methodical, combining the zeal of a psychopathic dictator with the mindset of a chief librarian. In addition to standardising calligraphy – so that all of China learned the written characters that are still in use today – he stipulated that all carts in his empire must have axles of identical widths (to minimise wear and tear on the roads) and that all bells must resound to the same pitch. Determined to open a new chapter in his country's history, he burned any book that expressed different opinions from his own and, in order to discourage Confucians who still wallowed in the glories of the past, he reputedly ordered 460 Confucian scholars to be buried alive. The emperor did not exactly take kindly to criticism.

To prevent rebellion, he ordered complete disarmament and the melted-down weapons were made into a dozen bronze giants, each weighing 30 tons, which stood in the courtyards of his imperial palace at Xianyang. The Xianyang complex housed replicas of the 270 palaces of the vanquished states and Shi Huangdi developed such a fear of dying that each night he slept in a different palace, using the network of tunnels to move secretly from one to the other. It became a crime punishable by death merely to reveal his whereabouts and when he did venture beyond the palace grounds, he always travelled with two carriages so that potential assassins would not know which one to target. On his grander expeditions he invariably wielded a huge repeater crossbow, specifically designed to kill sea monsters, which, according to a dream he had experienced, were endangering his life.

As it was, the actual attempts on his life were scarcely conventional. One was carried out by a blind musician who tried to beat the emperor about the head with his harp! There were strings attached to an earlier assassination attempt, too.

2

During the period when the states were at war a renegade Qin general was befriended by a potential killer from the neighbouring state of Yan. Both men wanted Shi Huangdi dead but knew that the only way to get near him was to take him a gift that he really wanted. And at that time the only gift Shi Huangdi really wanted was the head of the renegade general. Reasoning that it was all in a good cause, the general generously committed suicide so that his head could be sliced off and taken to Shi Huangdi in a box – the perfect gift for the man who had everything. The would-be killer duly presented the box to Shi Huangdi before suddenly producing a poison-dipped dagger that had been concealed in a map. However, the fatal lunge missed and the hitman suffered the ignominy of being seen off by a blow from the court doctor's medicine case.

These incidents heightened Shi Huangdi's obsession with death. To thwart his seemingly impending doom, he started to crave immortality. Encouraged by physicians, who believed that with the right diet and medicines it was possible to live for at least a thousand years and possibly forever, the emperor conducted an exhaustive search for the secret of eternal life. He consulted soothsayers, commissioned musicians to write songs about immortality and hired magicians to produce a suitable elixir. He also sent expeditions to find the fabled mountains of Penglai, on which the immortals were said to live, where all the birds and animals were white, trees bore pearls, and towers and palaces were made of gold and silver. Thousands of youths and maidens, selected for their beauty and purity, were despatched on fleets of ships to discover this promised land, but none ever returned.

Meanwhile, just in case he was unable to find the key to immortality, Shi Huangdi was taking steps to safeguard his exalted position in the next world. From the moment he became emperor he set about building the mausoleum that would ultimately serve as his most extraordinary legacy. Over the next 36 years – right up until his death – he supervised work on a giant terracotta army, which would be buried with him so that, in his mind if not his body, he would still have command of legions of troops. As many as 700,000 prisoners of war and slaves were employed on the project, which painstakingly created 8,000 life-size figures – warriors, horses and chariots – all arranged in strict battle formation to guard the emperor's tomb. The torsos of the clay soldiers were made from moulds, but the heads and hands were modelled individually. Thus each had a different face (probably the likeness of a real soldier) while many carried genuine spears or swords. And they were all positioned to face east, thereby protecting the emperor from the vanquished enemies who hailed from that direction. In addition Shi Huangdi created an entire miniature underground city – with walls, a palace, government offices and even a cemetery – intended to be his afterlife capital.

Although the terracotta army was uncovered in 1974, the tomb itself – said to contain flowing rivers of mercury and reproductions of the stars and planets in precious pearls – remains untouched, not least because it is reputed to be guarded by automatic crossbows to deter grave-robbers. When the emperor was buried, his son ordered that all of Shi Huangdi's childless concubines and all of the workers who knew the secrets of the tomb should be buried alive with him. Nothing was left to chance.

For all his fears of assassination and dread of homicidal sea monsters, Shi Huangdi's actual death was a disappointingly low-key affair. More deranged than ever, he had set off on an epic expedition with the intention of finally slaying an evil sea monster once and for all. He was accompanied by a posse of magicians, still seeking the herb of immortality, and an army of alchemists to distil it when it was found. He did find his nemesis – which turned out to be nothing more than a beached whale – but in the act of killing it he caught an illness. With the magicians unable to conjure up an on-the-spot remedy, Shi Huangdi involuntarily abandoned his quest for immortality.

MAD, BAD AND DANGEROUS TO KNOW

CALIGULA, EMPEROR OF ROME (AD12–41)

The Roman Emperor Caligula was an unlikely animal lover. Here was a man who, in one of his more cerebral moments, ordered a hapless individual to be flogged in his presence with chains for days on end, not allowing the poor wretch to be put down until he was offended by the smell of the gangrene in the victim's brain. Here was a man who passed a law making it illegal for anyone to look at him in the street, any transgressors who happened to glance in his direction being fed to the lions. Here was a man who delighted in devising new forms of torture, one of his favourites being to cover people with honey before setting loose an army of red wasps. Here was a man who championed the slow, lingering death so that the condemned could appreciate the experience of dying, who turned the imperial palace into a whorehouse, a bisexual deviant who had sex with all three of his sisters. Yet if you dig deep enough, even the most barbaric of despots has a redeeming feature. Caligula's was that he was kind to his horse.

Indeed, his devotion to his four-legged friend, Incitatus, went way beyond kindness. He bestowed lavish gifts upon the horse, including a collar of precious jewels, and housed it in a marble stable, complete with ivory manger, purple blankets and a team of servants to cater for its every need. Guests were asked to dinner in Incitatus' honour and the horse, too, was invited to dine at the emperor's table, eating golden barley

5

while Caligula drank to the animal's health from a golden goblet. Caligula was not finished yet, however, and announced that he was intending to make the horse a consul of the Roman Empire, responsible for imposing law and order on the masses. In doing so, he showed scant regard for the rule stating that the minimum age for a consul was 42. Perhaps Caligula calculated the eligibility by means of a conversion in horse years. Anyway, it was at this point that people quietly began to question Caligula's sanity.

In truth, his sanity had never been in much doubt. He was barking mad. As the Roman historian Seneca wrote: 'Nature seemed to have created him in order to demonstrate what the most repulsive vices in the highest in the land could achieve. You had only to look at him to see that he was mad.' The third emperor of Rome was born Gaius but was named Caligula after the child-size military boots he wore in camp, 'Caligula' meaning 'little boot'. Inevitably he detested the nickname and when he became emperor, punished anyone who used it. And Caligula's punishments were not to be taken lightly. In fairness, he had the sort of troubled childhood that would have warranted a Social Services file the size of Gaul. His father Germanicus, mother Agrippina the elder, and all of his brothers were either murdered or starved to death on the orders of his great-uncle the Emperor Tiberius. Although spared, Caligula spent much of his youth as a virtual prisoner of Tiberius on the island of Capri. Tiberius was not taken in by Caligula's show of loyalty and described him as a 'serpent'. However, the boy clearly learned a great deal from his illustrious relative, who himself indulged in all manner of fiendish tortures and sexual perversions, including sex with goats, donkeys and camels. No doubt the old man was proud when, even before coming of age, Caligula was caught in bed with his favourite sister Drusilla.

Then in March AD37 Tiberius fell ill and collapsed into a coma. The court officials thought he had died and were congratulating Caligula on his accession when Tiberius awoke. According to the popular rumour of the day, the frail Tiberius was quickly smothered with his bedclothes by Caligula's chamberlain Macro, thus allowing Caligula to become emperor.

Caligula had already inherited epilepsy from his father but then in October AD37 he was stricken with a serious disease, possibly encephalitis (inflammation of the brain) which, with symptoms similar to schizophrenia, could have been responsible for his increasingly erratic behaviour. Nor was his situation helped by the deaths of both Drusilla and his grandmother Antonia in the first year of his reign, although the former could hardly be said to have been a positive influence. Caligula had been so besotted with his sister that he had taken her as his mistress between wives and when she fell pregnant with his child it is said that his impatience for the birth grew to such an extent that he had Drusilla disembowelled in order to remove the baby from the womb. Regardless of whether the story is true, Drusilla died, whereupon Caligula had her deified.

Part of Caligula's problem was that he believed himself to be a god and therefore not restricted by the rules that governed mere mortals. One of the perks, he reasoned, was that he could sleep with whomever he wanted, including his sisters. Having announced his divinity, he established a special temple featuring a life-sized statue of himself in gold, which was dressed on a daily basis to reflect his own choice of clothes. By all accounts, he was an unlikely god. The historian Suetonius wrote: 'He was very tall and extremely pale, with an unshapely body, but very thin neck and legs. His eyes and temples were hollow, his forehead broad and grim, his hair thin and entirely gone on the top of his head, though his body was hairy.' So sensitive was the emperor about his lack of hair that it became a capital offence for anyone to look down from a high place as Caligula passed by. Sometimes he would even order the shaving of those blessed with a full head of hair. However, he was equally defensive about his excessively hairy body so that even a casual reference to 'hairy goats' in conversation was fraught with danger.

Despite his physical shortcomings, Caligula actively promoted himself as a god. He particularly identified with Jupiter and had a piece of machinery designed to simulate the thunder and lightning associated with his alter ego. Once he asked the actor Apelles whether Jupiter or Caligula were greater. When Apelles hesitated in his reply, Caligula responded by ordering him to be cut to shreds with a whip. While poor Apelles pleaded for mercy, Caligula, who made a point of attending as many punishments as possible, simply remarked on the beauty of the actor's groans. In Caligula's world that passed for compassion. By the summer of AD39 he had become convinced he was Neptune and in that guise he issued instructions for a three-mile bridge of boats to be constructed across the Bay of Naples. He intended demonstrating his ability to emulate Neptune's mastery of the sea by riding on horseback at breakneck speed across the makeshift bridge wearing the breastplate of Alexander the Great. New ships were built for the epic journey, merchant vessels were requisitioned and all went remarkably well until Caligula got hopelessly drunk. Having completed the ride and praised the soldiers who had built the 'bridge', the emperor rather spoiled the occasion by hurling many of his companions into the sea to their deaths and by launching into violent, unprovoked attacks on others. It was just one of his little mood swings.

Caligula's unpredictability became his one constant. For one who derived such pleasure from inflicting pain, it was ironic that he himself was such a tortured soul. An incurable insomniac unable to sleep for more than three hours at night, he suffered terrible nightmares. Instead of sleeping, he would dance at midnight to the sound of flutes before an audience of senators who had been dragged from their beds to witness the spectacle. More alarmingly, he took to prowling through the palace for hours on end crying out for dawn and daylight.

His domestic arrangements offered precious little stability. Between bedding his sisters and any other young woman or man who caught his eye, he had four wives. The first, Julia Claudilla, died young and then, shortly after becoming emperor, he achieved the role of wedding guest from hell when, at a ceremony he was supposed to be merely attending, he took a fancy to the bride and ran off with her. However he quickly tired of his conquest – a woman by the name of Livia Orestilla – and divorced her a few weeks later. His third wife, the wealthy Lollia Paulina, lasted only marginally longer before, in AD38, he married the older Milonia Caesonia despite the fact that she was already pregnant. Caesonia's rampant immorality made her a perfect match for the emperor who concluded that the daughter, Julia Drusilla, had to be his because she was such a savage child that she used to scratch the faces and eyes of any children who played with her. Caligula was a firm believer in keeping women in their place. Whenever he kissed the neck of one of his lovers, he would whisper tenderly: 'This lovely neck will be chopped as soon as I say so.'

Not that he saw any reason to limit himself to the fairer sex. He indulged in homosexual affairs with everyone from a pantomime actor to his own brother-in-law. The latter, Marcus Aemilius Lepidus, was married to Caligula's sister Drusilla while also having affairs with the emperor's other two sisters. Such debauchery clearly offended Caligula, who eventually had Lepidus murdered.

Keeping in touch with his feminine side, Caligula sometimes used to wear women's clothes. He thoroughly enjoyed dressing up and was often seen in garments of sumptuous silk, decorated with precious stones. He even wore jewels on his shoes, the overall effect leading to accusations – made out of earshot, naturally – that the emperor's mode of attire was a touch effeminate.

Such costumes did not come cheaply and after inheriting a healthy treasury courtesy of the careful housekeeping of his predecessor, it took barely a few months for Caligula's excesses and extravagances – such as building pleasure boats encrusted with gems and drinking pearls dissolved in vinegar – to bleed the coffers dry. To pay for his spending, he made it a capital crime for his subjects not to bequeath the emperor all their worldly goods. Exceptionally wealthy people who had been forced to leave their estates to Caligula but were slow to die had the process speeded up by the emperor's homicidal henchmen. He also introduced all manner of new taxes, including one on prostitution, and, showing commendable enterprise, he opened a brothel in a wing of the imperial palace where lofty senators were obliged to pay a thousand gold pieces to have sex with his ever-willing sisters. The senators were then commanded to send their wives and daughters to work in the brothel.

Caligula's ways did not exactly endear him to the people. When he was stricken with that serious illness in the first year of his reign, one citizen, Afranius Potitus, bravely vowed that if the emperor recovered he would surrender his own life. After Caligula pulled through, he had Afranius flung to his death. Not only did he punish treachery – suspects were either executed or driven to suicide – but he also failed to reward loyalty. Macro – the chamberlain who had smoothed the path to accession – had to sit and watch while Caligula embarked on a typically lusty affair with his wife. For good measure, the emperor then accused Macro of being her pimp and ordered him to commit suicide.

Caligula's grip on reality became increasingly tenuous. In AD39 he planned to invade Britain but the expedition foundered farcically in northern Gaul when he realised that he had forgotten to notify the bulk of his army. Instead the few soldiers he had at his command were ordered to collect sea shells from the shore. As his mental condition further deteriorated, he began talking to the moon and inviting it to join him in bed although it is unclear whether he intended consummating the relationship. Apart from sex, his other great passion was sport, particularly any pastime that ended with someone being mauled to death. Watching condemned criminals being thrown to the lions was a particular favourite and when, as occasionally happened, there were insufficient criminals to satisfy the emperor's bloodlust, he ordered innocent spectators to be dragged from the benches and hurled into the arena. It clearly didn't pay to sit too near the front.

By a twist of fate, after four years of tyranny Caligula was assassinated while celebrating the Palatine Games and, somewhat surprisingly for Roman times, the motive for murder was personal rather than political. The chief conspirators were two members of his own guard: Cornelius Sabinus, one of many whose wife had been debauched and publicly humiliated by Caligula, and Cassius Chaerea, whose high-pitched, effeminate voice had been cruelly mocked by the emperor and who had been made to dress in women's clothes and act as a prostitute. Revenge on their tormentor was sweet. Lying in wait, the guards ran a sword through Caligula's genitals, fatally stabbed his wife Caesonia, and smashed the head of their baby daughter against a wall. It was an extreme but by no means unpopular massacre. In fact, the Romans lived in such fear of Caligula and his black moods that for some days afterwards they refused to believe that he was really dead. The news just seemed too good to be true.

MOTHER LOVE

NERO, EMPEROR OF ROME (AD37–68)

Agrippina the Younger, one of Caligula's wanton sisters, was the ultimate stage mother, a ferocious harridan who would stop at nothing to ensure that her boy, Lucius Domitius Ahenobarbus (later known as Nero), became emperor of Rome. Lies, incest, murder: they all came the same to Agrippina. Her wicked scheming and sinister manipulation undoubtedly had a profound effect on shaping the character of the man reviled by historian Pliny the Elder as 'the poison of the world', the first emperor to be declared a public enemy by the senate.

Nero was born on 15 December AD37 to Agrippina and her husband Gnaeus. It was not an altogether promising start to life. Father was a drunken, adulterous bully who once deliberately rode down a child on the Appian Way for the sheer hell of it and whose idea of reasoned argument was to gouge out his critic's eyes. Mother had slept with her brother Caligula at the age of twelve and went on to have an affair with her cousin and brother-in-law, Lepidus. Not to be undone, Gnaeus was sleeping with his own sister. It brought a whole new meaning to happy families.

In AD39 Caligula had Agrippina exiled to the Pontian Islands where, following the death of Gnaeus from dropsy, she and young Nero were reduced to living in poverty. Upon Caligula's assassination, she was recalled by his successor, her uncle Claudius, and succeeded in persuading the wealthy Passenius Crispus to divorce his wife and marry her instead.

When her new husband had the decency to die quickly, Agrippina became a merry widow and set about wooing her uncle Claudius, still reeling from the treachery of the Empress Messalina who had been executed for cheating on him. Powerless to resist Agrippina's feminine wiles, Claudius married her in AD49. As the emperor's wife, Agrippina was now in a position to exert considerable influence towards securing the throne for her son. First, by casting aspersions on Messalina's issue, she steered Claudius into making Nero his immediate heir ahead of his own son Britannicus. But Agrippina knew it was a fragile hold, one which needed the blessing of Claudius's beloved daughter Octavia. So, stooping to new depths, Agrippina falsely accused Octavia's fiancé of incest with his sister. Claudius promptly broke off the engagement, the former fiancé killed himself and, almost seamlessly, Agrippina slipped Nero into his place. In AD53 Nero married his stepsister Octavia, thereby cementing his claim to the throne. Agrippina removed the final obstacle barring her son's way the following year, by having the gullible Claudius poisoned.

Having toiled so hard – if unscrupulously – to elevate her son to the top, Agrippina might reasonably have expected to reap the fruits of her labours, but instead she could only look on in horror as Nero soon dumped the gentle Octavia in favour of an ambitious servant girl by the name of Acte. Agrippina reacted with undisguised jealousy towards the new mistress, fuelling rumours that she had at one point enjoyed an incestuous relationship with her son. With her track record for keeping it in the family, such a notion was hardly inconceivable. Agrippina became more twisted than ever, threatening to resurrect the claim of the fourteen-year-old Britannicus. Nero acted swiftly. After having sex with his handsome stepbrother, he had him poisoned at dinner, although he told the outside world that the boy had suffered a fatal epileptic fit. Before anyone could argue, Nero arranged for Britannicus to be buried with indecent haste. Meanwhile Agrippina paid for her plotting by being forced to move out of the imperial residence and also suffered the indignity of seeing her head removed from the coinage. Her time was clearly up.

Released from Agrippina's apron strings, the teenage Nero started to run wild. Wearing a cunning disguise, he would venture out on to the streets of Rome as part of a violent gang, attacking and robbing passers-by. He developed sadistic tendencies, boiling some victims in hot oil and ordering executions often for no more heinous a crime than possessing a funny walk or a strange expression. As an alternative entertainment, he enjoyed watching women fight dwarfs.

As Acte's influence waned, she was replaced in Nero's affections by an older woman – the beautiful but formidable Sabina Poppaea – even though he was still technically married to Octavia. To be rid of Octavia, who steadfastly refused a divorce, he had her imprisoned on the island of Pandateria on a trumped-up charge of adultery. There, her wrists were slashed to make it look as if she had committed suicide and her head was brought back to Rome for Poppaea to gloat over. In the meantime Nero had also disposed of his domineering mother. His love for her had long since turned to hatred and he hatched a scheme whereby she would suffer a fatal 'accident' at sea by virtue of a booby-trapped boat. But although the lead canopy did collapse on her as planned, the resourceful Agrippina managed to swim ashore, forcing Nero to send a group of soldiers to finish her off. With mother and wife out of the way, all that remained was for Poppaea to gain a divorce from her husband Otho. When that was granted, Nero and Poppaea were married in AD62.

By now Nero had become obsessed with his singing career. He decided that he had a beautiful voice and would lie down with lead weights on his chest to strengthen his diaphragm. He staged huge feasts and festivals, at which he would perform his own compositions, accompanying himself relentlessly on the lyre. He even toured Greece, appearing on stage in fancy dress. His shows would last for hours on end, frequently stretching through the night, and audiences were forbidden to leave their seats until he had finished. Some women feigned death in order

14

to be carried outside; others were obliged to give birth in the theatre for fear of risking the emperor's wrath. Any male guest looking bored during a Nero 'gig' would be led outside to have his testicles hacked off, which, in view of the music on offer, was often deemed the lesser of the two evils. When Nero had at last concluded his interminable dirges, he would sometimes delight in serving his guests human excrement and forcing them to lick the plates clean. So after listening to six hours of shit, they now had to eat it, too.

Nero's musical ramblings received a resounding *nul point* from the people of Rome, who felt that the sight of their emperor performing on stage dressed like an early Elton John did not exactly convey the right image. Nero tried to justify himself by claiming that he was promoting the arts and indeed he did encourage talented young musicians until sulkily dropping them when he realised their efforts were being better received than his own. His popularity plummeted still further in July AD64 when a great fire swept through Rome, the blaze rumoured to have been started deliberately by the emperor to clear land for his latest self-glorifying project, the Golden House. With the fire at its height, Nero was said to have been exulting in the beauty of the flames while singing one of his own compositions in full stage costume. Hence he has gone down in history as the emperor who fiddled while Rome burned. Nero was quick to blame the fire on the small community of Christians, supporting his stance by ruthlessly persecuting them in the ensuing months. Some victims were burned as human torches to illuminate the city at night.

Nero soon began to take out his mounting frustration and anger on those closest to him. The year after the great fire, with his wife Poppaea pregnant, he flew into a violent rage and kicked her in the belly. She died shortly afterwards, but lived on in the form of one of Nero's songs in which he waxed lyrical about her long auburn hair. For once Nero was genuinely grief-stricken over his actions until he spotted a young slave, Sporus, who looked uncannily like his late wife. To assuage his guilt over Poppaea's death, Nero decided to recreate her. So he had

Sporus castrated, dressed him in the finery of an empress, renamed him 'Sabina' and went through a marriage ceremony with him; the pair kissed openly. Soon, however, Nero married another young slave, Pythagoras. It was said that he acted as husband to Sporus and wife to Pythagoras. The emperor also formed a homosexual attachment to the actor Paris, who promised to help the emperor master the art of stagecraft. However, Paris was put to death when it became apparent that he was a far better actor than Nero. Between these dalliances with young men, Nero did take on a more conventional wife, the beautiful and wealthy Statila Messalina . . . after first taking the precaution of having her husband executed.

For the most part, Nero's attendant sycophants shielded him from the true state of public opinion, leading him to believe that he was still adored by the masses, but the myth was shattered when a conspiracy to murder him at the chariot races came to light. As a result, nineteen people met their deaths, among them his former tutor Seneca who was ordered to commit suicide, this having supplanted execution as Nero's favourite method of capital punishment. Even the most inventive spin doctor would struggle to portray attempted assassination as a vote of confidence, and the incident led to Nero becoming more paranoid than ever.

Alongside singing, chariot racing was his great hobby and he used to build up his physique by taking the Roman equivalent of an anabolic steroid – drinking dried boar's dung in water. He endeavoured to restore his popularity by taking part in the AD66 Olympics in Greece and he won every event that he entered . . . thanks in no small part to bribing his rivals and the judges, who may also have been influenced somewhat by the presence of 5,000 imperial bodyguards. His finest moment was being declared victor of the Olympic chariot-race – despite falling out of his chariot.

In January AD68 Nero made a triumphant return to Rome, seemingly unaware that there was increasing unrest over the extortionate tax demands that he was now making. The empire was being crippled financially and in spring the Senate declared

Nero to be a public enemy and sentenced him to be flogged to death as a common criminal. As his army generals defected, Nero took refuge in a villa outside Rome. When soldiers arrived to arrest him on 9 June, he stabbed himself in the neck, the job being completed by his helpful private secretary. Deluded as ever, Nero's last words were: 'What an artist dies with me!'

Simon Cowell may just have disagreed.

THE PRIZE GLUTTON

VITELLIUS, EMPEROR OF ROME (AD15–69)

To say that the Roman Emperor Vitellius was fond of his food is like saying that Picasso was fond of painting. Described as a very tall man with a 'vast belly', Vitellius revelled in his reputation as a *bon viveur*, eating three or four large meals a day, invariably followed by a riotous drinks party at a different house each night. The news that Vitellius had invited himself round for supper was enough to send any host into a state of panic, and with an appetite that made Henry VIII look positively anorexic, he never disappointed. His trick was self-induced vomiting. For between courses Vitellius would stick a feather down his throat so that he could throw up and start feasting afresh. If nothing else, he was always a topic of conversation at any dinner party he attended.

Hidden within the glutton was an intelligent man trying to get out. The son of a consul, Aulus Vitellius himself became consul at the age of 33 and was later appointed proconsul of Africa. His first marriage had ended acrimoniously. His wife, Petroniana, had given birth to a son, Petronianus, who was apparently blind in one eye, but as the relationship between husband and wife began to suffer she agreed to make the boy her heir only on condition that he be released from his father's authority. Vitellius did not take kindly to this clause and, according to informed sources of the time, promptly murdered his son, although he tried to paint himself as the intended victim by claiming that Petronianus had accidentally drunk the poison that he had prepared for his father. In the circumstances it was not altogether surprising that Vitellius and Petroniana were divorced shortly afterwards.

Another accusation levelled at Vitellius was that he starved his mother to death. Of course, with Vitellius' appetite, this may not have been intentional – he simply ate all the pies.

Despite being well educated, Vitellius had little military experience and so it came as a considerable surprise when, in AD68, the new emperor Galba appointed him commander of troops in Lower Germany. By the start of the following year, the legions in Upper Germany were refusing to swear allegiance to the detested Galba, who had refused to reward them for earlier successes. The army in Lower Germany followed suit and immediately hailed Vitellius as the new emperor.

Keen to stake his claim, Vitellius joined his men on the march south towards Rome, although in his case it was more of a slow limp because of a permanently damaged thigh, the legacy of being run over by Caligula's chariot during a chariot race. Vitellius did not lead the troops – he left that to his trusted generals Caecina and Fabius Valens – and anyway, there were inns to visit. Vitellius was not fussy where or what he ate, so long as it was food. Calling at wayside inns, he was more than happy to eat the previous day's leftovers if nothing better was available and was known to snatch from the fire food that had already been thrown out. With Vitellius around, nothing went to waste.

Tacitus wrote of the emperor-in-waiting: 'If only he had been less addicted to high living. For rich fare he displayed a revolting and insatiable appetite. Delicacies were carted all the way from Rome and Italy to tickle his palate, and the routes which lead from the Tuscan and Adriatic seas were loud with the sound of traffic. Leading members of the various cities found the provision of sumptuous banquets a heavy drain on their pockets, and the very cities were reduced to beggary.'

The army had advanced just 150 miles when news reached them that Galba had been killed and that Otho (former husband of Nero's ill-fated Poppaea) had seized the throne. Nevertheless, they forged ahead over the Alps before meeting

Otho's troops near Cremona along the River Po. Thanks to the expertise of his generals and his own ability to keep out of the way, Vitellius won the day and 48 hours later the vanquished Otho committed suicide. When Vitellius put in a belated appearance at the corpse-strewn battlefield of Cremona, he tastelessly remarked that the smell of a dead enemy was sweet and that of a fellow citizen sweeter still. Such comments did not go down well with his Roman subjects.

For the time being, however, Vitellius was able to march to Rome in triumph – a journey marked by the constant feasting and drunkenness of his army, the men being only too willing to follow their leader's example.

Tacitus described the indecorous procession. 'With every mile travelled towards Rome, the emperor's progress became more riotous. It was joined by actors and gangs of eunuchs and all the other idiosyncrasies of Nero's court. For Vitellius was a personal devotee of Nero. He had been in the habit of attending the emperor's song recitals, not – like the better sort – under compulsion, but as a slave and hireling of pleasure and gluttony.'

Suetonius was equally damning, writing of Vitellius:

Having begun his march, he rode through every city in his route in a triumphal procession; and sailed down the rivers in ships, fitted out with the greatest elegance, and decorated with various kinds of crowns, amidst the extravagant entertainments. Such was the want of discipline, and the licentiousness both in his family and army, that, not satisfied with the provision everywhere made for them at the public expense, they committed every kind of robbery and insult upon the inhabitants, setting slaves at liberty as they pleased; and if any dared to make resistance, they dealt blows and abuse, frequently wounds, and sometimes slaughter amongst them.

The new emperor and his entourage entered Rome at the end of June AD69. The initial omens were good. There were few arrests and executions and, in conciliatory mood, Vitellius kept a number of Otho's officials in his administration and even granted an amnesty to Otho's brother. However, he upset many citizens of Rome by disbanding the existing Praetorian Guard and the city's urban cohorts and offering the positions to the German legions who had been responsible for his success. Vitellius knew that just as the legions had made him, so they could break him. He did possess a cruel streak – although by no means as marked as some of his predecessors – and enjoyed saving condemned men from execution so that he could have them murdered in front of him. He also had a pathological hatred for jugglers and astrologers! Yet it was not his targeting of minority groups, nor his dismissal of the old guard, nor even his occasional flashes of cruelty that brought about his downfall – it was his passion for extravagant entertainment. His betting on the races offended many but it was the non-stop partying and expensive banquets that really alienated the people of Rome.

During his brief reign he spent 900 million sesterces on banquets, one feast alone featuring 2,000 fish and 7,000 birds. His favourite dish – all his own concoction – was known as 'Minerva's shield' and was laid out on a silver platter the size of a large room. Arranged on the dish were delicacies brought back by the Roman navy at his request from lands and seas far and wide – peacock brains, pike livers, stuffed thrushes, flamingo tongues, pheasant brains and fried stork. While Vitellius stuffed his face, some of his regular supper companions began to feel the heat. After being forced to miss several days of eating and drinking through illness, Quintus Vibius Crispus, one of the emperor's dining cronies, commented: 'If I had not fallen ill, I should have died.'

Rumours about the emperor's scandalous behaviour quickly filtered through to all parts of the empire and by the start of July – barely a week after his grand arrival in Rome – the armies of the eastern provinces had set up a rival emperor in Palestine, Titus Flavius Vespasianus, a man who could consider himself lucky to be alive at all after once falling asleep during one of Nero's concerts. In October AD69 Vespasian routed Vitellius'

21

troops at the second battle of Cremona and although the emperor, with the assistance of the loyal Valens, tried to raise a new army, the men he sent forth surrendered to the enemy without a fight at Narnia in mid-December.

With the writing on the wall, Vitellius tried to abdicate in a desperate bid to save his own skin but his supporters forced him to return to the imperial palace. On 20 December Vespasian's sympathisers fought their way into Rome. Cornered in the palace and deserted by his aides, Vitellius tied a money-belt around his waist, disguised himself in dirty clothes and hid in the door-keeper's lodge, piling a mattress and a couch against the door to prevent anyone entering. However, a couple of items of furniture were no match for determined soldiers and within minutes they had smashed through the barricade. Vitellius was dragged out and hauled through the streets of Rome half-naked to the Forum where he was tortured, killed and thrown into the River Tiber. The condemned man was not even given the opportunity to enjoy a last hearty meal.

THE PROSTITUTE PRIEST

ELAGABALUS, EMPEROR OF ROME (204–22)

Even by the standards of Roman emperors, Elagabalus was an oddball. He only lived for eighteen years – ruling for just four – yet in that short time he succeeded in scandalising citizens who had become all too accustomed to imperial excesses and eccentricities. He was a mass of contradictions: an effeminate youth who got through five wives in four years; a high priest who raped a vestal virgin and posed as a female prostitute. Furthermore, he was arguably the only emperor to preside over a marriage between two rocks. There really was no one quite like Elagabalus.

He owed his accession to his ambitious grandmother, Julia Maesa. When the Emperor Caracalla was murdered in 217, Julia concocted a yarn that the fourteen-year-old Elagabalus was his illegitimate son when, in truth, he was his nephew. But the Roman legions bought the story along with the suggestion that the youngster's strong religious convictions would make him a better bet than his chief rival for the throne, the lawyer Macrinus. Naturally, nobody wanted to give any more power to a lawyer and so the troops switched their allegiance to Elagabalus. Macrinus paid for his claim with his life. He should have read the small print.

Originally known as Bassianus, the young emperor was born in Syria and took his new name from Elagabal, the Oriental sun god whom he worshipped. As a high priest of a weird, phallic-oriented, Syrian religious sect, Elagabalus saw it as his duty to sacrifice sheep and cattle every day at dawn. Hundreds of beasts were slaughtered, spread out on the altars of the cult's temples and soaked in fine wines. Then Elagabalus would dance gaily around the altar to the accompaniment of cymbals, flutes and drums. Elagabalus was keen to introduce the cult to Rome and had a special temple built on the city's Palatine Hill, where the locals were ordered to worship a huge stone phallus. They remained sceptical.

In his role as high priest, the strange and sensitive Elagabalus saw himself as the embodiment of his sun god and decided therefore that it was about time he married a goddess. He settled on Tanit, the Carthaginian moon goddess. Each deity had a large stone that was the focus of worship and while Elagabalus's stone was brought from Syria, the Tanit stone was being transported from Africa. The young emperor not only presided over this bizarre union of two inanimate objects, he also ordered his subjects to celebrate the 'marriage' and had the effrontery to demand a large sum of money for his dowry.

As his grandmother had anticipated, because of his youth and ethereal nature, Elagabalus was happy to leave the boring duties of government to her. Soon after he arrived in Rome, she sought to confirm his status by marrying him to Julia Cornelia Paula, a member of a highly influential family, but they divorced after barely a year, with Elagabalus claiming that his bride was 'bodily unsuitable' to be an emperor's wife. His second marriage was all his own work. In 220 he broke into the secret sanctuary of the goddess Vesta and raped Aquilia Severa, one of the chaste vestal virgins. Under Roman law, any vestal who had sexual intercourse was to be buried alive, but Elagabalus elected to marry her in the hope that they could produce 'god-like children'. However many Romans were greatly offended by his action and considered it sacrilege. The emperor's honeymoon period was over.

As if that were not sufficient to fuel doubts about Elagabalus' suitability to be emperor, he now began dressing as a woman. He hated Roman and Greek clothes because they were made of cheap wool, preferring instead expensive silk garments embroidered with gold. He took to wearing gold necklaces and had his cheeks rouged and his eyes painted, even plucking the hairs from his chin so that he could look more feminine. He actually considered undergoing a sex change by having his genitals removed and offered physicians large sums of money to provide him with a vagina by means of an incision, but in the end he contented himself with circumcision only. Cassius Dio wrote: 'He had planned, indeed, to cut off his genitals altogether, but that desire was prompted by his effeminacy; the circumcision which he actually carried out was a part of the priestly requirements of Elagabalus, and he accordingly mutilated many of his companions in like manner.'

His companions were certainly a rum bunch. Whereas homosexuality had been almost compulsory in the earlier days of the empire, it was frowned upon in third-century Rome. But the sexually rampant Elagabalus loved to surround himself with handsome young men and went through a form of marriage to an ex-slave, Hierocles, whom he tenderly referred to as 'my husband'. Their relationship was not without the occasional lovers' tiff. When the emperor's gaze settled upon Aurelius Zoticus, a youth with a reputation for being extremely well endowed, the jealous Hierocles administered a drug that sapped Zoticus' ardour. After struggling all night to obtain an erection, Zoticus was thrown out of the palace in disgrace by a frustrated Elagabalus. The emperor was also a committed masochist and arranged to be caught in compromising situations so that his lovers could thrash him as punishment for his infidelity. According to observers, his body was covered in marks from these willingly received beatings.

Cassius Dio added: 'He used his body both for doing and allowing many strange things . . . He would go to the taverns by night, wearing a wig, and there ply the trade of a female huckster. He frequented the notorious brothels, drove out the prostitutes and played the prostitute himself. Finally, he set aside a room in the palace and there committed his inde-cencies, always standing nude at the door of the room as the harlots do, and shaking the curtain which hung with gold rings, while in a soft and melting voice he solicited the passers-by.'

In addition Elagabalus created a public bath inside the imperial palace so that he could recruit the young men with the biggest penises. Perhaps this penis fixation was all part of his religious worship or maybe it was because God had apparently dealt him a lousy hand in that department, his own member being said to resemble a pickled sprout! What is certain was that to be well endowed was a life-saver. For whereas Elagabalus rounded up men with small penises and had them paraded naked through the streets to their execution, those whose equipment could bring a tear to his eyes were rewarded with posts in high office for no other reason than their impressive physique. Thus a barber, an actor, a cook and a mule driver all found themselves in positions of power simply because the emperor had taken a shine to them.

When it came to emperors with bizarre lifestyles, the Roman people had long been battle hardened. Consequently, Elagabalus might have got away with the transvestism, the prostitution, the homosexuality and the S&M, but the elevation of favourites to important government positions – coupled with the violation of a vestal virgin (Rome's most sacred law) – left a nasty taste in the mouth. He was living on borrowed time.

Undaunted, Elagabalus continued his perverted ways. He threw lavish feasts at which guests were forced to wrestle with lions and eat live parrots. Sometimes, as a diversion, he ordered dozens of live snakes to be thrown at the guests so that he and his friends could laugh at the scenes of panic as people were killed by snake bites or crushed to death in the throng as they tried to escape. An invitation to dinner from Elagabalus definitely warranted the plea of a prior engagement.

His servants fared little better . . . unless, of course, they were hung like donkeys. One of his favourite amusements was to send his staff on impossible missions. He once ordered a servant to find him 1,000lb of cobwebs and when the poor soul returned having failed in his task, he was thrown into a cage and eaten alive by hundreds of starving rats. Elagabalus liked to toy with his victims like a cat with a mouse. He would tie his enemies to a wall and stab them with a red-hot poker until they screamed for mercy. To inflict yet more pain, he would then peel the skin off their bodies and dip them in a vat of salt. When he wasn't butchering cattle and sheep, he was indulging in mass human sacrifice, slaying thousands of young boys and girls as part of his religion. Whenever he entered Rome he insisted on the priests greeting him with golden bowls filled to the brim with the intestines of recently sacrificed children.

By 221 even his grandmother was beginning to despair of Elagabalus. Her hold over him was clearly slipping. She tried to repair some of the damage by persuading him to divorce Aquilia Severa (their union having failed to produce the desired mini-god) and marrying him instead to Annia Faustina, a descendant of the psychotic Emperor Commodus, a man who used to round up all the dwarfs, cripples and freaks he could find in the city and bring them to the Colosseum where he watched them fight each other to the death with meat-cleavers. Although the newlyweds must have had much to talk about, the marriage did not last and Elagabalus quickly jettisoned her and, against his grandmother's wishes, remarried Aquilia Severa.

Discontent increased about the emperor's lifestyle. He responded by having his critics executed, but an army revolt forced him to remove many of his favourites from office. Sensing that Elagabalus was now a lost cause, Julia Maesa began promoting another grandson, Alexander, as an alternative ruler, claiming that he, too, was a son of Caracalla. Quite how many more she had hidden away was open to speculation. Elagabalus reluctantly agreed to adopt his cousin and invest him with the title of Caesar but he soon grew jealous of Alexander's popularity and tried to have him assassinated. However, the soldiers ordered to carry out the dastardly deed refused and turned on the emperor instead.

On the evening of 11 March 222, his equally detested mother, Julia Soaemias, was hunted down and murdered. Elagabalus hid in the toilet but was found and stabbed to death.

The two were beheaded and their bodies dragged on hooks through the city to the sound of widespread rejoicing before being dumped into the sewers that ran into the River Tiber. Hierocles and other imperial favourites were mutilated and stabbed up the anus 'so that their death fitted their lives', noted Cassius Dio. It was the end of one of the least glorious chapters in Roman history.

THE WICKED STEPMOTHER

FREDEGUND, QUEEN OF NEUSTRIA, FRANCE
(543–97)

On the death of King Chlothar in 561, four of his sons – Charibert, Guntram, Chilperic and Sigibert – divided between them the lands of the Franks, which were then under the Merovingian dynasty. Chilperic inherited Chlothar's own kingdom, Neustria, a region of northern France with Soissons as its capital. But it was not long before he began to covet Sigibert's territory, Austrasia, the area of modern-day France and Germany to the west of the Rhine.

Chilperic was not one for standing on ceremony. His supposed hatred of the church did not exactly endear him to the chronicler Gregory of Tours, who labelled him 'the Nero and Herod of our time'. Gregory's character assassination went on: 'Many a district did he ravage and burn, not once but many times. He showed no remorse at what he did, but rather rejoiced in it, like Nero of old who recited tragedies while his palace was burning. He frequently brought unjust charges against his subjects with the sole object of confiscating their property . . . He was extremely gluttonous, and his god was in his belly. It is impossible to imagine any vice or debauchery which this man did not practise. He was always on the lookout for some new way of torturing his subjects. Whenever any were judged guilty of some crime or other, he would have their eyes torn out of their heads.'

It was not exactly the most glowing of references, but Chilperic was a pussycat compared to his sometime wife Fredegund, the prototype Lady Macbeth.

Chilperic was born in 523. His first wife, Audovera, bore him three sons and a daughter but the marriage foundered when Chilperic fell under the spell of the queen's servant, Fredegund, a beautiful girl with an eye for the high life. Intending to take Audovera's place, she encouraged Chilperic to cast his wife aside and have her locked in a monastery. Fredegund immediately became the king's mistress with a view to securing a more permanent role, but her scheme was dashed when Chilperic instead married Galswintha, daughter of the King of Spain, principally for her splendid dowry. Fredegund was evidently not amused by the turn of events, nor at the prospect of being relegated back to servant girl, and persuaded Chilperic – over whom she still had a powerful hold – to have Galswintha murdered so that she could reclaim what she saw as her rightful place in the regal bed. Sure enough, within a few days of Galswintha being found strangled in bed in 568, Chilperic was sleeping with Fredegund again and soon they married.

It did not need Sherlock Holmes to work out who was behind the killing, and Galswintha's death sparked a bitter forty-year feud between the families of Chilperic and his brother Sigibert, the latter's wife, Brunhilda, being Galswintha's sister. Brunhilda wasted little time in vowing revenge on Fredegund.

Chilperic decided that attack was the best form of defence and sent his son Theudebert to ravage Sigibert's lands south of the Loire, killing clergy and raping nuns. However, Sigibert rallied strongly, killing Theudebert and forcing Chilperic to seek refuge in Tournai. In 575 Sigibert heard from a group of Chilperic's Franks that they would welcome him as their new king and he advanced on Tournai ready to slay his brother. But on the way Sigibert was stabbed to death by two assassins . . . who had been sent by Fredegund. The incident did little to restore family harmony.

Matters worsened when Merovech, Chilperic's son by Audovera, married the widowed Brunhilda. While Chilperic disowned his son and had him committed to a monastery, stepmother Fredegund, revelling in her role as queen, tried to him have killed as punishment for his betrayal.

During their reign, Chilperic and Fredegund imposed numerous crippling taxes and when two of their young sons, Chlodobert and Dagobert, died of dysentery, Fredegund felt that she and the king were being punished for their greed in extorting so much money in taxation from their subjects. In a rare moment of contrition, they threw the new tax lists into the fire, hoping to make amends for their sins. However, any sympathy for Fredegund quickly evaporated when, bitter at the loss of her own sons, she had her stepson Clovis (another of Audovera's boys) sent to the infected region around Berny in the hope that he, too, would perish from dysentery.

That particular plan failed but Fredegund had no intention of burying the hatchet . . . unless it was in Clovis's back. Clovis would soon learn that it did not pay to get on the wrong side of the queen. For hearing that he had fallen in love with the daughter of one of her woman-servants, Fredegund had the girl thrashed, ordered her hair to be cut off, and had her tied to a stake outside Clovis's window. Just in case Clovis didn't quite get the message, Fredegund then had the girl's mother tortured.

Clovis's mere presence on earth was like an itch that Fredegund could not scratch. So when word spread that he was plotting against her, it provided her with just the excuse she needed to have him murdered, although the official line was that he had committed suicide by stabbing himself to death. For good measure, she had his mother, Audovera, killed, too – murdered in the monastery after fifteen years of solitary confinement.

Fredegund may have been the stepmother from hell but she was scarcely any more loving towards her own offspring. The birth of a boy, Samson, left both mother and baby in poor health. Fredegund totally rejected the sickly infant and announced that she wanted him killed, only to be dissuaded by Chilperic. In the event the boy only lived until the age of four. Fredegund shed no tears at his death. However, she was uncharacteristically distraught when another young son, Theuderic, died, reputedly as a result of witchcraft. Determined to make someone pay for the tragedy, she had dozens of Parisian housewives rounded up and tortured. Gregory of Tours described the punishment: 'Fredegund then had these poor wretches tortured in an even more inhuman way, cutting off the heads of some, burning others alive and breaking the bones of the rest on the wheel.' Still not avenged to her satisfaction, she proceeded to have a prefect, Mummolus, tortured for allegedly being involved in Theuderic's death but just as she was about to order his decapitation by sword, she changed her mind and spared him.

In 584 Chilperic was assassinated on his way home from a hunt. Although nothing was ever proved, it was strongly rumoured that the killer had been hired by Fredegund. She now set about preserving the inheritance of their one surviving son, the infant Chlothar, by systematically murdering his rivals. Fortunately for the intended victims, the men she chose were not always up to the task. Both her arch enemy, Brunhilda, and Brunhilda's son, Childebert, escaped with their lives thanks to bungling assassins. When the cleric sent to despatch Brunhilda returned having failed to accomplish his mission, Fredegund repaid him by having his hands and feet cut off. She later sent two priests to assassinate Brunhilda but they were equally unsuccessful, owing their technique more to Laurel and Hardy than Brutus and Cassius. Seething with anger and frustration, Fredegund had the hapless duo executed.

She had better luck with another old adversary, Praetextatus, Bishop of Rouen, whom she arranged to have murdered in the middle of a service in his own cathedral. The killing prompted widespread outrage, however, one of the town leaders rebuking Fredegund: 'You have been the cause of much evil in this world, but you have never done anything worse than this, when you ordered one of the Lord's bishops to be murdered. May God be quick to avenge his innocent blood! We all propose to inquire closely into this crime, to prevent you from committing any more atrocities of this sort.' These were brave words but, given Fredegund's reputation, possibly a shade unwise. Understandably, the town leader was on his guard at their meeting and when, supposedly in conciliatory mood, she invited him to stay for dinner, he refused. She accepted his decision but insisted that as a peace gesture he have a drink before setting off on his journey. He weakened and downed a glass of absinth mixed with wine and honey, unaware that she had added an extra ingredient – poison. After leaving the royal household, he rode for less than half a mile before dropping dead to the ground. Another one bites the dust.

Although Fredegund did a sterling job ruling Neustria until Chlothar came of age, there were still fierce family rows with her headstrong daughter Rigunth, particularly over Chilperic's riches. One day the queen turned to Rigunth and said: 'You can take all your father's things which are still in my possession, and do what you like with them.' She then led her daughter into a strongroom and opened a vast chest full of jewels and precious ornaments. After handing a series of gems to Rigunth, Fredegund sighed: 'I'm tired of doing this. Put your own hand in and take whatever you find.' Rigunth should have known better. As the girl reached in, Fredegund suddenly seized the heavy lid and slammed it down on Rigunth's neck, pressing it with all her strength against her daughter's throat in an effort to choke her to death. Fortunately for Rigunth, her screams alerted the servants, who rushed to her aid.

Fredegund never changed. Right up until her death in Paris in 597, she was involved in plots and intrigues designed to silence anyone who made the mistake of crossing swords with her.

CAUGHT IN THE ACT

EDWY THE FAIR, KING OF ENGLAND (940–59)

By all accounts, Edwy the Fair was an amiable king. Indeed, he was given his nickname by his brother-in-law, Athelweard the Chronicler, because of his generally pleasant demeanour. Yet he is remembered solely as a lascivious youth who soured his coronation by cavorting so enthusiastically in his room with his future bride and mother-in-law that the crown rolled off his head and across the floor. Alas for Edwy, the sorry scene was witnessed by a prominent churchman who made no attempt to disguise his disgust. It was an inauspicious start to Edwy's reign and one from which he never recovered.

When King Edmund of Wessex and England died in 946 his two sons, Edwy (also known as Eadwig) and Edgar, were too young to succeed him, so his brother Eadred was elected king instead. Eadred died childless nine years later, as a result of which the claim passed back to Edmund's sons. As Edwy was two years older than his brother, the nobles approved him as king on the basis that he was the oldest of the children in the natural line of the House of Wessex. Edwy was not yet sixteen when he was crowned at Kingston upon Thames on 26 January 956 by Oda, Archbishop of Canterbury. But behind the scenes there were problems. For Edwy, still an impressionable teenager, had fallen hopelessly in love with his third cousin, Elfgiva, and it seemed that her mother, Ethelgiva, wanted a piece of the action too.

The coronation itself passed off without incident but during the following day's official celebration banquet, it was noticed that the young king had absented himself and retired to his quarters. An anonymous clerk who penned the life of Dunstan, Abbot of Glastonbury, wrote of Edwy's delicate situation: 'A certain foolish woman, noble by birth, with a daughter ripe and alluring, attached herself to him. She pursued him and enticed him into intimate relationships, clearly in order to ally either herself or her daughter with him in marriage. It is said that the king consorted with them alternately, and shamelessly. When the time came, as appointed, for him to be anointed and consecrated king after the common election of all the English nobles, on the very day after this solemn occasion, he suddenly rushed out, full of lust, leaving the merry banquet and those of his nobles who were sitting with him, straight for the arms of that whore.'

Archbishop Oda was appalled by Edwy's behaviour. Aware that the king had entered into what in presidential terms might be described as an inappropriate relationship, it did not take Oda long to work out why he had excused himself from the banquet. So he asked his fellow bishops and nobles to fetch Edwy and instruct him to return to his regal duties. Everybody was reluctant to undertake the mission for fear of incurring the wrath of the new king until Dunstan and Kinsige, Bishop of Lichfield, finally agreed to go. Even though he had been informed of the nature of Edwy's dubious dalliance, however, Dunstan could hardly have been prepared for the sight that greeted his eyes.

For as he and Bishop Kinsige entered the royal quarters, they found the king engaged in a threesome on the bed with mother and daughter. Dunstan's biographer recalled the clergymen's arrival: 'They entered, thus commanded, and they found the royal crown, which shone forth in a splendour of wonderful metal-work, gold, silver and gems, far from the king's head and lying carelessly tossed to the ground. The king was with them both after his evil custom, pressed close in with desire, like pigs wallowing in a pit.'

Trying to suppress their indignation and embarrassment, Dunstan and Kinsige announced diplomatically: 'Our peers have sent us in to ask you to come without delay to your seat at the decked table, and not to spurn your nobles by being absent from their joyful feast.'

They had asked nicely but the king, young though he was, knew that being ordered about was not part of his job description. So he refused to move. And who could blame him? A straight choice between two carnivorous women taking it in turns to ravish his body or eating something furry with a bunch of stuffy nobles and bishops. No contest.

However, Dunstan would not take no for an answer. His biographer continued: Dunstan dragged him [Edwy] from his adulterous repose, placed the crown back on his head, and led him by the hand back into the royal company, thus snatching him by force from his women.' According to the account of William of Malmesbury, not content with infuriating Edwy by his high-handedness, Dunstan also forced the king to renounce Ethelgiva as a 'strumpet'.

Edwy's response, no doubt encouraged by the wounded Ethelgiva, was to have Dunstan exiled from England. He vowed never to return until the king was dead. Realising that one powerful enemy was more than enough, Edwy set about appeasing Archbishop Oda in the wake of the coronation fiasco. In the first year of his reign alone he made over sixty land grants, mainly to the church, and Oda himself was granted extensive lands at Ely. However, this generosity backfired as it was seen by some as an indication of political weakness or inexperience.

Despite the misgivings of the clergy, Edwy duly married Elfgiva, thereby allowing her mother to acquire the status at court that she had always craved. The one-time 'strumpet' was now referred to as being among 'the most illustrious of women'. But Oda remained unhappy with the arrangement and, living up to his nickname of 'the severe', he and the exiled Dunstan engineered a coup. In 957 the councils of Mercia and Northumbria, enraged by the king's apparent bias towards Wessex, rejected Edwy in favour of his brother Edgar. Under the new regime, Edwy kept Wessex but surrendered Mercia and Northumbria to Edgar. One of Edgar's first acts was to recall Dunstan.

If this was a crushing blow to Edwy, worse was to follow. Despite loyally attempting to stand by his wife, he was powerless to prevent Oda annulling the marriage in 958 on the grounds that, as cousins, the king and his spouse were too closely related.

In September 959 Elfgiva died at Gloucester in suspicious circumstances. On 1 October Edwy died too, aged just eighteen. Some blamed excess for his death, others cited a hereditary illness, and a few sensed foul play, pointing the finger at Archbishop Oda, who made little secret of his desire for Edgar to rule the entire country.

Thus Edwy's brief, inglorious reign came to an end. He never accomplished anything of note except for making enemies in the church – and in tenth-century England that was definitely not the shrewdest move. Ultimately he was overthrown for the love of a good woman . . . and her mother.

A CHAIN OF TRAGEDY

MARGARET 'MAID OF NORWAY', QUEEN OF SCOTLAND (1283–90)

Misfortune dogged the Scottish throne in the second half of the thirteenth century. A series of untimely deaths left the succession in the hands of a three-year-old Norwegian girl but the bad luck did not end there, as she achieved the unwanted distinction of dying before ever setting foot on Scottish soil.

The early years of Alexander III's reign offered little hint of the tragedies to come, although his first queen, Margaret, was responsible for the unlucky death of a young courtier. One day she was walking beside the River Tay with a group of courtiers, among whose number was a pompous young squire. The queen soon tired of his arrogance, so when he knelt down at the riverbank to take a drink, she saw the opportunity to have a joke at his expense. With the man's attention focused on quenching his thirst, she playfully pushed him into the river, but could only watch in horror as the swirling current swept him away to his death before anyone could jump to his rescue.

Margaret died in 1275. Alexander was only 34 and, with two sons and a daughter, was under no dynastic pressure to marry again. Then in 1281 his younger son David died and within another two years his remaining children had also gone to their graves – Alexander following a lengthy illness and Margaret, wife of Eric II of Norway, in childbirth. Their baby daughter, Margaret, known as the 'Maid of Norway', was thus the only immediate heir to the Scottish throne unless her grandfather, King Alexander, sired more children. The Scottish nobles were concerned at the prospect of the country's first female ruler but in 1284 they acknowledged that Alexander's granddaughter would indeed succeed him in the absence of any male heir. However, with Alexander having taken a new and energetic young wife, Yolande de Dreux, the member of a prominent French family and a descendant of Louis VI, they were optimistic that a boy might yet arrive to avert any potential embarrassment.

Then, in 1286, the Scottish royal family were hit by yet another tragedy. On the wild, windswept night of 19 March, King Alexander, fortified by wine following a council meeting at Edinburgh Castle, impulsively decided to ride home to his young wife in Dunfermline Palace, a journey that meant negotiating the hazardous Firth of Forth. Alarmed by the prevailing weather conditions, the boatman at South Queensferry refused to take him across the water – until the king pulled rank. Despite travelling in the teeth of a blizzard, they safely negotiated the Firth of Forth, but the king was still faced with a treacherous ride along the northern shore. He was joined by three squires for company and two local men acting as guides but in the gloom and gales the king became separated from them and his horse stumbled on the edge of a cliff, hurling him to his death on the beach below. His body was found by courtiers the next morning.

On his death, Queen Yolande suddenly announced herself to be pregnant. Whether it was a genuine false alarm or just wishful thinking remains uncertain, but no baby ensued and the throne duly passed to the infant Margaret, who was living with her father in Norway. While the Scots waited anxiously for news from hundreds of miles across the North Sea, Edward I of England, the little girl's great-uncle, was also taking a keen interest. The six guardians who had been appointed to take control of Scotland pending Margaret's belated arrival quickly dissolved into warring factions, a situation that encouraged Edward to try and gain a long-awaited foothold north of the border. The country was threatening to disintegrate into civil war until Edward, capitalising on the chaos, hatched a plan whereby he would not only safeguard his son's future but also place himself as overlord of Scotland. In 1289 – three years after Alexander's death and still with no sign of the young queen – Edward announced that Margaret was to succeed to the throne under his custody and that she was to marry his son, the future Edward II. The Scottish nobles agreed the proposed marriage at the Treaty of Birgham. Under the terms of the treaty, Scotland would remain fully independent – at least on paper. For the overall effect was to give Edward the real power.

On 20 May 1290, Edward despatched a 'great ship' from Yarmouth to Norway with a view to bringing Margaret over to Scotland for the first time. Its luxurious provisions included sturgeon, rice, whale meat, sugar loaves, gingerbread, figs and raisins to comfort the young girl on the journey and to feed the dignitaries who would accompany her. The ship reached Bergen six days later but King Eric happened to be away fighting the Danes at the time and so it returned to England without its royal cargo. In August Eric announced that he would bring Margaret to Scotland himself . . . in a Norwegian ship. Instead Eric stayed at home while Margaret – a delicate child at the best of times – was despatched across the turbulent North Sea in the company of Bishop Narve of Bergen.

Their ship left the Norwegian port in September bound for Leith but a ferocious storm drove it off course to the Orkneys. According to Bishop Narve, Margaret was 'seized with illness at sea' and was believed to have been dead even before the vessel took refuge at a little harbour on South Ronaldsay. She had apparently succumbed to seasickness, the exertion of the journey proving too much for her frail constitution. Instead of arriving in triumph, she had arrived in a coffin. The Scots never did see their queen.

Her body was returned to Bergen where, somewhat bizarrely, King Eric ordered the coffin to be opened so that he could ensure that she really was dead. When he was satisfied that there was no sign of life, he had her buried beside the body of her mother.

Her demise marked the end of the line of Dunkeld and enabled Edward I to seize control. Styling himself 'Overlord of the land of Scotland', he installed Englishmen in Scottish castles and demanded that any successor to Margaret recognise him as their feudal superior. Fourteen claimants put their names forward to be the new King of Scotland, including Eric of Norway, Margaret's father, in an optimistic attempt at reverse inheritance. But the winner was John Balliol, a descendant from a daughter of David I of Scotland, and in 1292 he acceded to the throne.

The sad tale of Margaret, the young queen who never saw her country, was revived around 1300 when a woman from Leipzig claimed that she was the 'Maid'. However, since Eric had taken the precaution of checking the coffin, her claim was quickly disproved and she was burned as a witch. Incidentally, had Margaret's marriage to Edward II gone ahead, the crowns of Scotland and England would have been united three hundred years earlier than they eventually were, in 1603. But judging by her experiences in the North Sea, she would never have been able to ride the storm.

ROMEO AND JULIET

PEDRO I, KING OF PORTUGAL (1320–67)

The ill-fated love story of Dom Pedro, heir to the Portuguese throne, and his forbidden sweetheart, Inez de Castro, has passed into the country's folklore. It is a tale of murder, marriage by proxy, intrigue, secrecy – and the most peculiar coronation in history.

The story begins in the year 1336 when sixteen-year-old Dom Pedro married a Castilian noblewoman, Constança Manuel. She was obviously quite a catch as she had already rejected the offers of several crowned heads before accepting the hand of Dom Pedro, on the urging of his father King Alfonso IV. However, because Castile was at war, the bride was unable to travel to Portugal and so the marriage had to be performed by proxy, which may have saved on the cake but must have resulted in a fairly uneventful wedding night for the groom. Indeed, the war lasted for another four years and it was not until 1341 that Constança finally set off for Portugal to meet her spouse.

It must have been an unnerving experience for Dom Pedro waiting in Bragança to greet a woman to whom he had been married for nearly five years but had yet to set eyes upon. Many a fourteenth-century bride had given birth to three children and caught the Black Death in that time. Fortunately his first impressions were favourable: his bride appeared to be both attractive and amiable. Then his gaze strayed momentarily to Constança's entourage and took in the beauty of one of her ladies-in-waiting, her sixteen-year-old cousin, the graceful Inez de Castro. Their eyes met across the proverbial crowded room and Pedro immediately fell in love with the girl whose yellow hair gleamed like gold in the sunlight.

As befits a tale of tragic young lovers, Pedro pined for Inez from that very first meeting and went out of his way just to catch a glimpse of her. The feeling was obviously mutual because soon they began an affair, which, despite the Moorish-influenced moral laxity that prevailed in Spain and Portugal, caused quite a scandal at court. Alfonso warned his son to end the relationship and when he refused, the king forced Inez into exile at a convent in Coimbra. Undeterred, Dom Pedro sent secret messages on a small wooden boat by way of a water duct that led to the convent, and the pair would meet in nearby woods to continue their affair.

Then in 1345 Constança died after giving birth to a son, Ferdinand. Now free of his marriage, Dom Pedro wasted little time in making his true love more accessible and established Inez in a residential palace near the convent. For the next ten years they continued their affair openly. Time and again Dom Pedro petitioned his father for permission to marry Inez, but Alfonso, and indeed the entire court, was now more vehemently opposed to the relationship than ever. The cause of the increased hostility was Inez's father, Pedro de Castro, who had now become a powerful figure in Castilian politics. Her brothers, too, were politically active and were conspiring to overthrow the King of Castile. They asked Dom Pedro to join them in their revolution and to become the new ruler but since he and the Castilian monarch were related (sharing the same grandfather), he turned down the offer.

Desperate to find a suitable candidate to be the future Queen of Portugal, Alfonso tried touting his son's name around but Dom Pedro remained obstinate in his refusal to marry anyone except Inez. By the start of 1354 Inez had already given birth to three illegitimate children and, with a fourth on the way, Dom Pedro was keen to have at least one legitimate heir by the woman he loved. So on 1 January of that year the couple married secretly in Bragança and spent the next twelve months in clandestine matrimonial bliss.

Behind the scenes, disruptive forces were at work. Members of the royal council, envious of the Spanish influence at court, became concerned that Inez's children would usurp the legitimate sons of Constança, thus handing more power to the Castros. Unaware of the secret marriage, they advised Alfonso to eliminate Inez before Dom Pedro had the chance to legitimise the children. They also persuaded the ageing king that his throne was in danger from an alliance between Dom Pedro and the Castros. Alfonso listened, refused, wavered and finally yielded to the pressure. Inez was to be murdered.

On 7 January 1355, while Dom Pedro was away on a hunting trip, Alfonso and three royal councillors – Pero Coelho, Diogo Lopes Pacheco and the Chief Justice Álvaro Gonçalves – travelled to Coimbra with the intention of assassinating the unsuspecting Inez. They found her near a fountain on the estate where, according to popular legend, Alfonso was so moved by her beauty and tears that he had a change of heart and turned to leave. However, his accomplices had come too far to back down and convinced the king of the need to kill Inez. While Alfonso vacillated once more, they seized the initiative and stabbed her to death with their swords. Her body was quickly and quietly buried in the cemetery of Santa Clara Church.

Returning from the hunting trip, Dom Pedro was aghast to learn of the dreadful deed. Some say that he was so grief-stricken that his sanity departed along with his beloved Inez. Encouraged by her outraged brothers, he immediately declared civil war on his father and was only appeased by the concession of a larger role in government. The three assassins had already fled to Castile and as part of the reconciliation with his father, Dom Pedro agreed not to pursue them. In reality, he was merely biding his time.

Two years later, King Alfonso died and Dom Pedro succeeded him as Pedro I. One of his first moves was to rescind the promise and order the extradition of the assassins from Castile. Lopes managed to escape but the other two were brought before the king. In a public execution, carried out in the king's presence, the two killers were subjected to a horrific death. After being tortured, their hearts were pulled out while they were still alive – one through his chest, the other through his back. Finally they were put to death with a lack of mercy that mirrored their disposal of Inez.

Even this bloody revenge could not compensate for the loss of Inez and Pedro continued to brood over her, contemplating various ways in which he could make his sons by her his rightful heirs. So he announced publicly that they had been secretly married. The royal councillors expressed a degree of disbelief but having seen what he had done to two of their former members, thought it best to keep their opinions to themselves. Nevertheless it was suggested that the children could only have been considered legitimate heirs if Inez had been recognised by papal authority in the form of a church coronation.

Ordinarily King Pedro would have accepted the impossibility of the situation and gone back to his brooding but, his senses still impaired by grief, he saw no reason why Inez should not be crowned . . . even though she had been dead for five years. To the horror of the councillors, Pedro ordered that the body of Inez be exhumed from its resting place in Coimbra, dressed in royal robes and brought to the monastery of Alcobaça by a splendid procession. The event was described by Ferno Lopes, the royal archivist of Portugal: 'And he brought her corpse from the monastery of Santa Clara de Coimbra, where she had been laid, in the most exalted procession that could be arranged. She came in stages, a procession with extremely correct protocol for the time, carried by great cavaliers, accompanied by gentlemen of noble birth and many other people, and ladies, and damsels and a great number of clergy. By the side of the road stood many men with great candles in their hands, organised in such a way that, wherever the corpse went, along the entire route, it travelled between lit candles . . . And that was the grandest funeral procession which had been seen in Portugal as of that time.'

According to legend, once the corpse had arrived at the monastery, Pedro ordered it to be placed on a throne, anointed and crowned. The king is said to have sat enthroned next to his late queen while the nobles of Portugal stepped forward one by one to lift her withered hand and kiss it. At the end of this decidedly unusual coronation ceremony, Pedro had the newly crowned corpse and the throne sealed in a marble sarcophagus. When the king himself died in 1367, he was buried, as he had requested, in an identical sarcophagus next to that of Inez. After all that effort, Ferdinand I, his son by Constança, succeeded him.

Inez's tomb resisted centuries of curiosity until in 1810 invading French soldiers opened it in search of souvenirs and hacked her yellow hair from her skeleton. Even in death she was not allowed to rest in peace. All things considered, she had paid a heavy price for catching the eye of the heir to the throne.

HEART OF GLASS

CHARLES VI, KING OF FRANCE (1368–1422)

With wars to fight, plagues to conquer and peasants to subjugate, fourteenth-century rulers had to be made of stern stuff. Unfortunately, Charles VI of France was convinced he was made of glass and that any physical movement would cause him to shatter into a thousand pieces. This did not bode well for his ability to govern through difficult times and it is therefore no coincidence that his reign witnessed one of the sorriest episodes in French history – Agincourt.

The son of Charles V and Jeanne of Bourbon, Charles came to the throne in 1380 at the age of twelve, although the real power initially resided with his four uncles – the Dukes of Anjou, Burgundy, Berry and Bourbon. While the amiable young king indulged in his favourite pursuit of hunting, this cunning quartet set about feathering their own nests by raising taxes and looting the treasury, policies that did not go down well in a country still recovering from the financial drain of the Hundred Years War. Rebellions sprung up in towns and cities all over France until Charles exerted his authority by crushing the insurgents.

In 1385 he married Isabeau, the fourteen-year-old daughter of the Duke of Bavaria. Before the wedding, prominent members of the French court had insisted that the princess be examined naked to ensure that she could bear children – at least, that was the excuse they gave. She clearly passed the test with flying colours because Charles was so besotted that he brought the marriage forward, the anticipation of enjoying full-blooded sex with the fair Isabeau having prevented him from sleeping properly at night. She was said to be a beautiful, sensuous nymphet while Charles himself was also quite a catch. An accomplished horseman and archer, he was taller than average with a sturdy physique and a genuine compassion for his subjects, even the lower ranks. Whereas many a monarch would ride haughtily past humble peasants, Charles made a point of stopping to greet them. In modern parlance, he was a man of the people. At first the marriage was truly harmonious, not least perhaps because she spoke no French and he did not understand German. It is, after all, difficult to sustain an argument when neither party has any idea what the other is saying. However, in time it became apparent that, for all her physical attributes, Isabeau was a mite shallow, her principal interests being herself and spending money. She certainly did not treat her role as queen with the reverence it merited and did not even bother to learn French.

By contrast, Charles appeared a conscientious ruler and in 1388, with the assistance of his brother Louis, Duke of Orléans, he removed his four uncles from power and replaced them with a group of his father's counsellors. At this stage there was no indication that Charles would soon become as mad as a hatter.

Then in April 1392 he was stricken by a mysterious illness – possibly encephalitis or the hereditary blood disease porphyria – that caused his hair and nails to fall out. The symptoms of porphyria include hallucinations, delirium and severe weakness of the limbs, and Charles was still exhibiting worrying traits – feverish fits and incoherent behaviour – when he learned of an assassination attempt on one of his favourite advisers, Olivier de Clisson, in the streets of Paris. Although far from fully recovered, in August an irate Charles led an expedition against the chief suspect, the Duke of Brittany.

In doing so, the king ignored the strongest medical advice, the royal doctors having declared him to be 'feverish and unfit to ride', but he was determined to avenge his friend and besides he felt as comfortable on a horse as he did on his wife.

48

On the journey north few in the party could have been unaware that the king was not quite himself. His behaviour had become decidedly irrational, and he lapsed into sentences of nonsensical gibberish. Furthermore, this most mild-mannered of monarchs began making rude gestures at people and trees alike. To berate a fellow human in the heat of a long ride is perhaps understandable but to direct torrents of verbal abuse at an oak sapling suggests a particularly fragile temperament.

The uneasy peace suddenly exploded on a hot day in a forest near Le Mans after Charles, riding at the head of a group of knights, was approached by a wild-looking individual muttering ominous forebodings. The king, who had been drinking heavily, was greatly disturbed by the incident. Shortly afterwards, the royal party had just emerged into open countryside when an exhausted page accidentally dropped the king's lance, causing it to land noisily on a colleague's helmet. Startled by the sound, Charles immediately drew his sword and, shouting 'Forward against the traitors!', began lashing out at everyone within reach. Within a matter of seconds he had killed four of his own knights. Overpowered before he could wipe out his entire entourage, he was lifted from his horse and placed on the ground, where he lay motionless and speechless, his eyes rolling wildly from side to side. His attendants found an ox-cart to transport him to a place of safety but for two days he lay in a coma, hovering between life and death. When he eventually came round he talked only nonsense at first but, with the help of a physician, he made a partial recovery. However, when he learned that he had killed four of his own men, he wept inconsolably. He was never the same again.

The following January, in a valiant attempt to lift the king's spirits, Isabeau threw a masked ball at which Charles and a group of his courtiers dressed up like lepers in linen costumes. Alas, they were accidentally set alight by a torch and four of them were burned alive. While the queen fainted in shock, the king was saved by the quick-thinking Duchess of Berry, who smothered him beneath her voluminous skirts – an action guaranteed to make many a man faint too. The episode dealt another blow to the king's deteriorating mental health.

Thereafter his attacks of insanity became increasingly frequent and of longer duration. He used to run screaming through the royal palace, claiming that he was escaping from unseen enemies, until he collapsed from sheer exhaustion, or he would prowl the corridors, howling like a wolf. To prevent the news reaching the outside world, his attendants had the doors walled up. His mood alternating alarmingly between passive listlessness and hyperactive jollity, he would smash furniture in fits of rage and urinate in his clothes. On other occasions he would flatly deny that he was king or that he was married with children, insisting instead that his real name was Georges. When presented with his wife's coat of arms, he maniacally tried to erase it.

Most famously he went through a period of believing that he was made of glass and that if anyone approached too closely he would break. He refused to travel by coach for fear that the vibration would cause him to shatter into pieces and demanded that iron rods be inserted into his clothing to stop him from breaking. By then it was a little too late to prevent Charles from cracking up.

His courtiers didn't know what to make of the glass king. A vase, perhaps, or a nice little candle-holder?

The royal physicians were equally puzzled. At first they tried conventional methods of dealing with madness and a surgeon drilled some holes in the king's skull in an attempt to relieve the pressure on his brain. Initially, the operation seemed to have been successful, but Charles soon suffered another relapse. Tortured by his condition and dreading a repeat of the slaughter at Le Mans, he begged that his dagger be removed before he could inflict injury on himself and others. When the initial treatments failed, medics began to search for another explanation for the king's illness and concluded that he was a victim of sorcery. One of the most respected sorcerers in the land diagnosed that the king was possessed by the devil and attempts were made to exorcise him. In what appeared to smack of desperation, a pair of friars were introduced wailing magic incantations and carrying a potion of powdered pearls. However, when their bid to ward off the evil spirits proved ineffective in bringing about an improvement in the king's condition, rather than admit that they were frauds, they accused the king's brother of poisoning his mind. It was a costly miscalculation and one that they paid for with their heads.

The king was becoming ever more distraught and during one particularly bad attack he screamed: 'If there is any one of you who is an accomplice in this evil I suffer, I beg him to torture me no longer but let me die!'

For several months in 1405 Charles refused to change his linen, bathe or be shaved. Quite apart from the state of his personal hygiene, he began to suffer from skin trouble and lice. Having exhausted all other options, his physicians decided that the only cure was a radical form of shock treatment. So one day in November they arranged for ten men with blackened faces to sneak into the royal apartments and frighten him. When the king entered, they all jumped out, shouting words that were at the forefront of medieval medical science, such as 'Boo!' Incredibly the ruse worked and for the next few weeks Charles agreed to be washed, shaved and dressed.

Deranged though he was, Charles's sexual vigour showed no sign of flagging and an exhausted Isabeau gave birth to no fewer than twelve children. However, as his illness worsened and his behaviour became more schizophrenic, he turned against the queen, even failing to recognise her in his less lucid moments. Having nobly put up with years of his uncontrollable urges – some of which left her in fear of her life – not to mention the lice and the howling, she finally reached the end of her tether. So she arranged for her place in the king's bed to be taken by a young lookalike, Odette de Champdivers, who, as the daughter of an impoverished horse-dealer, was only too pleased to acquire the trappings of royalty. Each night Odette, wearing Isabeau's clothing, was placed in the king's bed to satisfy his animal lusts. Such was his mental state that – for the first few years at least – he apparently failed to spot that the substitute had been brought

51

on. By Odette, who came to be known as *la petite reine* ('the little queen'), Charles had a daughter, Marguerite.

In the meantime Isabeau was enjoying her new-found freedom, notably in the arms of her brother-in-law, Louis of Orléans, who had been pursuing her with a stalker's zeal. In truth, their affair had been going on for ages and as they became more open about the relationship, rumour began to spread concerning the legitimacy of some of the queen's children.

By now Charles was little more than a puppet ruler, and when it came to making important state decisions he tended to side with whoever spoke loudest. The battle to win the king's ear developed into a bitter power struggle between brother Louis and John the Fearless of Burgundy, until, in 1407, Louis was murdered at the instigation of his rival. Queen Isabeau quickly overcame her grief at her lover's death by joining forces with his killer but the Duke of Burgundy was soon opposed by a new enemy, Bernard of Armagnac. With the country divided and the king powerless to intervene, France was at the mercy of foreign invaders and in 1415, Henry V of England pressed his own claim to the French throne by defeating a numerically superior Gallic army at Agincourt.

While the country continued to disintegrate around him, Charles had more pressing matters on what remained of his mind. Bernard of Armagnac informed him that Isabeau, who was now so overweight that she was unable to get around without the aid of a wheelchair, had been unfaithful. In a rare burst of activity, Charles rode to confront her and had her formally banished. Odette, it seemed, satisfied all his needs.

But Isabeau continued to be a thorn in his side and declared that the king's heir, Charles, the Dauphin, was illegitimate. For good measure, she arranged for her daughter Catherine to marry Henry V and recognised them as the true heirs to the French throne. By the Treaty of Troyes of 1420, Henry would act as regent for the incapable king while he lived and would succeed him on his death. Charles, who had been reduced to living in a state of neglect at Senlis, was brought back to Paris on Henry's orders, but the following year he was taken ill with fever. He recovered after devouring copious amounts of oranges and pomegranates and seemed physically, if not mentally, indestructible.

Then, in the spring of 1422, Henry V died, leaving his ten-month-old son – and Charles's grandson – as his successor, Henry VI. Six months later Charles finally succumbed, too. It was a merciful release – not least for Odette de Champdivers.

Henry VI inherited some of his grandfather's insanity in short spells of delusion while the discredited Dauphin, Charles VII, who eventually took the French throne with a little help from Joan of Arc, developed a morbid phobia of bridges after witnessing John the Fearless being hacked to death on one. But really these were just minor eccentricities compared to the crystal-crazy Charles VI.

VLAD THE LAD

VLAD THE IMPALER, PRINCE OF WALLACHIA
(1431–76)

Vlad the Impaler was a man's man. He had no interest in the arts or wearing fancy costumes; he preferred war games. Above all, he loved to inflict pain and misery on as wide a scale as possible, and, according to legend, to suck blood. Today, he would undoubtedly have enjoyed a long and distinguished career with the Inland Revenue. But back then his chosen method of torture was impalement. In the course of his reign, it is estimated that he had between 80,000 and 500,000 men, women and children murdered, the vast majority of them brutally impaled so that they endured a slow, lingering death. Feared and revered by his subjects in equal measure, he was nevertheless a man who would not flinch at protecting his kingdom from the threat of outside attack, no matter how overwhelming the odds. For Vlad, the stakes were never too high . . . or wide . . . or sharp.

Vlad's life is indeed the stuff of which legends are made, the most notable, of course, being that of Count Dracula. He is generally held to be the inspiration for Bram Stoker's infamous vampire and as such has posthumously spawned a worldwide tourist industry. It is arguably his only charitable act.

The part of modern-day southern Romania then known as Wallachia had been founded in 1290 by a character called Rudolph the Black and successive rulers fought to keep the country independent from the rising threat of the Ottoman

Empire. The throne of Wallachia was not necessarily passed from father to son. Instead the prince was elected by the boyars, or land-owning nobles, a situation that provoked bitter hostility among the rival factions. When the ageing Prince Mircea died in 1418, he left behind a number of illegitimate children, among them the Impaler's father, also named Vlad. It appears that Vlad senior grew up in the court of Hungary's King Sigismund who, as Holy Roman Emperor, founded a secret fraternal order of knights called the Order of the Dragon to uphold Catholicism and fight the Turks. The order's coat of arms was a dragon and so Vlad, in his role as a knight with the order, was known as Vlad Dracul, 'dracul' meaning 'dragon' (or sometimes 'devil') in Romanian. Sigismund appointed Vlad senior the military governor of Transylvania, a post that he held from 1431 to 1435. During that time he lived in the Transylvanian town of Sighisoara and it was there in 1431 that he fathered a son, to whom he gave the family name of Vlad. As the son of Dracul, Vlad junior was known as Dracula.

Unwilling to remain a governor for ever, Vlad Dracul set his sights on seizing the throne of Wallachia from Alexandru I, a feat he accomplished in the time-honoured tradition of having his rival assassinated. To protect Wallachia's interests, he switched sides, now favouring the Turks instead of the Hungarians. The Sultan of Turkey, no stranger to the complex world of international politics, sought to ensure Vlad Dracul's continuing support by ordering that his two youngest sons – Vlad Dracula and Radu – be held hostage in Turkey. Under this arrangement young Vlad was kept captive for a period of four years. In 1447 both his father and his elder brother, Mircea, were murdered and a member of the rival Danesti clan – backed by the Hungarians – was elevated to the Wallachian throne. The Turks bitterly resented a Hungarian puppet being in charge of Wallachia and so the following year they released the seventeen-year-old Vlad Dracula and placed an army at his disposal.

With the help of his Turkish army, he seized the Wallachian throne to become Prince Vlad III but he lasted only two months before being driven into exile by the Hungarians. The ensuing years saw countless assassinations, executions and changes of allegiance, with Vlad ruling for three separate periods, totalling around seven years. During this turbulent period he established his reputation as the most fearsome tyrant in Europe.

Vlad's murderous exploits have passed into Romanian folklore, particularly his penchant for impaling his enemies and leaving them to rot in the sun. Some folk collect stamps, others watch birds, but Vlad had a genuine passion for impalement. And there was a real art to it. To the uninitiated, it appeared to involve nothing more than hammering a sharp wooden stake into the ground and sticking the victim on it, like a piece of rejected copy on an editor's spike. But Vlad was a perfectionist who revolutionised the world of impalement in the same way that Dick Fosbury forever changed the face of the high jump . . . although fortunately without impaling himself on the bar. Traditionalists in impalement opted for the sharp stake for a quick death, but Vlad wanted to prolong the enjoyment . . . or agony, depending from whose perspective the punishment is seen. So instead of having the stakes sharpened, he preferred the wood to be rounded and oiled at the end in order that the death be long and drawn out, lasting for hours, sometimes even days.

Now to some this may seem like a selfish, barbaric deed, but in fact Vlad was thinking of his guests. For he often used a mass impalement as dinner-party entertainment. It lasted longer and was considerably cheaper than a minstrel and, to Vlad at least, was more amusing than a jester. So he would arrange for the preparation of a row of stakes, each the thickness of a strong man's arm and often arranged in nice geometric patterns, and for the victims, still alive, to be impaled somewhere around their chest. The height of the stake indicated the rank of the victim, although top billing must have been small consolation to the recipient at that particular point. Then the stakes were hoisted upright and as the condemned were hung suspended above the ground, the weight of their bodies would slowly drag them downwards, causing the sharpened end of the stake to pierce their internal organs. And all the while Vlad and his friends would be tucking into a banquet at a table specially laid out for the occasion, enjoying a leisurely supper amid the pitiful sights and sounds of the dying. Heartless and horrifying as it was, impalement may just have inspired the local taste for kebabs.

One such hideous feast took place at Brasov in 1459 after the local merchants had refused to pay taxes despite receiving repeated warnings. In response Vlad led a typically ruthless assault on the town, burning an entire suburb and impaling his prisoners on a nearby hill. The scene was immortalised in a gruesome woodcut that appeared in a German pamphlet around the end of the century. It depicts Vlad tucking into a hearty meal while impaled victims are dying all around him before anyone could even say, 'How do you like your stake?' As he eats, his henchmen are hacking off the victims' limbs right next to his table. The narrative opens: 'Here begins a very cruel frightening story about a wild bloodthirsty man Prince Dracula. How he impaled people and roasted them and boiled their heads in a kettle and skinned people and hacked them to pieces like cabbage. He also roasted the children of mothers and they had to eat the children themselves.'

During that episode a squeamish dinner companion made the mistake of holding his nose in an effort to avoid the smell of blood and flesh. On seeing this, Vlad considerately had him impaled higher than the rest so that he might be above the stench. Vlad himself resisted the temptation to chew the flesh of dissidents, presumably on the basis that he didn't want to eat something that might disagree with him.

One of Vlad's earliest revenge missions was conducted against the nobles of Tirgoviste, whom he held responsible for the deaths of his father and brother. According to an early Romanian chronicle, Vlad invited the nobles and their families to an Easter feast. After the guests had finished their meal, his soldiers surrounded them, rounded up the able-bodied and marched them fifty miles up the Arges River to Poenari, where they were forced to build his mountain fortress. These prisoners toiled away for months in atrocious conditions. As the clothes fell from their bodies, they were forced to work naked. Many died; those who survived were impaled. It was Vlad's idea of justice.

Even when imprisoned in Hungary for a time, Vlad could not resist indulging in a spot of impalement and a number of small animals and birds were subsequently found impaled upon miniature stakes near his place of captivity.

He was by no means selective about whom he impaled. A fifteenth-century German pamphlet recounted: 'He devised dreadful, frightful, unspeakable torments, such as impaling together mothers and children nursing at their breasts so that the children kicked convulsively at their mothers' breasts until dead. In like manner he cut open mothers' breasts and stuffed their children's heads through and thus impaled both. He had all kinds of people impaled sideways: Christians, Jews, heathens, so that they moved and twitched and whimpered in confusion a long time like frogs.'

He needed little excuse for an impalement, punishing women who had affairs, merchants who cheated their customers and one lazy woman for the sole reason that her husband's shirt was too short. He even impaled some Saxon merchants because they refused to give him a discount. Afterwards he would display the bodies in public to teach everyone a lesson, the decaying corpses often being left up for months.

He also had something of an obsession with female chastity. As well as adulterous wives, maidens who lost their virginity and unchaste widows were also targets of his cruelty. Such miscreants invariably had their sexual organs cut out or their breasts hacked off. Alternatively a red hot stake would be inserted through the groin so that it protruded through the mouth. One unfaithful wife was executed by being skinned alive, mutilated and impaled. Her skin was then placed beside her on a table.

His care for the less fortunate members of society also left something to be desired. One day he invited a number of elderly people, sick people and beggars to a banquet at his castle. After they had eaten their meal and drunk a toast to their gracious host, he asked them: 'Would you like to be without cares, lacking nothing in this world?' 'Yes,' they answered enthusiastically. At which Vlad had the castle boarded up and set on fire. None of the guests got out alive – but, as Vlad had promised, it was an end to their problems. He later explained: 'I did this so that no one will be poor in my realm.'

A Romanian account related how he plundered Transylvanian towns where residents were suspected of supporting the rival Danesti faction:

In the year 1460, on the morning of St Bartholomew's Day, Dracula came through the forest with his servants and had all the Wallachians of both sexes tracked down, as people say outside the village of Humilasch, and he was able to bring so many together that he let them get piled up in a bunch and he cut them up like cabbage with swords, sabres and knives; as for their chaplain and the others whom he did not kill there, he led them back home and had them impaled. And he had the village completely burned up with their goods and it is said that there were more than 30,000 men.

It would be wrong to assume that Vlad was nothing more than a psychotic impaler. He enjoyed other forms of capital punishment too. A German pamphlet describes some of his proudest moments:

He had some of his people buried naked up to the navel and had them shot at. He also had some roasted and flayed . . . He captured the young Dan (of the rival Danesti clan) and had a grave dug for him and had a funeral service held according to Christian custom and beheaded him beside the grave . . . He had a large pot made and boards with holes fastened over it and had people's heads shoved through there and imprisoned them in this. And he had the pot filled with water and a big fire made under the pot and thus let the people cry out pitiably until they were boiled quite to death . . . About three hundred gypsies came into his country. Then he selected the best three of them and had them roasted; these the others had to eat.

When a group of emissaries from the Ottoman Empire angered him by failing to remove their turbans in his presence, Vlad demanded to know why. They replied that it was part of their religion to keep turbans on at all times whereupon, to ensure that they were able to do exactly that, he had their turbans nailed to their heads. On another occasion he ordered 400 young apprentices to be burned alive

Vlad soon realised that his terrible reputation could be used in psychological warfare against potential invaders. Having switched sides to support the Hungarians, he inevitably came into conflict with the Turks. In 1462 the Turks drove deep into Wallachian territory against woefully outnumbered forces. Vlad tried every trick in the book – poisoning wells as he retreated, even initiating a form of germ warfare by deliberately sending victims of infectious diseases into the Turkish camps. But the Sultan pressed on until he reached the outskirts of Vlad's capital city, Tirgoviste. A Greek historian described the sight that greeted the invaders:

> *He [the Sultan] marched on for about five kilometres when he saw his men impaled; the Sultan's army came across a field with stakes, about three kilometres long and one kilometre wide. And there were large stakes on which they could see the impaled bodies of men, women, and children, about twenty thousand of them, as they said; quite a spectacle for the Turks and the Sultan himself! The Sultan, in wonder, kept saying that he could not conquer the country of a man who could do such terrible and unnatural things, and put his power and his subjects to such use. He also used to say that this man who did such things would be worthy of more. And the other Turks, seeing so many people impaled, were scared out of their wits. There were babies clinging to their mothers on the stakes, and birds had made nests in their breasts.*

The Sultan chose to withdraw.

Not surprisingly, fear of impalement kept crime in Wallachia at a minimum. It really was just about the ultimate deterrent, sufficient to satisfy even the most severe magistrate. And for all his little quirks, Vlad was a firm believer in law and order and in honesty in general. The story goes that one day two monks visited him in his palace and were shown the row of corpses in the courtyard. Asked what they thought of the atrocities, the first monk told Vlad: 'You are appointed by God to punish evil doers.' But the second was more honest and condemned Vlad for his actions. According to Russian literature, Vlad rewarded the second monk for his honesty and impaled the first for lying. Another to pay for her dishonesty was Vlad's mistress who, after falsely telling him that she was pregnant, paid for her deception in the worst possible way. When an examination exposed the lie, he slit the poor woman open from her groin to her breasts, leaving her to die a slow, horrible death.

Whilst there is no eyewitness evidence that Vlad ever actually drank the blood of his victims, let alone that he was a vampire, such exaggerations could hardly be said to be a slur on his character.

Little is known about his private life, except that his first wife was reputed to be 'kind and humble with a heart of gold', and that after she had apparently committed suicide to escape the approaching Turks, he married a Hungarian princess as part of the deal to restore him to the throne of Wallachia. His wives bore him a total of three sons. There is no record of Vlad having impaled any members of his own family – he obviously didn't bring his work home with him.

With the help of the King of Hungary, Vlad seized the Wallachian throne for a third time in 1476. But a few months later the Turks attacked yet again and Vlad was killed while fighting near Bucharest. Some say he died at the hands of a Turkish assassin posing as a servant; others claim he was accidentally killed on the battlefield by his own men after he had disguised himself as a Turk to confuse the enemy. Either way, the joyous sultan displayed his head on a pike in Constantinople (the old name for Istanbul) to prove that the feared Vlad was finally dead.

For all his faults – and they included the small matter of wiping out ten per cent of the population of Wallachia – Vlad the Impaler (or Vlad Tepes as he is known in Romania) was admired by many for imposing his own brand of law and order and for his bravery in keeping enemy forces at bay. And he may just have been misunderstood. An American physician recently suggested that Vlad's murderous actions might have been prompted by an allergy to blood. The medic claimed that in some allergic reactions, sufferers also develop an addiction to the same substance, and if deprived they can react in a bizarre and deranged manner. So for the price of a couple of sessions of counselling, Vlad the Impaler could instead have gone down in history as Vlad the Wellbeloved or Vlad the Thoroughly Decent Bloke.

DEARLY DEPARTED

JUANA I, QUEEN OF CASTILE (1479–1555)

Juana the Mad. The nickname handed down over the centuries leaves little room for ambiguity. Unusually, the cause of Juana's insanity was love – the love for her husband Philip, which showed no sign of abating even after his death. On the contrary, she remained so infatuated by him that wherever she travelled, she insisted on being accompanied by his coffin. She opened it regularly, sat next to it at dinner and lay beside it on her bed at night. Even allowing for her loss, these were not the actions of a rational woman. Declared unfit to rule by her own family, she was kept hidden away from public gaze for over forty years, mostly confined to a darkened room in a gloomy castle: alone with her confused thoughts and the memory of her beloved Philip.

Juana was the third child of Queen Isabella I of Castile and King Ferdinand II of Aragon, whose marriage had united Spain. A restless, tearful baby, she grew to become a sullen, somewhat timid child, one who cared for little company but her own and was prone to dark, melancholic moods. These sombre phases were all too reminiscent of her grandmother, Isabel of Portugal, who spent much of her life in seclusion and depression and ended up being chased by ghosts and not recognising anybody, least of all herself.

Juana's desire for solitude would have made Greta Garbo seem positively gregarious. Nevertheless she was intelligent, well read, thoughtful and diligent and approached her religious

63

duties with the same devotion that she tackled everything else in life. She also had a talent for dancing and playing the clavichord and was able to speak fluent Latin.

But at heart she was a typical teenage girl and, as such, her dedication to study and God went out of the window the moment she encountered boys. For at the age of sixteen she was betrothed to the modestly titled Philip the Handsome of Austria, the only son of the Emperor Maximilian I. In 1496 she set off to the Low Countries to meet her prospective husband for the first time. For once she was not alone, being part of a fleet of ships manned by some 22,000 Spaniards. The path to true love was far from smooth. Three ships were lost on the voyage and Juana herself fell victim to seasickness. When she finally embarked she was green from the seasickness and blue with a heavy cold. Recognising the symptoms, Philip did not rush to meet his turquoise bride, sending instead his sister Margaret. By the time they did meet, Juana had recovered fully from her ordeal and was looking at her best, a dark-haired Spanish beauty. For his part, Philip was cheery, athletic and confident. It was lust at first sight.

In that instance Juana forgot all her inhibitions and pious upbringing and practically threw herself at Philip, who responded with similar enthusiasm. Even though neither spoke the other's language, they found a method of communicating and ordered the nearest cleric to marry them on the spot. Before the ceremony had been properly concluded to unite this marriage of different tongues, the pair fled to the royal bedroom, tore off their clothes and made passionate love. The earth movement could probably have been felt back in Spain. The wedding was formally completed in church the following day, by which time both parties had managed to control their carnal urges . . . at least for the time being.

However, it quickly became apparent that Philip wanted Juana solely for her body. He was certainly not interested in her mind, her intensity clashing alarmingly with his frivolity. Whereas her interests lay in education and the arts, his were eating, drinking and chasing women. And he had no intention of amending his philandering ways simply because he was now married – after all, having a supply of willing girls on tap was surely one of the perks of royalty. Some things never change.

Whereas Philip was happy to continue leading the life of a bachelor gay, Juana's sheltered childhood had led her to expect more from marriage – even a politically arranged one. Whenever she saw her husband enjoying the company of another woman, she flew into a jealous rage. She began sinking into depression and suffering anxious fainting fits. She became fiery and temperamental, haughty and obstinate. Philip's response was to punish her by steering clear of her bedroom for days, leaving her to cry herself to sleep and to bang her body against the wall in frustration. Yet in spite of his unsympathetic behaviour, she remained hopelessly – madly – in love with him.

Two years into their marriage, Queen Isabella sent an emissary to question Juana but she flatly refused to tell him anything. He reported back to her mother that Juana appeared miserable, tense and unstable.

As her Spanish entourage gradually drifted away, Juana felt increasingly isolated. The solitude she had craved as a child now seemed like torture. She trusted no one, least of all her husband, whose absences grew ever more frequent but who entered the marital bed long enough to father a daughter, Eleanor, in 1498 and a son, Charles, two years later. If she hoped that the births would turn Philip into a responsible, caring father, she was sadly mistaken. Where there was fun to be had and pretty girls to be fondled, Philip's name was first on the list.

The deaths of her elder siblings had left Juana as heiress of Spain, Mexico, Peru and the Caribbean and, following the birth of another daughter in 1501, Juana and Philip were summoned to Spain, their children staying behind in Flanders. On arrival back in her homeland, a relieved Juana hurled herself histrionically into her father's arms, hugging and kissing him with a fervour quite unbecoming of a royal family. Isabella was more frosty, however, and showed little sympathy for her daughter's plight – a rejection that merely served to heighten Juana's neuroses.

Philip quickly tired of Spanish life. He hated the incessant heat, the interminable religious services and the gloomy court life, not to mention the fact that the Spaniards either kept their women hidden away or guarded by formidable chaperones. Feeling restrained under the watchful eyes of his wife and in-laws, he yearned for the freedom of Flanders. His discontent was not helped by a bout of the measles, but once he had recovered he vowed to get out of Spain as soon as possible. However, by then Juana was pregnant again. Deserting her at such a time seemed inconceivable but after a bitter and violent quarrel, he set sail without her. Mortified, she begged to be allowed to ride off after him, but when her mother, agitated by Juana's mental state, had her locked up in the Castle La Mota at Medina del Campo for her own safety, she plunged into an even deeper depression.

Life with Philip was bad enough, but life without him was unbearable. Juana was now totally unhinged and spent days on end wandering around mumbling incoherently, almost childlike, unable to eat or sleep. And those were her good days. On her bad days, she turned into a she-devil, screaming obscenities at servants and clerics alike, her anger boiling over at the thought of all the women her errant husband was bedding back in Flanders. With her mother refusing to allow her to leave Spain, citing first a tense political situation and then the winter storms, Juana decided to take matters into her own hands. On a cold, winter's night, she tried to escape, half-naked, from the castle, but when the city gate closed before her, she hurled herself against its iron bars, yelling abuse. Nobody could reason with her. She swore at her mother and threatened to torture and execute the bishop for keeping her locked up. Her ranting subsided only when she was overcome by exhaustion, whereupon she spent the rest of the night and half the next day sitting morosely in the open courtyard with no protection against the biting winds.

Seeing their daughter falling apart before their eyes, Isabella and Ferdinand finally agreed to let her go and in 1504 she returned to Flanders. The prospect of being reunited with Philip had temporarily lifted her melancholy, but it returned with a vengeance when she learned that the husband on whom she still doted had taken a mistress. Now when Juana was riled, it was always advisable to keep some distance between her and her foe – say, a hemisphere. But Philip made the error of allowing the two women to meet. Snorting fire and spitting blood, Juana grabbed a pair of scissors and hacked off her love rival's flowing locks. When the woman tried to defend herself, Juana stabbed her in the face with the scissors and ordered the hair to be chopped back to the roots. Usually one to shy away from confrontation – particularly where Juana was involved – Philip felt moved to intervene and slapped his wife around the face in an attempt to bring her to her senses. It simply had the effect of driving her to her room, where she remained for several days.

Determined to win back her man, Juana had her Moorish serving maids devise a series of love potions designed to make her irresistible, but Philip dismissed these as sorcery, had the maids sacked and ordered that Juana be confined to her room. Juana protested at her treatment by going on hunger strike, forcing Philip to relent. The pair were briefly reconciled, only for the bitter arguments to start up again within a matter of days. Her volatile nature and his unfaithfulness and lack of sensitivity were straining the marriage to breaking point. Philip became so alarmed by her behaviour that he instructed her treasurer, who was responsible for administering Juana's meagre income, to keep a diary of the queen's actions in case she was losing her mind. As was always the case with Philip, however, the move was not instigated out of concern for his troubled wife, but with a view to safeguarding his own interests.

In 1504 Queen Isabella died, allowing Juana to become Queen of Castile, but Ferdinand seized upon her delicate mental state to take control. Philip, too, had designs on her inheritance and, backed by her treasurer's notes regarding her erratic behaviour, tried to persuade Juana to hand over the reins of government to him. Thus the bemused Juana found herself in the middle of a power struggle between her father and her husband. In January 1506 Juana and Philip sailed for Spain, purportedly to enable her to claim her crown, but on arrival he entered into secret arrangements with Ferdinand with a view to power-sharing. Excluding Juana from the negotiations, they declared her mentally unfit to rule and divided the spoils between themselves. Their joint statement said of Juana: 'Should she wish to participate this would lead to the utter destruction and annihilation of our kingdom, owing to the maladies and passions which it would be indecorous to describe.'

In September of that year Philip caught a fever. Juana, pregnant again, never strayed from his bedside over the next six days as he bravely fought the illness, but in the end her tender nursing proved in vain. At 28 the man she loved with all her heart was dead. Pregnancy had always unsettled Juana but now, with the sudden death of Philip, she became completely overcome with grief.

For the remaining 49 years of her life, she wore nothing but black. Unable to bear the torture of being parted from her beloved, she refused to allow his body to be buried, declaring: 'We must remain together for eternity.' Having been separated from him for such long periods during their marriage, she resolved to make up for lost time. And at least now she knew where he was.

She did eventually agree to let Philip be buried temporarily in a monastery near Burgos but even then she had the coffin opened so that she could gaze upon him one last time. When the wrapping was removed from the corpse, she began passionately kissing its feet and had to be forcibly removed from the vault. Following the outbreak of a virulent epidemic in the Burgos region, Juana decided to move to Torquemada; naturally the coffin went too, guarded by an armed escort and travelling only by night. To ensure that she finally had him all to herself, she issued stern orders that all women and girls be kept away from the coffin. Again she opened it, this time on the pretence of ensuring that his body was still there. In death as in life she liked to check on him.

Four months after Philip's death, she gave birth to their daughter, Catalina. While she did so, Philip's coffin was placed in a nearby church. But soon Juana and her husband's coffin were off on their travels again. Over the ensuing weeks she became even more attached to it, never letting it out of her sight, whether in bed or at the dinner table; they were the ultimate odd couple. Occasionally she would lift the lid of the coffin to talk to Philip and stare lovingly at his decaying remains. However, she knew that such macabre behaviour would certainly result in the loss of her inheritance. So what should she do? Take the money or open the box?

On his return from Italy in 1509, King Ferdinand made the decision for her and had her imprisoned in the fortress palace of Tordesillas. With her older children still living in the Netherlands, Juana channelled her love into Catalina as a constant reminder of her dead husband. Not that Philip was ever far away. He was buried just outside her window, from where she would gaze at his grave for hours at a time.

Juana made sure that the young Catalina never strayed from her side. The child even slept in an alcove that could be reached only via her mother's room and was not allowed to venture beyond their quarters. With just two female servants for company, it was a miserable upbringing. Juana's frugal existence extended to her diet. Meals usually consisted of nothing more than bread and cheese, which had to be left outside the door because Juana la Loca ('Juana the Mad') as she was now known, would not eat if anyone other than her daughter were present.

When Ferdinand died in 1516, he was succeeded by Juana's eldest son, Charles V. Five years later Juana became the unwitting figurehead of a plot to unseat Charles and the rebel forces briefly released her from her imprisonment. However, she was too confused to capitalise on the situation and, suspicious as ever, refused to sign the necessary documentation. After initially siding with the rebels, she disowned them. Charles repaid her support by returning her to Tordesillas, where she would spend the rest of her life until her death in 1555 at the age of 75, kept under constant observation and forbidden to leave the palace. Indeed, the only time she left her darkened room was to attend Mass occasionally.

Now and then she would blame her predicament on evil spirits. In her more coherent moments, she would protest that she was the queen, Spain's true ruler, but by then nobody was listening to her – except, she hoped, her darling Philip, out there beneath the window.

PLAYING AT SOLDIERS

ZHENGDE, EMPEROR OF CHINA (1491–1521)

When the tenth emperor of the Ming dynasty – Zhu Houzhao, who took the name of Zhengde – came to the throne in 1506 at the age of fourteen, it was with a less-than-glowing reference. His father, Hongzhi, adored the boy but was not blind to his faults and on his deathbed urged the Grand Secretaries to look after him. For, as Hongzhi himself put it, whilst there was no doubting his son's intelligence, he also 'loved ease and pleasure', two qualities not necessarily recommended for a Chinese emperor.

The warning proved well founded. Zhengde showed minimal interest in state affairs, found organised ritual tedious, and cast aside the advice of wise officials in favour of the flattery of eunuchs. Lazily allowing the eunuchs at court to take control of government, the emperor preferred to focus on a life of leisure. He enjoyed riding, hunting, archery and music and filled the court with wrestlers, acrobats and magicians – anyone who could entertain him and take his mind off matters that required serious thought.

Whereas his father adhered strictly to the teachings of Confucius, Zhengde firmly believed in the mystical powers of wine, women and song. He was often drunk for days on end and ordered prostitutes to be brought to the palace and paraded for imperial inspection. Guards were ordered to abduct the most beautiful girls in Beijing for the emperor's use and when the production line slowed or he simply fancied a

71

change of scenery, he would sneak out of the palace – clumsily disguised – and visit the city's brothels. Although these excursions brought the court into disrepute, they also earned the emperor a reputation among his subjects as a great lover. Arguably, it was the only thing at which he excelled.

He was fascinated by fire and when a palace went up in flames during a lantern pageant, he remarked, oblivious to the tragedy unfolding before his eyes: 'What a magnificent display of fireworks.'

A shallow youth who became a shallow man, Zhengde did little more than play at being emperor. He also played at soldiers, having suddenly developed a passion for the military following a series of uprisings in the provinces. He began toying with explosives – much to the concern of the court – and took to drilling a group of eunuchs in the palace. He adopted 127 young officers as his sons, giving them the imperial family name, and promoted favoured military commanders to high posts in government, conveniently overlooking their absence of political expertise. He insisted that all at court wear military dress and, imagining himself as a fearless commander, announced that he was heading off on a dangerous campaign, which, in truth, amounted to nothing more than a camping trip. Nevertheless his officers were obliged to play along with the charade, staging a triumphant torchlight return as their glorious leader, in full military uniform, sword glistening, rode home proudly claiming that he had decapitated a barbarian. To many experienced officials, the only person losing his head was the emperor.

Zhengde then had the bright idea of sailing south down the Grand Canal in the guise of Supreme Military Commander. This extravagant gesture (140 officials were flogged, some to death, for protesting at the expense) saw him arrive in Nanjing in 1520. The joy at seeing their emperor was marred somewhat when, in one of his rare policy-making decisions, he forbade the people to raise hogs because the Chinese name for them sounded like his family name of Zhu. That just about summed up Zhengde's contribution to Chinese politics.

But his grand tour backfired when, on the return journey, the imperial boat capsized and Zhengde was taken ill, spitting blood and fainting at a ceremony. Three months later he died, having accomplished precious little of note in his fifteen-year reign.

THE BUTCHER OF NOVGOROD

IVAN IV, TSAR OF RUSSIA (1530–84)

A graduate of the Vlad the Impaler school of diplomacy, Ivan IV of Russia raised the art of barbaric cruelty to new heights. If anyone incurred his displeasure, his only dilemma was whether to have them boiled alive or roasted. His most ingenious punishments were hatched during his all-too-frequent violent rages, which, as one observer noted, turned his mind 'into the nature of a wild beast'. But to compare Ivan to a wild animal would be to risk a lawsuit from the National Association of Wolves and Bears. For even wild beasts don't kill their mate or their young.

And the Russian imperial family cannot say they weren't forewarned. When Ivan's father, Vasily III, had jettisoned his first wife in order to marry Yelena Glinskaya, the patriarch of Jerusalem had apparently told him: 'If you do this evil thing, you shall have an evil son.'

Yet it could all have turned out so differently for the man who came to be known to the world as Ivan the Terrible. An intelligent, sensitive child with an insatiable appetite for books, his mind was scarred by the atrocities that went on around him, some of them witnessed at first hand, as feuding boyars sought to capitalise on the young tsar's vulnerability by waging a bloody power struggle.

Ivan became tsar at the age of three on 3 December 1533, following the death of his father. On account of his tender years, his mother Yelena assumed control in conjunction with

74

her lover, Prince Ivan Obolensky, but only after they had seen off a challenge from the boy's uncle Yuri, who claimed the throne for himself. Yuri was thrown in a dungeon and left to starve to death. Another uncle was also eliminated but then in 1538 Yelena herself died, almost certainly poisoned. A week later Obolensky was arrested and beaten to death by his jailers. The nation was in turmoil.

The war between the rival Shuisky and Belsky families continued to escalate. Armed men rampaged through the imperial palace, often bursting into Ivan's quarters in search of enemies. Murders, beatings and rapes became part of everyday life in the Kremlin. The ruthless boyars treated the young tsar with disdain. His nurse was packed off to a convent and he was often left hungry and without clothes. Powerless to act, he took out his frustration on defenceless creatures, tearing feathers off birds, piercing their eyes and slicing open their bodies. It was a sign of things to come.

In 1539 the Shuiskys cranked up the pressure by raiding the palace and seizing most of Ivan's few remaining confidants. As a demonstration of their power, they had the loyal Fyodor Mishurin skinned alive and left on public view in a Moscow square.

The deeply traumatised Ivan sought to drown his sorrows in drink. He became increasingly unruly, joining a gang who terrorised the streets of Moscow, beating up bystanders and raping women. He loved to ride his horse full tilt into crowds of innocent Muscovites and would drop dogs and cats to their deaths from the top of the Kremlin's towers, purely for fun. Yet all the while he eagerly pursued his studies, poring over religious and historical texts for hours on end. Only too aware of his Jekyll and Hyde personality, he would sometimes bang his head repeatedly on the floor during prayer, thereby sustaining a minor scar on his forehead.

In December 1543, Ivan elected to fight fire with fire. In his first political initiative, he ordered the arrest of Prince Andrew Shuisky and had him thrown to a pack of starved hunting dogs. Another thirty rebel boyars were hung on roadside gibbets.

Other ringleaders were beheaded, thrown to the dogs or, if their crime had merely been one of insolence, had their tongues cut out. It was the only language they understood . . . even if they could no longer speak it. By acting swiftly and brutally, Ivan finally established control.

The success of the purge seemed to heighten his cruelty. Rape victims of his gang were disposed of by being hanged, strangled, buried alive or thrown to the bears. And when he went hunting, animals were not his only quarry – he grabbed the opportunity to rob and attack farmers too.

In 1547, he was crowned. One of the first tasks facing the new tsar was that of acquiring a wife, and, as befitted his status, he set his sights on finding the most desirable girl in the whole of Russia. To this end, he issued a circular to all nobles ordering them upon pain of death to send their eligible daughters to Moscow for inspection. Around 1,500 turned up, each subjected to examination by midwives to check that they were still virgins. It really was a beauty contest with a difference. Then Ivan scrutinised each girl closely – presumably rejecting those whose ambition was to travel, meet people and relieve world poverty. Eventually he was captivated by the beauty and charm of Anastasia Zahkarina Koshkina and duly married her.

Surprisingly, perhaps, in view of his method of finding his bride, Ivan grew to love Anastasia, whom he referred to affectionately as his 'little heifer'. By Ivan's standards, that was a compliment. Over the next thirteen years she bore him six children, only two of whom survived infancy, and generally had a calming effect on him. Instead of inflicting terror on a daily basis, he concentrated on working for the benefit of his country. Under wise advisers, he reduced corruption and introduced key reforms to government, the church and the army. He conquered fresh territories in the Baltic, established trade links with England and was generally perceived as a hero by his people.

However, during this spell of relative tranquillity there occurred an incident that was to shape Ivan's attitude over the remainder of his reign. In 1553 he was taken ill with a life-threatening fever and, in order to safeguard the position of his son Dmitri should he fail to pull through, he demanded that the nobles swear an oath of allegiance to the baby boy. Convinced that Ivan was on his deathbed, the majority of the boyars refused to commit themselves to the support of his family. Ivan did eventually recover but he never forgave the boyars for their treachery and resolved to set up a powerful centralised state that was capable of crushing all enemies with ruthless efficiency.

But before he could implement his new policy, his family was hit by tragedy. He and Anastasia were visiting a monastery to give thanks to God for Ivan's recovery from the illness when a nurse accidentally dropped little Dmitri into the river. The baby drowned. It is not recorded what happened to the clumsy nurse.

Ivan's cruelty began to bubble dangerously below the surface. In 1555 he ordered the construction of St Basil's Church in Moscow. Delighted with the result, he is said to have had the architects blinded so that they would never be able to design anything more beautiful. If they were flattered, they probably did not feel like expressing their gratitude.

Then in 1560 Ivan suffered another family blow. Anastasia, his calming influence, died after a long illness. Ivan broke down completely, banging his head on the floor in full view of the court and smashing furniture. Many of the boyars had opposed the marriage to Anastasia because she did not come from a titled family and now, in his desperation to blame someone for her death, his bitterness and anger were directed once more at the nobles, whom he suspected of poisoning her. Although he had no firm evidence to support his theory, this did not prevent him ordering wholesale executions.

Ivan's old rages started to return, causing him to 'foam at the mouth like a horse' and tear out his own hair. His mood swings between violence and contrition became ever more marked. In one breath he would excitedly listen to prisoners being tortured and in the next he would beat his head in penitence, praying for those whom he had mutilated and murdered.

Near the end of 1564 he suddenly quit Moscow and announced his intention to abdicate, but the populace, fearing the consequences of civil war, begged him to return. Following lengthy negotiations, Ivan, who almost certainly used the abdication ruse as a means of strengthening his hand, bowed to the people's wishes, but only on condition that he be given absolute power to punish anyone he deemed disloyal and to dispose of their estate as he desired. Ivan now had *carte blanche* to hammer the boyars into submission and even extinction.

The men chosen to carry out Ivan's reign of terror were the *Oprichniki*, a handpicked private army who had to swear a personal oath of allegiance to the tsar and were empowered to rob and torture with impunity. Dressed all in black and riding black horses, they struck fear into the heart of the sturdiest citizen; they made the most zealous members of the Spanish Inquisition look like a pack of Boy Scouts. When Ivan and his not-so-merry men approached one castle in Livonia, the occupants blew themselves up rather than fall into his hands.

Many of the *Oprichniki* were hardened criminals anyway and so they had no compunction about slaying at random. They thought nothing of bursting into a church during Mass and killing a priest before the altar. Ivan himself assisted the *Oprichniki* in executing his enemies and took a pathological delight in human suffering. Wherever he went he carried a metal-pointed staff, which he used to lash out at anyone who offended him. He set bears on people for fun, had victims plunged beneath the ice for being disrespectful (he once had several hundred beggars drowned in a lake) and had peasant women stripped naked for use as target practice by his *Oprichnik* marksmen. A chronicler described how Prince Boris Telupa, 'was drawn upon a long sharp-made stake, which entered the lower part of his body and came out of his neck, upon which he languished a horrible pain for fifteen hours alive, and spoke to his mother, brought to behold that woeful sight. And she was given to one hundred gunners, who defiled her to death, and the Emperor's hungry hounds devoured her flesh and bones.' Vlad the Impaler would have been proud of him.

Ivan's sense of humour could best be described as warped. When a group of women had the effrontery to laugh at him, he ordered them to his palace and made them undress. He then instructed his servants to throw 45 bushels of shelled peas on to the floor and watched in amusement as the naked women were forced to pick up the peas one by one. On another occasion he ordered the residents of a city to deliver to him a cart full of live fleas. After a prolonged effort and dreading the consequences, they reluctantly had to admit their failure but mentioned that they were now infested with the insects, whereupon Ivan roared with laughter and fined them 7,000 roubles. His 'jokes' were not always so kind. Once for a laugh he tipped boiling soup over a jester and when the poor man failed to see the funny side and cried out in pain, Ivan callously stabbed him to death.

The *Oprichniki* became a symbol of Ivan's brutality. He formed a quasi-monastic order with himself as the 'abbot' and them as the 'monks', but the order was nothing more than an excuse for a further round of rape and torture. Ivan would often act as master of the rituals, watching gleefully while men's ribs were ripped from their chests with razor-sharp, red-hot pincers.

Such was his paranoia that even Ivan's closest advisers were not exempt from the butchery. Members of his own councils whom he suspected of colluding with enemies abroad were savagely slain. The imperial chancellor, Ivan Viskovaty, was strung up on a gallows while members of the *Oprichniki* took turns to hack pieces off his body, starting from the ear. And the royal treasurer, Nikita Funikov, was tortured to death by being doused alternately in boiling and cold water until his skin peeled away.

But Ivan reserved his most monstrous atrocity for the citizens of Novgorod. Suspecting that they were about to hand the city over to the Poles, he conducted a brutal purge of the townsfolk. First he built a wooden fence around the city to prevent escape and then he erected an execution platform. He singled out the city's archbishop for special treatment, having him sewn into a bearskin and then hunted to his death by a pack of hounds. A thousand people a day were executed and when this proved too slow for Ivan's liking, he ordered mass drownings in the Volkhov River. Men, women and children were tied to sleighs, which were then run into the freezing waters. Any who managed to break free and surface were pushed back under the ice with long poles. Almost the entire population of 50,000 were killed in this way, the sheer mass of corpses causing the river to flood its banks. Later the city of Pskov suffered a similar fate.

And yet this cruellest of tyrants still insisted on having a bedtime story read to him every night and kept three infirm old men on the payroll to act as storytellers.

In 1572, to the relief of all Russians, he suddenly disbanded the *Oprichniki*. In the same year, he curiously abdicated for a second time and placed one of his generals, Simeon Bekboelatovitch, on the throne while he himself retired to a country estate. After paying frequent visits to Moscow to pay homage to the new tsar, however, Ivan changed his mind once more and resumed power.

His unpredictable behaviour mirrored his unstable home life. He is thought to have married a total of eight wives, four of whom died before him (one on his orders) and two of whom were banished to convents. A year after the death of his beloved Anastasia, he married Maria Temrukovna but she soon died. When it came to choosing a third wife in 1569, Ivan's reputation had become such that the young girl he picked promptly collapsed and died from shock at the dread of meeting him! Instead he married a merchant's daughter, Martha Sobakina, who died two weeks later, either from poisoning (according to Ivan) or as a result of her husband's excessively physical foreplay (according to some other sources). His fourth bride, Anna Koltovskaya, was accused of conspiracy and despatched to a monastery while the fifth, Anna Vasilchikova, mysteriously disappeared. She was replaced by Vasilisa Meleteva, who made the mistake of taking a lover, Prince Ivan Devtelev. When Ivan learned of the betrayal, he had the prince impaled on a stake beneath Vasilisa's bedroom window. She could count herself lucky to be sent to a convent. His seventh wife, Maria Dolgorukaya, was less fortunate and on discovering that his bride was not a virgin, Ivan had her drowned the day after the wedding. His final wife, Maria Nagaya, whom he married in 1581, went on to outlive him.

That year witnessed an incident that was to haunt even the tsar. Over the years friends had come and gone (often to the scaffold), as had wives, but he had always maintained a reasonably close relationship with his eldest son Ivan, who had watched enthusiastically at Novgorod while his father speared defenceless bystanders to death. Then in November 1581 the tsar flew into one of his terrible rages, the object of his venom being young Ivan's third wife, the pregnant Yelena. Objecting to the clothes she was wearing, the tsar knocked her to the ground and began kicking her, whereupon young Ivan rushed to her defence, only to be felled by a blow to the head from the heavy iron staff that his father always carried. Yelena lost the baby and young Ivan lay in a coma with a fractured skull. He died a few days later. The tsar was so overcome with grief at his actions that he banged his head violently against the coffin and started tearing out his own hair and beard.

With his long straggly white hair and hunched figure, Ivan looked considerably older than his years. His body had swollen and his skin was peeling off, emitting a vile smell. He had become addicted to mercury, which was kept bubbling in a cauldron in his room, and which may have contributed to his aggression.

In 1584 he was taken seriously ill. He summoned sixty astrologers to predict the exact date of his death and was told that he would die on 18 March. On 17 March, with Ivan seemingly on the road to recovery, he warned them that if they were wrong about the date, he would have them burned to death. There must therefore have been a collective sigh of relief when he suddenly collapsed and died the following day as he was preparing for a game of chess.

His violent temper meant that he was succeeded not by the capable Ivan but by the feeble-minded Fyodor. But surely the greatest irony was that a man responsible for so many acts of torture and slaughter should die while contemplating which pawn to move. It was the one time in his life when 'taking the bishop' did not have murderous connotations.

LOVE'S LABOUR'S LOST

ERIC XIV, KING OF SWEDEN (1533–77)

Until 1520 Sweden had been under Danish rule but in that year Gustav Vasa led a nobles' rebellion against the cruel Danish king Christian II. As a result Gustav was installed as the first king of an independent Sweden and became a national hero, revered for his strength and wisdom. He did have a darker side, though, and sometimes exhibited a homicidal temper. Dagger in hand, he once chased a terrified secretary round the castle courtyard and when a goldsmith took a day off without seeking permission, the king beat him so savagely that the man died. Even so, Gustav Vasa was a tough act to follow.

That task fell to his 27-year-old son Eric, a scholarly sort who unfortunately inherited his father's black moods but not his ability. In the end, the duties of monarchy proved too much for him.

For Eric was a paranoid schizophrenic with a bee fixation. Apart from getting a buzz out of keeping insects, he was a fluent linguist and an accomplished lute player who also composed music. He was also passionate about astrology and allowed himself to be guided by the stars.

Like England, Sweden was a Protestant country and this persuaded Gustav Vasa to try and marry his eldest son to the young English princess Elizabeth. Accordingly, Eric's tutor, Dionysius Beurreus, was sent to London in 1557 to open marriage negotiations, arguing that a union between the two nations would be beneficial for trade. However, Elizabeth's fiercely Catholic sister, Queen Mary, had no time for Protestants and was furious that the envoy approached Elizabeth before her. So she rejected the idea on her sister's behalf.

The following year Elizabeth succeeded Mary as Queen of England, prompting renewed optimism from the Swedes, but she politely but firmly informed Gustav Vasa that she could not marry his son because God had imbued her mind with such a love of celibacy that she could not possibly allow herself to be diverted from that path. At least she didn't say she was washing her hair.

A despairing Eric promptly wrote back insisting that he loved her . . . despite the fact that they had yet to meet. He was nothing if not persistent and forced Elizabeth to repeat her rebuttal six months later to the Swedish ambassador. Eric then sent his half-brother John to reason with her but his pleas, too, fell on deaf ears. Eric now decided that the only solution was to meet Elizabeth in person. His father consented to the trip but on 29 September 1560, just as Eric was about to set sail, Gustav was inconsiderate enough to die. Although his heart lay across the North Sea, Eric felt obliged to remain in his homeland for his coronation, but as soon as he was crowned, he left on his voyage of discovery. Alas, halfway to England a terrible storm broke, and the journey had to be abandoned. Was God trying to tell him something?

Eric was haunted by his father's shadow from the very start, his desperation to be a worthy successor undermined by his own paranoia and insecurity. As king, he demanded to be taken seriously – his coronation was an extravagant spectacle – but his inferiority complex and deep-rooted suspicion led him to believe that people were constantly laughing at him behind his back. He saw conspiracies everywhere. If anyone smiled or whispered in his presence, Eric thought he was being ridiculed. An ill-timed cough was seen as a clear sign of plotting while a sudden movement or gesture could send him flying into a rage. He ordered the execution of two of his guards simply because they had placed a jug, a cloak and a halter in the royal privy 'to annoy the king'. For hours on end, he roamed the corridors of the royal castle looking for someone to berate. Smartly dressed servants and pages were put to the sword because Eric concluded that they were 'obviously intent on seducing the ladies of the court'. The king was a restless spirit.

Central to his desire for respect was the securing of a suitable royal bride. Despite Elizabeth being far from overwhelmed by his advances (she wasn't even whelmed), he became dangerously obsessed with winning her hand. Saddened though he was by the abortive voyage, he thought that at least it would have shown Elizabeth that he was serious in his intentions, and he vowed to try again the following spring. In this respect, he was encouraged by his envoy in London, Nils Gyllenstierna, who told him how excited Elizabeth was about his impending visit. This was not so much an exaggeration as an outright lie. Nevertheless, the English public were sure that a royal wedding was in the offing and London street traders, ever alert to a business opportunity, began selling commemorative woodcuts depicting Elizabeth and Eric side by side on separate thrones. Eric played his part by sending Elizabeth tender love letters in Latin, but she remained singularly unmoved. A lot of woodcuts would remain unsold.

Now that it appeared that his finest prose had turned the queen's stomach rather than her head, Eric suspected that someone must be poisoning her mind against him. His paranoia settled on the queen's favourite, Robert Dudley, Earl of Leicester, and he became so jealous of Dudley that he considered challenging him to a duel. Fortunately, Gyllenstierna managed to convince Eric that such behaviour was unbecoming of a monarch.

Eric was starting to get desperate. He had marriage contracts drawn up, but still received nothing remotely akin to a favourable response. He then embarked on an insane course of action designed to make Elizabeth jealous by suddenly opening negotiations for the hand of her detested cousin, Mary, Queen of Scots. Not surprisingly, this hardly endeared him to Elizabeth.

When his move for Mary failed, the luckless Eric turned to Christina, daughter of the German prince Philip of Hesse.

Meanwhile, in the hope of keeping his options open with Elizabeth, he wrote to the English queen explaining that he had approached Mary not for himself but for his half-brother John, and that his attempt to woo Christina was simply to test Elizabeth's love. It is highly doubtful whether such a witless strategy would have impressed Elizabeth had she received the letter, but any speculation was rendered immaterial when the missive containing these sentiments was intercepted by Eric's enemies, the Danes, who promptly sent it to Philip of Hesse. Outraged to read that his darling daughter was, at best, third choice in Eric's affections, Philip wasted no time in marrying her off to Adolf of Holstein. As a final insult, Philip promised to 'wipe the Swedish noses in the dust'. Eric had now succeeded in alienating half of the eligible princesses in Europe.

Despite not receiving one ounce of encouragement, Eric refused to take the hint and persisted with his fruitless attempts to seduce Elizabeth in writing. But by now she had tired of his flattery and sought other diversions to amuse herself.

Eric's schizophrenia was worsening. When John, whom he had always resented for being his father's favourite, defied him by marrying a Polish princess and invading Livonia, he was imprisoned and his servants were executed. Strangely, Eric now became convinced that he had been deposed and was being held captive by John, whereas in truth it was the other way round. When John was eventually released, the two men knelt to each other, Eric thinking that he was John's prisoner and John that Eric was his master!

Meanwhile Eric continued to suspect the nobles of plotting against him . . . if only because the stars told him. Having been advised by his trusted astrologers that the Swedish crown might be conferred on a 'light-haired man' (a description that fitted most of Sweden), Eric felt that it pointed to Nils Sture, one of the most powerful nobles in the land . . . despite the fact that Sture's hair was actually ginger. Eric blamed the nobles for sabotaging his efforts to marry a foreign princess and when Sture was involved in a failed attempt to marry the king to Christina of Lorraine, he became even more convinced that the aristocracy was plotting against him. Unconcerned by the total lack of evidence, he ordered the arrest of a number of nobles who were sentenced to death. Nils Sture and his father Svante were thrown in prison and charged with treason.

Eric then summoned the Swedish estates to a crucial meeting, at which he intended to demonstrate once and for all that he was not a man to be trifled with. Sadly, he lost the notes of his speech and immediately blamed his scheming servants for stealing the speech in a bid to discredit him. His paranoia was now rampant. Even the bogeyman was after him.

In May 1566 Eric announced that he was going to seek reconciliation with the Stures at Uppsala Castle. Instead he went straight to the cell where Nils Sture was imprisoned and, without saying a word, stabbed him to death. He then ordered the guards to kill all the other prisoners immediately except for 'Herr Sten'. No one knew who he meant but Sten Leijonhufvud and Sten Baner were spared. Meanwhile, Eric had run from the castle, jumped on his horse and ridden off into the nearby woods to escape imaginary attackers. Sensing that all was not right with the king, his loyal ex-tutor, Dionysius Beurreus, followed him in an attempt to calm him down. But Eric suddenly turned on him and stabbed him to death. Horseless, Eric wandered alone through the woods. Filled with remorse, he hid for a couple of days before attempting to make amends by arranging a grand funeral for the Stures. For the next few months the king was afflicted by mental depression and withdrew to the Castle of Svartsjö, outside Stockholm, completely neglecting affairs of state.

Unable to obtain a royal bride, Eric had embarked on an affair with a commoner, Karin Mansdolter. In 1568 they married and he had her crowned as his queen in July of that year. The nobles were outraged at what they perceived as a snub to their own daughters, while Eric thought that people were laughing at him over his choice of bride.

Queen Karin did not have long to enjoy her new-found status. Before the year was out, the nobles had deposed Eric and proclaimed John as the new king of Sweden. Early in 1569 Eric stood trial for his crimes. He denied that he had ruled tyrannically but the nobles insisted that his periodic insanity was merely a cover for his misdeeds and he was formally deposed and imprisoned along with his wife and son. Over the next few years Eric was kept in increasingly harsh conditions and, separated from his family, descended into total madness. Even so, as long as he remained alive, he represented a threat to the king until, in 1577, John had Eric poisoned with arsenic mixed in his pea soup – a murder apparently sanctioned by leading members of the Swedish parliament, the Riksdag. The official statement simply said that he had died 'after a long illness'.

Eric never did leave the mark on Swedish history that he had hoped, but with his insecurity and mental illness his reign was doomed from the outset. If only his astrologers had been able to warn him in advance . . .

WILD CHILD

DON CARLOS, PRINCE OF SPAIN (1545–68)

The Spanish prince Don Carlos did not enjoy the most auspicious of starts in life. His grandmother, Juana the Mad, was still imprisoned in the palace of Tordesillas, his mother, Maria Manuela, died four days after his difficult birth, and he himself was born seriously deformed. This may have helped to explain why he developed into a troublesome youth who enjoyed torturing animals and children and would fly into a furious, homicidal rage at the slightest upset. He was not someone to beat at medieval Scrabble.

His young father, Philip II of Spain, had been married to Maria for barely a year when she fell pregnant. The birth was painful and problematic, the situation exacerbated by the fact that the delivery was supervised by an inexperienced midwife. Maria survived just a matter of days and when physicians examined the baby Don Carlos, they did not expect him to reach adulthood either. For he was born with one shoulder higher than the other, a withered right hand, a spindly right leg that was noticeably shorter than the left, and a hunched back. Nor was he blessed with a strong constitution. He had a sickly, pallid complexion and was prone to fevers. In later years he sought to remedy this frailty by eating vast amounts.

Philip was a distant father – physically and emotionally. He spent much of his time abroad and when he was at home, he was cold and austere – a fanatical Catholic more interested in honing the technique of the Spanish Inquisition than in casting any affection in the direction of his shambling, stuttering son. As a result Don Carlos withdrew into himself with just his governess, the devout Leonor de Mascareñas, for company. Philip's youngest sister Joanna took over the regency during the king's foreign jaunts, but even her patience and charm failed to penetrate the boy's defence mechanism.

Don Carlos had given notice of intent at an early age. When he was three he used to delight in biting the breasts of his wet-nurses and at least three of them nearly died from the wounds he inflicted. He was not able to talk until the age of five and even then he did so falteringly (apart from his severe stammer, he could not pronounce the letters 'r' and 'l') and in a somewhat effeminate tone. He could have been bullied mercilessly, but Don Carlos was determined to get his retaliation in first.

By the time he was nine he had perfected his cruel streak, torturing little girls, servants and especially animals. He would roast small animals alive, maim dogs' genitals and he even bit the head off a harmless ring-snake. His temper became sadistic and uncontrollable. Once he sneaked into a stable and lashed out at the horses, causing such appalling injuries that twenty of them had to be put down. On another occasion he took a liking to a horse of which the king was particularly fond and persuaded Philip's master of the horse to let him ride it. He then rode the animal so cruelly that it died of its wounds. Grandparents traditionally dote on their grandchildren but the Emperor Charles V could not help but make an exception in the case of Don Carlos, describing him as, 'A very turbulent young man; his manners and his humour do not please me.' The Venetian ambassador did not pull his punches either, calling Don Carlos 'ugly and unpleasing', and adding: 'When he passed from infancy to puberty, he took no pleasure in study nor in arms nor in horsemanship nor in any virtuous things, honest and pleasant, but only in doing harm to others.' It was hard to argue with these assessments.

Lacking both maternal love and paternal discipline, Don Carlos ran wild . . . although running became an increasingly difficult task once he had decided that the way to improve his frail health was by eating vast amounts. Devouring food with an enthusiasm usually only seen on the plains of the Serengeti, he put on weight at a considerable rate. Sadly, his appetite for food was not matched not by his appetite for learning. He never recovered from his slow start to life and, despite assurances from courtiers that the Habsburg children were always late developers, Philip soon realised that his wilful son had no interest in education. And there was more chance of Philip turning Protestant than of getting Don Carlos to do something he didn't want to.

One of Don Carlos's favourite pastimes was ordering young girls to be whipped in his presence, as a result of which the royal court was obliged to pay regular sums of compensation to the girls' irate fathers. Such behaviour hardly indicated that he would make a great catch for a wealthy princess but in those days political expedience, rather than any suggestion of attraction, was the sole criterion for most high-level marriages. For that at least, Don Carlos had reason to be grateful. However, not only was the heir to the Spanish throne physically unappealing and mentally repellent, but court gossip hinted that he was impotent to boot. Around 1556, the eleven-year-old misfit was touted around Europe in the hope of being paired with a likely bride. Among the names mentioned was his cousin, the Archduchess Anna of Austria, but, along with every other eligible European princess, she apparently managed to find a get-out clause.

Rebuffed by royalty, Don Carlos lowered his standards and began scouring the streets in the hope of picking up a girl. Most found themselves fulfilling nothing more than his masochistic fantasies. By 1562, he had finally agreed to go to university, but probably more in the hope of collecting women than a proper education. There he formed a strong passion for the daughter of one of the servants, but any hopes of a relationship were ended when he suffered a crashing fall down a flight of stairs, the impact opening up a hideous head wound and knocking him unconscious. As his condition worsened dramatically, his head swelled to gigantic proportions and he started raving deliriously. The physicians bled him over and over again but he was not expected to survive. Philip rushed to his bedside and prayed for a recovery, and, through a miracle attributed to a religious relic brought by a group of Franciscan monks, Don Carlos stabilised and slowly began to respond. Within two months he was able to walk – albeit unsteadily – into the next room but the blow had made him even more deranged than before. At first this manifested itself in long silences, punctuated by nonsensical questions, before giving way to tantrums and rages of renewed intensity.

During these bouts of unrestrained fury, Don Carlos would attack his servants and even high-ranking court officials. On one occasion he tried to hurl a member of staff out of a window; another time he launched a ferocious dagger attack on a cardinal, forcing the churchman to sink to his knees and beg for mercy. He also menaced the Duke of Alba with a sword and was only prevented from carrying out his threat when the duke managed to disarm him. Anyone who annoyed him was liable to the most violent retribution. When water thrown from the balcony of a house accidentally splashed him, he immediately ordered the culprits to be executed. And a poor shoemaker who presented Don Carlos with a pair of boots that did not meet with his approval was forced to cut up the boots and eat them!

Two years after the near-fatal accident, plans were afoot to revive the proposed marriage to the Archduchess Anna. But to see whether he would make a suitable husband (in other words one capable of providing an heir) it was first decided to try and cure him of his believed impotence. Physicians and apothecaries prescribed a series of treatments, at the end of which Don Carlos was subjected to a physical test to prove his manhood. This involved procuring the services of a young girl, who was rewarded with the gift of a house for herself and her mother plus a cash prize in return for spending some quality time in the prince's bedchamber. Although Don Carlos then rushed to the Austrian delegation to boast that he had passed the test 'five times over', the medics remained unconvinced. Anna must have been a relieved archduchess for, as the French ambassador noted of Don Carlos: 'He is usually so mad and furious that everyone here pities the lot of the woman who will have to live with him.'

Following the abdication of Charles V, Philip now ruled the Netherlands and parts of Italy as well as Spain. And Don Carlos was his heir. Naturally the prospect of a raving madman undoing all his good work caused Philip considerable disquiet. The Spanish Empire could have been wiped out at a stroke.

Frustrated at being sidelined from state affairs and at seeing his dreams of ruling over the Netherlands diminishing with each passing scandal, Don Carlos started to develop an intense dislike of his father. In December 1567 Philip decided to test the water by allowing Don Carlos to preside over the state council. Instead, Don Carlos seized the opportunity to try and involve his illegitimate uncle, Don Juan, in a plot against Philip, but Don Juan informed the king. Philip's suspicions intensified when Don Carlos told his confessor that he wanted to kill someone. The intended victim was interpreted – rightly or wrongly – as being his father. When Philip rushed back to Madrid and held an emergency meeting with his advisers, Don Carlos feared the worst.

Alarmed for his own safety, he employed a French engineer, Louis de Foix, to build a device that enabled him to open and shut the door to his chamber from his bed. A weight was placed on top of the door to crush any intruder to death. He also kept a battery of weapons in his room for protection. However, these safeguards were unable to prevent Philip from forcing an entry. Through the darkness, Don Carlos was just able to make out the figure of his father (wearing full armour) in company with his adviser and confessor. Falling to his knees in abject surrender, Don Carlos begged the king to kill him. When Philip showed no sign of doing so, Don Carlos tried to throw himself on to the fire and had to be forcibly restrained. 'If you kill yourself,' snapped Philip icily, 'that will be the act of a madman.' To which Don Carlos replied, in a line that has led to his portrayal as a tragic antihero, 'I am not mad but desperate.'

Philip could see that Don Carlos was now beyond salvation
and had him incarcerated in the dark forbidding tower of
Arévalo Castle, shut off from the outside world. The king
decided that his son no longer existed – nobody was permitted
to talk about, or even pray for, Don Carlos. The Florentine
envoy remarked: 'The prince of Spain is so forgotten that he
appears truly never to have been in this world.' And a foreign
ambassador commented: 'They speak of the prince as if he
were dead.'

In a private letter to the Pope, Philip explained his actions:

*It has been God's will that the Prince should have such great
and numerous defects, partly mental, partly due to his physical
condition, utterly lacking as he is in the qualifications
necessary for ruling, I saw the grave risks which would arise
were he to be given the succession and the obvious danger
that would accrue; and therefore, after long and careful
consideration, and having tried every alternative in vain, it
was clear that there was little or no prospect of his condition
improving in time to prevent the evils which could reasonably
be foreseen.*

Involuntary isolation did little for Don Carlos's mental state.
The man who loved his food went on hunger strikes and had to
be force-fed with soup. He tried to take his own life by
swallowing various objects, including a diamond ring because
he thought diamonds were poisonous. In the summer of 1568
he was accused of plotting to kill the king and of conspiring to
take over as sovereign of Flanders. Refused any opportunity of
defending himself, he was inevitably found guilty of treason
and sentenced to death. Concerned about public opinion,
Philip was reluctant to approve the execution, hoping instead
that if his strict diet were relaxed, Don Carlos would quickly eat
himself to death.

A week or so later Don Carlos was seized with a raging fever
marked by incessant vomiting. On a baking hot Madrid day he
ordered a layer of ice to be placed on his bed so that he might

lie naked on it. Snow was brought in to keep him cool. For days he ate only fruit but then, feeling a little stronger, he asked for something savoury and was brought a huge chunk of paté, made from four partridges. Unable to resist the temptation set before him, he devoured the lot, washing it down with over ten litres of iced water. He was immediately taken violently ill once more. When the last sacrament was administered, he vomited the host. On 24 July Don Carlos's troubled life came to an end. The official line was that he had 'died of his own excesses', but many suspected that his food had been slowly poisoned on the orders of his father.

The tragic story of Don Carlos has subsequently been romanticised in literature and opera, and Philip II's attempts to airbrush his always difficult, and often violent, son from history have rebounded on him. For in the long term the temperamental and perhaps wronged prince will invariably attract more sympathy than the cold-hearted king.

THE BLOOD COUNTESS

ERZSÉBET BÁTHORY, COUNTESS OF TRANSYLVANIA (1560–1614)

A member of the Hungarian royal family, Erzsébert Báthory has entered European folklore as a bloodsucking vampire who slaughtered some 650 young women in order to improve her complexion and seek to maintain a failing grasp on her youth and vitality. Whilst these stories may have been slightly exaggerated, there seems little doubt that she was a cruel woman whose mistreatment of her staff resulted in a number of unexplained deaths.

As a niece of the King of Poland and Prince of Transylvania, Erzsébert enjoyed a privileged upbringing, although some of her other relatives were less desirable. An uncle was said to be addicted to rituals and worshipping Satan; her aunt Klara was a sadomasochistic bisexual who enjoyed torturing servants; and her brother was a drunkard and lecher. They made the Munsters look like the Waltons. As a child, Erzsébet witnessed the torture and execution of a gypsy who was sewn up inside a horse and left to die there. Whereas most children would have viewed the incident as a horrific nightmare, she saw it as an inspiration.

Her appearance belied her nature. She was tall and beautiful with delicate features and a gloriously creamy complexion, so stunning that it was often remarked upon. She had long dark hair, a voluptuous figure and amber eyes that were described as almost catlike. She was a fit and active girl and learned to read and write in Hungarian, Greek, Latin and German.

At the age of ten she was officially engaged to the wealthy Count Ferenc Nadasdy and was sent to live at Castle Sarvar with her future mother-in-law. In 1574 Erzsébet was rumoured to have given birth to an illegitimate daughter fathered by a peasant boy, but the baby was smuggled away. The following year, when she was fifteen, Erzsébet duly married Count Nadasdy and consequently became the lady of Csejthe Castle, a gloomy fortress situated high in Transylvania's Carpathian Mountains. Ferenc was not given to domesticity and spent much of his time away fighting the Turks, leaving his wife to amuse herself as she pleased. In his absence, she played with fashionable sex toys imported from Italy and she bleached her hair in the Venetian fashion. More alarmingly, she began experimenting with herbal brews, potions, powders and drugs, and welcomed those who shared her unusual interests into her home. Among her lodgers at the castle were people claiming to be witches, sorcerers, seers, wizards and alchemists who taught her their crafts in intimate detail.

She became increasingly fascinated by black magic and torture, paying particular attention to a device used occasionally by her husband to extract information from Turkish prisoners – a pair of silver claw-like pincers, which, when fastened to a stout whip, would rip human flesh to shreds. Ferenc, a hardened soldier known as the 'Black Bey', was so appalled by the contraption that he left it behind at the castle before setting off on his next adventure. His wife did not share such inhibitions and would soon put it to evil use.

She paid regular visits to weird Aunt Klara, who introduced her to the delights of women's orgies and flagellation. Above all, Erzsébet relished the opportunity to inflict pain on others and, equipped with her husband's heinous silver claws, began pleasuring herself at the expense of the miserable debtors from her own dungeons. The more shrill their screams and the more copious the blood, the more orgasmic her amusement. She preferred to whip her naked victims on the front of their bodies so that she could watch their faces contort in pain. Her sadistic leanings were encouraged by

Dorothea Szentes (also known as Dorka), a servant at the castle. In a letter to her husband, the countess wrote of a trick she had learned to (allegedly) put a curse on a foe: 'Dorka has taught me a lovely new one. Catch a black hen and beat it to death with a white cane. Keep the blood and smear a little of it on your enemy. If you get no chance to smear it on his body, obtain one of his garments and smear it.'

With the help of three trusted female servants and a retarded manservant named Ficzko, Erzsébet rounded up buxom servant girls at the castle to fulfil her latest fantasies. She had a ferocious temper and used the slightest mistake by a girl employee as an excuse to inflict terrible corporal punishment. The countess called it 'discipline' but it was nothing more than gratuitous sadism. Taken to an underground room known as 'her Ladyship's torture chamber', girls were whipped until they bled and then thrashed with stinging nettles. Among her implements of punishment were branding irons, razors, torches, knives, molten wax and, of course, the silver pincers. She sewed up the mouth of one girl who chattered too much while another was stripped naked, covered with honey and bound to a tree where she was left at the mercy of woodland insects. Beatings with a heavy club became commonplace and indeed almost preferable to some of the punishments administered. Whenever Erzsébet suspected a servant of stealing money, she would make her undress before burning her body with red-hot coins. Often she would stick sharp pins into the girls' lips and under their fingernails or drag them out into the snow where she or her partners-in-crime would pour cold water on their bodies until they froze to death. There was rarely a week without a 'Situations Vacant' advertisement at Csejthe Castle.

In 1604 Ferenc died, and Erzsébet, now in her early forties, started to fear the passing of time. The mirror showed that the years had taken their toll on her appearance and to a vain and beautiful woman this came as a mortal blow. At first she tried to conceal her decline through cosmetics and fine clothes but these would not cover the spreading wrinkles. One day it is said that a servant girl was attending to Erzsébet's hair when she committed some minor misdemeanour, as a result of which the countess reacted with characteristic fury, slapping the girl with such force that blood spurted from her nose. The blood also splashed on to Erzsébet's face and when she later looked in the mirror, she was convinced that in the areas where the girl's blood had dropped, her skin somehow looked younger and fresher. At the suggestion of a member of her close entourage, a sinister woman by the name of Anna Darvulia, Erzsébet apparently came to believe that bathing in the blood of young virgins would restore her youth. According to legend, the countess had her torturers kidnap young virgins, slash them with knives and collect their blood in a large vat. She then took a bath in their blood. In the case of a really beautiful girl, the countess would actually drink some of the blood. Occasionally she would attack the girls with her teeth, biting chunks of bloody flesh from their necks, cheeks and shoulders. Erzsébet Báthory was, it seemed, a vampire.

Whilst there is some dispute as to the precise nature of the countess' bloodlust, there is no doubt that the death rate among her servants was alarmingly high. She procured peasant girls by inducing their poverty-stricken fathers to send them off to 'a life of security in the service of the mighty House of Báthory'. Instead of a career with prospects, the girls could look forward to having their genitals burned with candle flames or a red-hot poker. At her house in Vienna, the countess installed a new torture device – a cylindrical iron cage suspended from the ceiling. The girl was placed inside the cage and as it was raised, a series of spiked hoops contracted mechanically, piercing the captive and condemning her to a slow, agonising death.

Despite the rapid turnover of peasant girls, Erzsébet was unable to stop the ageing process. Erzsi Majorova, a widow whom she had befriended from a neighbouring town, told her that she was using the wrong type of blood and that the virgins should be of noble birth. So from 1609 she began taking in aristocratic girls, 25 at a time, 'to teach them social graces'. The girls suffered the same fate as their impoverished predecessors, but for the first time the countess became careless and during a frenzy of lust, four bodies drained of blood were thrown over the castle walls. Before the blunder could be rectified, the villagers had collected and identified the bodies. In fact, a village priest had begun to suspect the awful truth about the mysterious disappearance of so many local girls when Countess Báthory ordered him to bury some bloodless corpses in secret. The authorities were notified and in December 1610 Erzsébet's cousin, Count Thurzó, arrived at Csejthe Castle to arrest her and her accomplices. The underground torture chamber was discovered . . . piled high with the mutilated bodies of young girls.

The trial opened in January 1611 but because of the countess's rank it was held behind closed doors and she never attended, choosing instead to remain at the castle and admitting nothing. Balkan law at that time permitted a mistress to do as she wished with her servants and so the prosecution focused on the treatment of the girls of noble birth. Tortured into confession, her accomplices described how fifty girls had died of mistreatment. One witness testified that one some days the countess had naked girls laid flat on the floor of her bedroom and tortured them so much that the blood could be scooped up by the bucketful. To conceal the pools of blood, the countess ordered the servants to bring up cinders. One young maid who did not endure the tortures well and died very quickly was dismissed by the countess in her diary with the comment: 'She was too small.' Another witness recounted how Erzsébet would sink her teeth into girls' breasts and bite off chunks of flesh. Most sensationally of all, one witness, identified only as 'the maiden Zusanna', revealed a register in the countess's chest of drawers and in her own handwriting that put the overall death toll at 650.

All of the accused were found guilty as charged. The wicked Darvulia had died before the start of the trial but two other female accomplices (Helena Jo and Dorothea Szentes) had their fingers torn from their hands by red-hot pincers before being burned at the stake as witches. The authorities ensured that the punishment fitted the crime. The manservant Ficzko got off lightly – he was merely decapitated because of his comparative youth and complicity in fewer crimes. Erzsi Majorova was eventually tracked down and she, too, was executed.

Purely because of her royal status, Erzsébet Báthory was never convicted of any crime, but she was ordered to be kept in the confines of a cramped tower room at her castle for the rest of her days with just a slit or two in the walls to allow for air and the passage of basic food and water. On 21 August 1614 one of her jailers, wanting to obtain a close look at her out of curiosity, peered through the hole in her cell and saw her lying face down on the floor. The Blood Countess was dead.

The unreliability of many of the witnesses at the trial means that it is impossible to say for certain whether Erzsébet Báthory deliberately murdered hundreds of young girls or whether they died accidentally as a result of her hideous punishments. Either way, she was not exactly the most considerate of employers.

A GOVERNMENT HEALTH WARNING

MURAD IV, SULTAN OF TURKEY (1612–40)

Contrary to popular belief, no sooner had tobacco arrived in Europe than there was firm evidence that smoking could seriously damage your health. At least it could in Turkey. For the manic Sultan Murad IV ordered that anyone caught smoking should be executed on the spot and their body left where it lay as a deterrent to others. Perhaps not surprisingly Murad's legislation had a more profound effect than a few words on a packet.

It was not just the man in the street who was at risk. Even on the battlefield Murad would punish any of his own soldiers caught smoking by having them beheaded or hanged and quartered, their corpses left to rot in no-man's-land. Consequently, the sultan often represented a greater danger to his army than the enemy. And when he caught one of the palace gardeners and the gardener's wife lighting up, Murad ordered their legs to be amputated and had the two miscreants wheeled through the streets till they bled to death.

In truth there were a lot of things that Murad didn't like. He was one of the least tolerant rulers in history. He once had a party of female picnickers drowned because they were making too much noise; he had a musician beheaded for playing a Persian tune; and he ordered the hanging of a man who had added an extra storey to his house because Murad thought the extension was to enable him to peer over the palace walls into the sultan's harem. He also banned the consumption of alcohol

101

and coffee throughout the Ottoman Empire, once again on pain of death. But here there was a certain method in his madness, as coffee houses, wine shops and taverns were meeting places where, in Murad's suspicious eyes, dissidents could meet to criticise the government. Yet whilst coffee drinkers, alcohol consumers and smokers faced instant execution, Murad himself indulged in all three pastimes – often in the company of favoured Persians! The word 'hypocrite' springs to mind.

Murad became sultan at the age of eleven following the second dethronement of his insane uncle, Mustafa I. His youth left him under the influence of his domineering mother, Sultana Kösem, who sought total control over him, even encouraging him to sleep with boys in the hope that no woman would ever take her place in his life. Murad struggled with his sexuality for the rest of his days and his resentment of his mother probably triggered his violent behaviour towards women.

Although crowned in 1623, political intrigue, wars and widespread revolts prevented him exercising his full prerogative for another nine years. His half-brother, Sultan Osman II, had been assassinated by the janissaries – the sultan's elite infantry corps – in 1622. When, in 1631, they again broke into the royal palace, killing the Grand Vezir (the Turkish equivalent of a prime minister), the Grand Mufti (the senior religious leader), Murad's favourite page and thirteen other high officials, he was forced into appointing a Grand Vezir of their choice. However, within six months Murad had flexed his military muscles and taken full command of the government. He had the unwanted Grand Vezir executed and took revenge on the army by ordering the strangulation of over 500 of their leaders. No fewer than 20,000 revolutionaries in Anatolia were executed and, with the sultan's spies scouring the streets of Constantinople, many more rebel leaders were murdered on the spot. Murad had made his mark.

A powerful, dark-eyed figure who emphasised his menace by wearing black silk, Murad lacked any form of finesse. In some respects he was little more than a savage, but his bravery in battle and cruel domestic regime made him a national hero and helped restore royal authority after years of unrest. Following the siege of Baghdad in 1638 he slaughtered 30,000 soldiers and a similar number of civilians before proceeding in triumph through Constantinople, trailed by the humiliated captured Persian chiefs in chains. As a demonstration of his power, it was awesome.

Murad consolidated his position by having most of his brothers killed, including his younger brother Bayezid, who committed the cardinal sin of defeating the sultan in a joust by knocking him off his horse. A proud sportsman, Murad did not take kindly to defeat, seeing it as a personal affront to his position, and shortly afterwards, in an act prompted purely by revenge and spite, he ordered the slaying of his popular sibling.

Invoking an ancient royal prerogative, which apparently allowed the sultan to do anything he pleased, Murad set himself a target of killing ten people a day. For this purpose he carried an arquebus (a portable gun) to take pot shots at passers-by, particularly those who strayed too close to his bedroom window. Sometimes he would wander the streets incognito in company with his chief executioner Kara Ali, looking for people to murder. Once he had found a suitable victim, he would select the tool best suited to the job. If he could not find a good club or nail on the executioner's belt, he would settle for a canister that contained powder for blinding. Before long, corpses hung at every street corner. In the early years of his reign, he focused his attentions on known troublemakers but as he became increasingly power-crazed and addicted to alcohol, he simply killed people for fun, cutting down anybody who irritated him. Wearing a loud shirt in a public place was sufficient to incur the sultan's wrath and he derived particular pleasure from beheading men with fat necks. It was one way of tackling obesity . . .

Murad's nocturnal raids were particularly terrifying. The Moldavian chronicler, Dimitri Cantemir, wrote of the sultan: 'Very often at midnight he stole out of the women's quarters through the private gate of the palace with his drawn sword, and running through the streets barefooted with only a loose gown around him, like a madman, killed whoever came his way.' When a French diplomat broke one of Murad's numerous laws – one forbidding foreigners to associate with Turkish women – the sultan had him impaled. He forced one of his doctors to swallow an overdose of opium and celebrated the birth of his own daughter by impaling a courier. The hapless messenger's crime had been to inform Murad that he had become the father of a boy.

His complex relationship with his mother meant that no woman was safe and while out riding with his bow he would use passing women for target practice. Yet he jealousy guarded the privacy of his harem and routinely executed anybody who came too close. When a boat full of ladies drifted towards the harem walls, Murad ordered his gunners to open fire, sinking the boat and drowning the entire party. It is estimated that his reign of indiscriminate bloodshed accounted for 25,000 of his subjects.

In 1640 the sultan who banned alcohol died from cirrhosis of the liver following a particularly heavy drinking session. On his deathbed, he called for the murder of his brother and successor, the mentally unbalanced Ibrahim, who had been confined to a specially designed cell, known as the 'Cage'. Only when his mother said the deed had been done was Murad able to die in peace. It is said that in a last act of vengeance Murad struggled to rise from his bed so that he could view the corpse of Ibrahim and then 'grinned a horrible ghastly smile' in the belief that he was the last of his line. However, his mother had tricked him. Ibrahim had been saved and went on to rule Turkey for a chaotic eight years. For Murad, he was the one that got away.

AN UDDER FIXATION

IBRAHIM I, SULTAN OF TURKEY (1615–48)

When murderous Murad IV ordered the execution of his brother Ibrahim, it was because he could not bear the royal dynasty to continue with what he called 'insane seed'. Those who thought he was cruelly exaggerating Ibrahim's mental incapacity quickly had to reconsider. For after a lifetime locked in the dreaded 'Cage', fearing that every day would be his last, Ibrahim greeted his accession with a caution that spilled over into paranoia. As a throng tried to enter his cell to proclaim him sultan, Ibrahim, fearing that it was another of Murad's evil tricks, was so terrified that he barred the door and refused to come out until his brother's corpse had been brought before him. Even then his mother, Sultana Kösem, had to 'coax him out as if cajoling a frightened kitten with food'. This did not bode well for the future stability of the Ottoman Empire. Having finally been convinced that Murad was no more and that he was a free man, Ibrahim danced like a dervish through the harem, screaming: 'The butcher of the empire is dead! The butcher of the empire is dead!' His sobriquet of 'Ibrahim the Mad' was not given lightly.

More than twenty years of imprisonment had left Ibrahim with a lot of catching up to do, particularly where women were concerned. Skipping through the harem, he was like boy in a sweetshop. While her son indulged himself in episodes of unbridled debauchery, Sultana Kösem was perfectly content to take on the day-to-day grind of government. He had a particular fondness for obese women, the bigger the better, and his mother saw to it that he was given a constant supply of overweight virgins. Unfortunately his long period of confinement had scarred him emotionally, leaving him frequently unable to rise to the occasion. Given his state of mind, it would surely have been better if Ibrahim had remained childless but his mother wanted to cling to power as long as possible and so arranged for a variety of aphrodisiac potions to be prepared for his use. As a result he churned out six sons, one after the other, by assorted concubines.

Newly invigorated, Ibrahim possessed a voracious sexual appetite and, armed with the seventeenth-century version of Viagra, was said to be able to entertain – and satisfy – one of his harem on the couch every hour. He particularly liked to engage in prolonged bouts of horseplay, frolicking among his harem like a stallion at stud and neighing as he galloped among them. The women in turn were expected to pretend to be his mares, kicking and bucking at his every fumble. The sultan certainly got his oats on a regular basis.

Ibrahim's enthusiasm for sex knew no bounds. He collected books that illustrated the various methods of intercourse and even invented a few positions of his own. He took a shine to the daughter of the Grand Mufti, Turkey's most eminent religious leader, but the cleric, having heard about the scandalous goings-on at the harem, strongly advised her to reject the marriage proposal. At this, an angry Ibrahim had the girl kidnapped and kept her as his sex slave for a couple of days before returning her to her father. The sultan also had a profound fetish for fur (the French called him *Le Fou de Fourrures*) and all of his rooms were lined in fur from floor to ceiling. He even had his cats shaved so that they could wear sable coats. His clothes were made of fur, his pillows were stuffed with it, and he loved nothing more than making love on sable skins . . . to a really fat woman.

To Ibrahim, size was everything. Supermodels would have been wasting his time. He preferred the brandy-glass figure to the hourglass. If he could have found a woman built like a

Turkish wrestler, he would have been in seventh heaven. Then, one day, he happened to notice the private parts of a cow – clearly a new experience for him, having spent so much time in a darkened cell – and was immediately struck by their beauty. Unable to get the thought of that magnificent udder out of his mind, he instructed his agents to scour the globe in search of a woman of bovine proportions. A suitable candidate was found in Armenia and introduced into the harem. Her name was Sechir Para ('Sugar Cube') and she tipped the scales at around 150 kilograms. Ibrahim was so pleased with her that he awarded her a handsome pension and made her Governor General of Damascus.

As the sultan's favourite, Sechir Para attracted considerable envy from the other girls in the harem and soon they were to have good reason for their animosity. For she passed on to Ibrahim a rumour that one of his concubines – she did not know the name – had been 'compromised by an outsider'. Ibrahim immediately flew into an uncontrollable temper that raged for three days. When his son and heir, Mehmed, made an ill-advised joke on the subject, the sultan grabbed his dagger and thrust it in the young boy's face, scarring him on the forehead for life. After the chief black eunuch had tried in vain to discover the girl's identity by torturing some of the harem, Ibrahim, driven mad by the uncertainty and suspicion, decided upon drastic action. Sparing only his informant, Sechir Para, and Mehmed's mother, Turhan Hadice, he ordered the remaining 278 women in his harem to be thrown into the Bosphorus, tied up in weighted sacks. They all drowned with the exception of one girl whose sack had not been tied up properly and whom the crew of a passing French ship pulled from the water.

The episode did nothing to increase Sechir Para's popularity and Sultana Kösem, jealous of her increasing influence, elected to eliminate the rival for her son's affections. Inviting her to dinner, she had her strangled. She then told the distraught Ibrahim that Sechir Para 'had died suddenly of a powerful illness'.

Throughout his reign Ibrahim had shown little interest in affairs of state, leaving everything to his mother. He cared only for his own luxuries, and taxes were increased dramatically to pay for his crazy excesses. Glittering diamonds hung from his beard, which was also drenched in expensive and heady perfumes, procured from European merchants. So greedy did he become that he threatened to stuff his Grand Vezir with straw unless he recovered presents donated by previous sultans to a holy shrine. Government offices were sold to the highest bidder or awarded to favourites while the sultan's erratic behaviour succeeded in alienating every political faction. But now that he had fathered successors, he was expendable.

In 1648 the janissaries rebelled over their low pay and, backed by the Grand Mufti's desire to exact revenge for the deflowering of his daughter, they demanded the sultan's head. As a warning they hacked the Grand Vezir to death and sold the pieces of his body in the street. Sultana Kösem tried to reason with them and refused to hand over Ibrahim until she received an assurance that he would not be killed but merely put back in the 'Cage'. Confined once again and without a cow in sight, he deteriorated rapidly, his cries of anguish piercing the thick walls day and night. Ten days later Ibrahim the Mad was put out of his misery when, on the orders of the Grand Mufti, he was strangled with a bowstring. The drowning of the harem had been the last straw. Really, for Ibrahim, it was all over once the fat lady 'sang'.

A MIXED INFANT

PHILIPPE, DUKE OF ORLÉANS (1640–1701)

The younger brother of Louis XIV, Philippe, Duke of Orléans, was known to all as 'Monsieur'. In many respects his nickname was the only masculine thing about him, for whereas Louis earned a reputation as France's most glorious monarch, Philippe was the skeleton in the cupboard (or perhaps closet), the acute family embarrassment that in recent years has become an essential ingredient of every American presidency.

That Philippe preferred to go where the Sun King didn't shine was scarcely surprising. After all, what hope was there for a strong, handsome boy when his mother insisted on dressing him as a girl?

Philippe's father, Louis XIII, died when the boy was just two and as the future Louis XIV was only four, their mother Anne of Austria acted as regent. Philippe was a beautiful, strong child with dark eyes and black hair but right from the outset Anne put him in a girl's dress. In those days it was customary for boys to wear dresses until the age of five but Philippe was dressed as a girl way beyond that period. Anne's emasculation of the infant Philippe did not stop with clothing. She treated him more like a daughter than a son (continually referring to him as 'my little girl'), she encouraged him to play with dolls, and in matters of education, designed a far less rigorous learning programme than that laid out for his brother.

Not surprisingly, Philippe's unusual upbringing soon had an effect on his character. A court confidante, Mme de Motteville, said young Philippe 'liked to be with women and girls, to dress them up and to arrange their hair; he knew more about the style of feminine dress than most women, and his greatest joy was to adorn them'. And when Philippe was allowed to play with boys, it was invariably with François-Timoléon de Choisy, who was also being raised by his mother as a girl and who later became a notorious transvestite. According to the chronicler Lescure, Mme de Choisy 'made her son a living doll, dressing him as a woman and giving him the spirit and nature of a woman'. Suffice to say, the two boys did not play soldiers.

François-Timoléon himself recalled: 'They dressed me as a girl every time the little Monsieur came to play and he came at least two or three times a week. I had my ears pierced, diamonds, beauty spots.' Of his playmate, he added: 'His jacket was removed so that he could put on the coats and skirts of women.'

So why did Anne persist in dressing Philippe as a girl? The general consensus of opinion is that by rendering him effeminate, she could make him submissive to, and therefore no threat to, her favoured Louis. There is little doubt that Louis was her chosen one. When the six-year-old Philippe fell ill with measles complicated by dysentery, Anne left him in Paris and instead went off to Fontainebleau with Louis for a change of air. She only returned to Paris when Philippe's condition deteriorated alarmingly and even then she stayed just three days because Louis was pining for her. The illness temporarily left Philippe so pale and thin as to be nearly unrecognisable, yet she abandoned him again the following year when he contracted smallpox. By contrast, when Louis had caught smallpox in 1647, Anne rushed to his side and remained day and night until he was out of danger – even though Philippe was still recovering from measles and dysentery. And when Louis pulled through, she ordered public rejoicing. Philippe was lucky to receive a 'Get Well Soon' card.

Philippe's childhood left him with a profound distaste for physical activity. Unlike brother Louis, he preferred to play with girls than play sport. Puerile and self-indulgent, Philippe was prone to temper tantrums. Once while ballet dancing, he tripped over his partner's skirt and when a lady at court laughed at the incident, he angrily slapped her. On another occasion he flew into a rage after Louis threw soup over him, soaking his precious hair and clothes. Philippe reacted by hitting the king. Hearing of the fracas, Daniel de Cosnac decided to apply for the post of Philippe's chaplain. 'I had thought that the prince was nothing but a pretty boy,' said de Cosnac at the time, 'but now I see he has it in him to be a man.' Not if his mother could help it.

By the age of seventeen, while Louis was attending to matters of state, the frivolous Philippe was frolicking in the river with the court's female attendants. Although he had once been caught lifting the petticoats of the ladies-in-waiting, presumably to see what all the fuss was about, this was very much an isolated foray into masculine territory and he was now a perfumed dandy who dressed in silks and ribbons at court and had a string of homosexual lovers, particularly favouring young men who bore a striking physical resemblance to his elder brother. His first male lover was the Duke of Nevers, nephew of Anne of Austria's closest adviser, the all-powerful Cardinal Mazarin, a liaison which adds weight to the theory that Anne had actively sought to castrate Philippe emotionally. Ironically, Mazarin used to complain about Philippe's effeminate habits.

One court observer, Mme de la Fayette, wrote of the nineteen-year-old Philippe: 'His inclinations were as close to the ways of women as those of his brother were far removed from them. He was beautiful and well built, but of a beauty and a build more befitting a princess than a prince. Also he was more concerned that his beauty should be admired by everyone than to use it to win the hearts of women, although he was continually in their company. His vanity seemed to render him incapable of attachment to anyone but himself.'

Although no longer given to wearing overtly feminine clothes in public, Philippe did not miss an opportunity to try on his favourite dresses behind closed doors. As his old friend François-Timoléon remarked: 'He showed me a thousand kindnesses because our tastes were the same. He would have

111

wished to be able to dress as a woman also, but he dared not because of his high position . . . but in the evening he put on a mob cap, earrings and beauty spots and sat contemplating himself in the mirrors, idolised by his admirers.' Masked balls were a godsend for anyone in society with a penchant for cross-dressing. Philippe adored them and would spend hours in front of the mirror applying his make-up and fixing his earrings before putting on his mask and entering the ballroom. There he would sit with real women before finally removing his mask so that he could reveal his beauty. At one ball, his latest lover, the Comte de Guiche, pretended not to recognise him and kicked him repeatedly in the backside, to Philippe's obvious delight.

In 1661 he was created Duke of Orléans but, more alarmingly, in the same year a marriage was arranged to Henrietta Stuart, sister of Charles II of England. Whatever his private thoughts on the subject, Philippe behaved impeccably towards his wife in public, only to be humiliated twice in the cruellest fashion. For whilst he did his utmost to appear the doting husband, it soon became apparent that she had eyes only for the king. Louis and Henrietta embarked on a scandalous affair and the gossip swiftly circulated around the royal court, to the acute embarrassment of Philippe. Once again his brother had upstaged him. Then, to add insult to injury, Henrietta seduced Philippe's lover, the Comte de Guiche. The woman had no shame. Poor Philippe was now an object of ridicule. He tried to prove his worth by taking a greater interest in affairs of state, but once again Louis blocked his progress at every turn. And when Louis chose to send Henrietta to England to negotiate an alliance with her brother (a job Philippe had yearned for), Philippe responded angrily by having sex with her several times a day in the hope of making her pregnant and preventing her departure. It must have been the ultimate punishment for them both.

In 1670 the duplicitous Henrietta died suddenly. Poison was suspected, with Philippe as the chief suspect although nothing was ever proven. He did, however, admit that he had ceased to love her after just fifteen days of marriage. Many were surprised his interest had lasted that long.

Purely because royal etiquette dictated that he had to have a wife, Philippe was married again the following year, this time to a German princess, Elizabeth Charlotte von der Pfalz, known to her friends as Liselotte. Philippe appeared genuinely fond of his new bride and, initially at least, they enjoyed an unexpectedly healthy sex life despite the fact that she was eighteen inches taller than him. As a result she often fell off the bed during, after – or perhaps instead of – lovemaking. Even so she bore him three children, Philippe later confessing that on each occasion he had rubbed his penis with a holy medal for luck. In the meantime Philippe had found an even more unlikely outlet for his energies by joining the army, thus setting a precedent for Charles Hawtrey in *Carry On Up the Khyber*. It was all part of Philippe's attempts to prove that he was capable of making a positive contribution to France, although it could be that he just liked wearing the uniform. Yet there was no doubting his gallantry in battle and he fought with distinction in the Dutch War, his finest hour being at the Battle of Cassel in 1677, where he defeated William of Orange. Indeed, a jealous Louis was so worried in case Philippe became too popular that he immediately had his military career terminated.

Thwarted by his brother once again, Philippe lost the will to fight for recognition. His marriage to Liselotte crumbled and after six years of heterosexual relations with her, he returned to his old homosexual ways. In later years he became little more than a parody of himself. In a withering attack, the Duke de Saint-Simon described the ageing Philippe as 'a little man propped up on heels like stilts; gotten up like a woman with rings, bracelets, and jewels; a long wig, black and powdered, spread out before; ribbons wherever he could put them; and exuding perfumes of all kinds.'

Monsieur's mother had a lot to answer for.

THE BEWITCHED KING

CARLOS II, KING OF SPAIN (1661–1700)

Carlos II was not so much a king, more a health warning. From birth to death he suffered from a horrific range of ailments, which made it difficult for him to speak, chew food, walk, see, hear, have sex or concentrate for any length of time. Consequently his short life was one of prolonged infancy and premature senility with precious little in between. His constitution was so frail and his mind so feeble that almost every day was expected to be his last. Court physicians laboured in vain to find suitable treatments until a priest came up with his own reason for the king's condition: Carlos, he said, was bewitched.

A more plausible explanation was that Carlos was the monstrous result of centuries of inbreeding by the Habsburgs who, rather than take a chance on outsiders, made it a policy decision to marry within the family. First cousins married each other; uncles married nieces. With every Spanish king being descended from Juana the Mad, her mental and physical characteristics were thus multiplied through the generations, culminating in the human freak show that was Carlos II, the last Habsburg king of Spain.

Carlos's father, Philip IV, took the French princess Isabella as his first wife but the union produced no surviving heir. When Isabella died, Philip, then aged 45, married his fifteen-year-old niece, Mariana, in a desperate attempt to produce an heir. Interestingly, Mariana had originally been earmarked as a wife for Philip's son Baltazar Carlos before his death from smallpox, but it seemed a pity to waste a good bride so Philip took her for himself. Philip quickly set about testing Mariana's fertility and she fell pregnant almost immediately, but the resultant daughter was not what Philip needed. He wanted a son. Seven years later, in 1656, his prayers appeared to have been answered with the birth of a prince, Felipe Prospero, but the boy was sickly and died young. With Philip's physical clock ticking down fast, he was hugely relieved when, in November 1661, Mariana gave birth to another boy, Carlos. The news prompted widespread rejoicing on the streets of Spain . . . until it became apparent that the heir to the throne was both physically and mentally retarded.

The distinctive Habsburg jaw is a curious feature even in its mildest form but Carlos's wasn't just pronounced, it was enunciated. It was so elongated that it jutted out from the rest of his face like Cornwall. He looked to have been conceived in a fairground hall of mirrors. Quite apart from the fact that it gave him an enormous misshapen head, his huge jaw prevented his two rows of teeth from meeting, which meant that he was unable to chew food. Consequently he had to swallow everything whole, rather like a python. Indeed, his mouth was something of a disaster area all round, because inside lurked a tongue so large that he was barely able to speak. He had to be breast-fed for four years by a small army of nurses and his legs were too frail to support him. As a result it was some years until he walked and even then he regularly fell over.

He became King Carlos II in 1665 on the death of Philip. His mother acted as regent but she was naïve in matters of government and was frequently undermined by the king's ambitious half-brother, the charismatic Don Juan, who, unlike all of Philip's legitimate children, enjoyed robust health. The intrigue and backstabbing at court sailed way over Carlos's head, as indeed did the alphabet and the ability to write his own name. For he was considered too weak to undergo the rigours of education, with the result that by the age of nine he remained unable to read or write. The following year he caught gastric fever but defied the experts by making a recovery although he still cut a far from imposing figure. The papal nuncio later wrote of him:

> *His face on the whole is ugly; he has a long neck, a broad face and chin, with the typical Habsburg lower lip . . . he has a melancholic and faintly surprised look . . . He cannot stand upright when walking, unless he leans against a wall, a table or somebody else. He is as weak in body as in mind. Now and then he gives signs of intelligence, memory and a certain liveliness, but not at present; usually he shews himself slow and indifferent, torpid and indolent, and seems to be stupefied. One can do with him what one wishes because he lacks his own will.*

When he came of age he did briefly try to assert his authority by refusing to sign a document that would have extended his mother's reign on the grounds of his own incapacity. In a bid to free himself from her control, he secretly appealed to Don Juan for help, only to be thwarted by Mariana's firm hand. Carlos was summoned to a meeting with her and left two hours later in floods of tears. Mother knew best.

Although for the most part very little stirred within Carlos's body, there was sufficient activity below the waist to suggest that it was about time he acquired a wife. But here, too, the Fates had conspired against him for, in addition to his other conditions, he suffered from potentially the most damaging of all: he was incapable of producing an heir. Understandably, the precise nature of his problem was not for public consumption, but it appears that he experienced premature ejaculation with the result that he was unable to achieve penetration. The spirit was willing but the flesh was weak. The question was: which European princess would draw the short straw and be nominated as Carlos's bride?

That dubious honour went to seventeen-year-old Marie Louise of Orléans, a niece of Louis XIV. Word had already reached the French court that Carlos was a good catch only in as much as his face resembled that of a pike, meaning that Marie Louise was guarded in her enthusiasm for the forthcoming nuptials. Uncle Louis tried to sell the arrangement to her by insisting that he could not have done more for his own daughter . . . to which Marie Louise replied icily: 'But you could have done more for your niece!'

Marie Louise resolved to make the best of a bad job, but it was no easy matter for a vivacious French girl to acclimatise to the sombre Spanish court and an imbecilic husband. When no child was born to the union, the Spanish people, ignorant of their king's shortcomings, suspected that Louis was supplying abortifacients to his niece in order to prevent her producing an heir to the Spanish dominions. With one eye on the future, Louis certainly took an unhealthy interest in Carlos's bedroom ratings, until, after ten barren years, the French ambassador Rébenec reported back:

> *She [Marie Louise] was anxious to confide in me something she had never wanted to tell anyone, namely that she was not really a virgin any longer, but that as far as she could figure things, believed she would never have children. Her modesty prevented her explaining any more fully, and my respect prevented me asking questions, but I gathered from what she said that there was a natural debility which was attributed to much vivacity on the king's part.*

The resourceful Rébenec then had Carlos's undergarments examined by surgeons for traces of sperm, but apparently the findings were inconclusive.

As Marie Louise's popularity diminished, her weight moved in the opposite direction. To inject a little pleasure into her miserable existence she began consuming vast amounts of sweetmeats and became so bloated that for Carlos to mount her in his frail state probably required the help of several servants and a stepladder. She began suffering gastric illnesses, which she attributed to poison, until in February 1689, at the age of just 27, one proved fatal. Carlos was so upset by her death that he ordered the opening of his ancestors' coffins, although his motives for doing so remain unclear.

With heirs to produce, there was little time for mourning and within two months another bride had been found for Europe's least eligible monarch. Sadly, Maria Ana of Neuberg was no more successful in providing the desired child. The king's health continued to give hope only to the local undertaker. At 35 his teeth and bones were diseased, his eyesight was failing, his hair had fallen out, he could still barely walk, and he suffered from ulcers, dizzy spells and epileptic spasms. Following another illness, the English ambassador, Stanhope, said of Carlos in 1697:

His constitution is so very weak and broken much beyond his age that it is generally feared what may be the success of such another attack. They cut his hair off in his sickness, which the decay of nature had almost done before, all his crown being bald. He has a ravenous stomach, and swallows all he eats whole, for his nether jaw stands so much out, that his two rows of teeth cannot meet; to compensate which, he has a prodigious wide throat, so that a gizzard or liver of a hen passes down whole, and his weak stomach not being able to digest it, he voids in the same manner.

Some thought him insane but he was more likely the victim of congenital syphilis, brought on by his father's regular visits to the brothels of Madrid. And, of course, his states of mind and body were exacerbated by the Habsburg inbreeding programme. Those who didn't think he was insane had a different explanation for his ill health, particularly his impotence; they said he was possessed. Carlos, himself, adhered to this theory, saying: 'Many people tell me I am bewitched and I well believe it; such are the things I experience and suffer.' The royal confessor, Froilan Diaz, also believed this and contacted a friend, Antonio de Arguelles, a chaplain who had enjoyed a degree of success in exorcising a group of nuns that had been possessed by demons. In an effort to ascertain the source of the king's bewitchment, Father Arguelles was told to write the names of the king and queen on a piece of paper, which he was to keep hidden in his breast while exorcising the afflicted nuns. He then asked Satan whether either of the names on the slip of paper was bewitched, to which the Devil apparently replied in the affirmative, adding that the king's bewitchment 'was due to destroy his generative organs, and to render him incapable of administering the kingdom'. Further questioning revealed that the spell had been administered to the king in a drink when he was aged fourteen.

Armed with the Devil's testimony, the intrepid Arguelles and Diaz tried to track down the witch responsible, but had no luck apart from a mad woman who burst into the palace and claimed that she and her friends kept the king locked in a small box in their room. Meanwhile, the king's condition showed little improvement. Arguelles urged him to eat his food more slowly, to drink half a pint of olive oil a day and to have all food and drink blessed before consumption. The queen was exorcised in a desperate bid to encourage her fertility but was angered by rumours implying that she had been responsible for bewitching the king. A new exorcist was then brought in from Germany to try and cure Carlos. The royal couple took to hiding small bags of charms, hair and nail clippings under their pillows to ward off evil spirits, but all of these measures proved in vain. The king's epileptic fits became more frequent and from 1698 he was rendered deaf. Doctors treated his attacks by placing freshly killed pigeons on his head to prevent dizziness and applying the steaming entrails of mammals to his stomach in order to keep him warm. During his final debilitating illness of September 1700 he passed more motions than the Spanish parliament – nearly 250 in just nineteen days.

For 35 years the crowned heads of Europe had waited for this travesty of a king to die and now they started to squabble over the carcass. The opportunist Louis put his grandson, Philip of Anjou, on the Spanish throne as Philip V, prompting the War of the Spanish Succession. Ironically, it soon became apparent that Philip had demons of his own.

AN EXTENDED FAMILY

AUGUSTUS II, KING OF POLAND (1670–1733)

The greetings card industry would have loved Augustus. For in the course of his life he fathered an estimated 355 children – a birthday for virtually every day of the year. Even more remarkably, only one of that number was born legitimate. Few people have been responsible for so many bastards.

Augustus himself struggled to keep track of them, with the result that at least one of his daughters subsequently became his mistress. There is no evidence to suggest that the discovery of this blunder troubled him; he probably viewed it as nothing more than an occupational hazard. Anyway, scruples were not exactly his forte.

A tall, burly, convivial man with thick black eyebrows and dark eyes, his sheer physical power earned him the sobriquet of 'Augustus the Strong', although his ability to procreate at will also did little to diminish his reputation. He was arguably the most sexually potent monarch in European history, a man never happier than when in the company of his extensive harem of beautiful women. Among his legions of illegitimate children was the renowned soldier Maurice de Saxe, an ancestor of the novelist George Sand. Augustus fuelled his carnal marathons by eating heartily and consuming colossal quantities of wine, neither of which caused him to put on an excessive amount of weight. Then again, he did burn the calories off regularly. To impress dinner guests, he used to pick up two of his state trumpeters, one in each hand, and hold them out at arm's length for five minutes, while they played a fanfare.

He may have been physically strong but he displayed precious little fortitude as a ruler. Having become Elector of Saxony in 1694, he conveniently changed his religion to Catholicism three years later so that he could also acquire the title of King of Poland. Previous electors had been Protestant, but the dishonourable behaviour of Augustus meant that Saxony now had a Catholic sovereign ruling over an almost entirely Protestant country. This in itself was sufficient to create discord, without his costly wars against the youthful Charles XII of Sweden, which proved so crippling financially that he was forced to pawn or sell off large districts of his ancestral electorate. A patron of the arts, Augustus made Dresden his capital city and transformed it into a centre of culture. He bought works of art, built museums and established the Meissen porcelain factory, but these projects, on top of his wars, dealt a further blow to Saxony's finances.

He was no more popular in Poland than in Saxony and was forced to renounce the throne in 1706 following his defeat by Charles XII. However, he regained the crown three years later with more than a little help from his Russian allies.

His subjects may have suffered at his hands, but the greatest humiliation was reserved for his queen. He married Christiane Eberhardine in Bayreuth in 1693 but his attentiveness did not last much beyond the birth of their son, Augustus – his sole legitimate heir. For the rest of her reign – right up until her death in 1727 – she could only look on helplessly while her sex-crazed husband romped with the members of his harem and fathered enough sons to form a private army. The future Augustus III did not share his father's appetite for – or choice in – women. After falling in love with and marrying the squat and undeniably plain Archduchess Maria Josepha, he brought his new bride to Dresden to meet her in-laws. On their arrival, Augustus the Strong mistook a pretty lady-in-waiting for the bride and embraced her warmly with more than a hint of lechery. Discovering his mistake, he turned to his son and snapped: 'Sir, I would have thought you would have had better taste.' To console the lady-in-waiting, the king quickly added her to his list of mistresses.

Augustus the Strong outlived his queen by six years, finally expiring at the end of a particularly heavy drinking session in Warsaw. One chronicler aptly described him as 'Lutheran by birth, Catholic by ambition and Mahometan in his habits.'

THE END OF THE LINE

GIAN GASTONE DE' MEDICI, GRAND DUKE OF TUSCANY (1671–1737)

The Medici family had ruled Florence since 1434 but by the start of the eighteenth century the great city, like the once proud family, had fallen into decline. The reigning Grand Duke, Cosimo III, and his wife, Marguérite Louise of France, were spectacularly incompatible. He was sour and passionless with a deep-seated aversion to physical contact because he thought sex would ruin his health; she was beautiful, lively, witty and refined but grew to despise her husband. Worryingly, they had to produce an heir to ensure the continuation of the dynasty.

Cosimo certainly had no intention of overextending himself in the bedroom. He only slept with his wife once a week and even then it was under the strict supervision of a doctor, who, one presumes, stood by, stopwatch in hand, ready to tell the Grand Duke that he had exercised sufficiently. It was surely not what Marguérite Louise had envisaged by 'three in a bed'. She became so bored with the arrangement that she withdrew her services completely for several months and was exiled from court. When she did reluctantly return to the fold, she fell pregnant twice more (she had already given birth to a son Ferdinando), but an indication of her continued unhappiness can be gauged from the fact that on all three occasions she tried unsuccessfully to induce a miscarriage. And while pregnant with her third child, she even attempted to starve herself. Yet every baby went the distance – Ferdinando, Anna Maria and lastly

Gian Gastone. Marguérite Louise did not, however. When Gian Gastone was four, she fled to France, never to return, living thereafter on a pension provided by her estranged husband.

Neglected by his grandmother, mother, father, brother, sister and even the court, Gian Gastone was a lonely, melancholy child. So deep was his gloom that some began to question his sanity. Nevertheless he was intelligent, excelling at languages and literature, and developed a keen interest in botany, spending much of his time in a refuge in the Boboli Garden, where he studied plants and flowers and various precious objects that he had collected. His father rewarded his academic ability by appointing him Governor of the University of Pisa. The one thing he inherited from his father was a dislike of sex with women, but whereas Cosimo abhorred intercourse with anyone, Gian Gastone, rather like Pisa's famous tower, had a different leaning. So it came as an unpleasant surprise to the homosexual 26-year-old when his father arranged for him to marry Anna Maria of Saxe-Lauenburg, a wealthy widow with a daughter. Anna Maria's first husband had drunk himself to death, so her expectations of marriage were not high . . . which was just as well.

Even her own father would have struggled to describe Anna Maria as being easy on the eye. And as Gian Gastone discovered, she looked no better in the flesh – even though there was plenty of flesh to look at. She was described as 'appalling and immensely fat' with 'ungainly massive limbs' and a 'coarse ill-favoured aspect'. In another world she would have been a star of *Big Brother*. Nonetheless, Gian Gastone dutifully obeyed his father's wishes and the marriage went ahead.

They had nothing in common. Anna Maria loved hunting and horses whereas Gian Gastone was practically allergic to all sporting pursuits. Furthermore, she had no intention whatsoever of leaving her Bohemian estates, forcing him to travel hundreds of miles north for the dubious pleasure of being with his new bride.

Gian Gastone took to Bohemia like a duck takes to oil. He hated the country, he hated the smell of his wife's horses, but above all he hated his wife. He found her bossy, overbearing, uncouth and physically repellent. In return, she thought he was effeminate and accused him of being impotent. Then again, Anna Maria could have made Casanova impotent.

She knew that the sole purpose of the union was to provide an urgently needed Medici heir and, to her credit, she did attempt to lose some weight in a bid to raise a little interest from her reluctant spouse. It proved to no avail and after ten months of lacklustre probing, Gian Gastone threw in the towel. His seeds remained firmly in the packet.

To help him forget his domestic misery, Gian Gastone turned to alcohol, gambling and young men. He acquired a residence in Prague and visited the city's taverns in search of company, his quest aided by one of his entourage, Guiliano Dami, who introduced him to young students and footmen. He travelled to France to see his mother, who greeted him with what barely even amounted to apathy, and occasionally, under renewed pressure from his father to beget an heir, he made the ultimate sacrifice and returned to his wife. But Anna Maria was perfectly happy renovating her castle and could muster little enthusiasm for her part-time spouse, leaving him to sink further into depression and spend most of his days staring blankly out of the window. The chances of conception were considerably slimmer than Anna Maria's thighs.

In 1705 the unhappy Gian Gastone returned to Florence, but the move did little to lift his spirits initially. He rarely ventured out by day and his eccentric behaviour led people to conclude that he was going mad. Once, in what was thought to be a thinly veiled hint at the need to clean up city corruption, he bought a peasant broom-seller's entire stock and had it delivered to the municipal offices 'for future use'.

In 1713 Gian Gastone's brother Ferdinando suffered a miserable and prolonged death from syphilis and eight years later his mother died, too. Displaying her customary love for her children, she left them nothing, instead bequeathing everything to a distant relative. When his father Cosimo died in 1723 at the age of 81, Gian Gastone succeeded him as Grand

Duke of Tuscany. Gian Gastone himself was now 52 although, bloated with alcohol, he looked considerably older. He and Anna Maria would have made a good pair of bookends. Free at last from the paternal pressure to sire an heir, Gian Gastone let himself go completely. He had no wish to be involved in government and instead devoted what little energy he still had to drunken debauchery. Fuelled by an excess of alcohol at one official reception, he began shouting all manner of obscenities and had to be ejected. As he was pushed into his coach, he threw up and used his dirty wig to wipe the vomit from his face. Sometimes he was so drunk that he fell off his horse.

But Gian Gastone's most notorious behaviour was reserved for his bedroom, where he entertained legions of young men (and occasionally women) known as the *ruspanti* because they were paid a fee of between one and five ruspi for their services. His friend Dami acted as recruiting officer for these orgies, scouring the streets of Florence in search of likely lads, and proved so successful that at one time Gian Gastone had as many as 370 *ruspanti* from which to choose. As the Grand Duke was almost permanently drunk, his role was mainly observational, loudly encouraging the young men with the cries of a demented huntsman, although he did derive satisfaction from coercing them into giving him a sound beating. For added amusement, he named the young men after Florentine dignitaries and watched in delight as a duke crudely had his way with a marchioness. From time to time he hired his own *ruspanti*, including a Bohemian bear-leader, Michael Henzchemic. One night Gian Gastone decided that only Henzchemic could cater for his lusts but by the time the man had been located, he was, like the Grand Duke, exceedingly drunk. Brought back to the palace, he downed more wine with the Grand Duke until the latter, as was his wont, vomited on Henzchemic's face and chest. Henzchemic was so angry that he lashed out at Gian Gastone, whose cries alerted the guards before serious damage could be done.

Besides a high sex drive, the other chief requisite for the *ruspanti* was an impaired sense of smell. For after taking to his bed suffering from a sprained ankle in 1730, Gian Gastone scarcely left it for the last seven years of his life and was unable, or unwilling, to dress himself properly. The sheets were soiled and the whole room stank of tobacco, drink and excrement. His dogs slept with him in bed and even a donkey bearing peaches for his lunch was ushered into the bedroom. Lunch was usually taken around five o'clock in the afternoon, followed by supper at two in the morning . . . always in bed. As he grew older, fatter and smellier, he became nearly blind and could hardly walk. His fingernails, toenails and beard were allowed to grow unchecked. In June 1737 the now senile Grand Duke fell seriously ill from a large stone in the bladder and died inside a month.

Although the people of Florence had seen precious little of him, they greatly mourned his passing, not least because he (or rather his ministers) had abolished the death penalty and lowered the price of grain.

With no heir to succeed him, Gian Gastone was the last of the Medici. On his death, the Grand Duchy passed into the hands of the Duke of Lorraine and Florence became part of the Austrian Empire.

A COLLECTOR OF CURIOSITIES

PETER THE GREAT, TSAR OF RUSSIA
(1672–1725)

Peter the Great was a man of many parts. An enthusiastic amateur surgeon and dentist, he liked to carry out a beheading before dinner in order to whet his appetite. He enjoyed shipbuilding, carpentry and testing explosives (although not at the same venue) and went through numerous fads and phases, but the two great loves of his life were alcohol and freaks of nature. He founded a notorious drinking club and had a bizarre fixation for dwarfs, the result being that the most frequently heard words from the tsar's lips became: 'Mine's a short.'

As a child he played with dwarfs, who would pull him along in a miniature cart, and the fascination for them never left him, although with Peter himself standing nearly seven feet tall in adulthood, most of the Russian population must have seemed dwarf-like to him. Whereas he was capable of terrible cruelty to anyone who incurred his wrath, he always treated his dwarfs with great kindness. When two of his favourites got married, he invited 72 more to come from the farthest provinces of his empire. The wedding feast was held at the royal palace, at which Peter went to the trouble of providing small tables for the dwarfs and large tables for the other guests. When one of the same dwarfs died, Peter staged a lavish funeral ceremony. The tiny coffin was placed on a tiny hearse, drawn by small horses with black trappings while at the head of the procession walked a priest, selected for his unusually short stature. All of the choristers at the ceremony were children but, as a striking contrast, Peter had the procession flanked by fifty tall grenadiers.

Indeed, Peter was also attracted to giants. He had returned from a trip to France with a 7ft 6in colossus by the name of Nicolas Bourgeois and married him to a Finnish woman of similar proportions in the hope that they would produce huge children. The plan failed but Peter continued to pay the couple an annual salary of six hundred roubles and to include Bourgeois in his weird ceremonies, often dressing him up like a baby and having him paraded on strings by a team of dwarfs. On his death, Bourgeois was stuffed for inclusion in Peter's remarkable Museum of Curiosities.

Housed in St Petersburg – which, from 1713, the tsar had declared to be the new capital of Russia – the museum represented his lifelong passion for abnormalities of nature. Items on display included a man without genital organs, a child with two heads, a sheep with five feet, a deformed human foetus, and the corpses of Siamese twins. But his prize exhibit was a pickled phallus, donated by the King of Prussia, Frederick William. The item had caught the tsar's eye on a trip to Berlin and Peter thought it would be a fun idea to persuade his wife, Catherine, to kiss it. Catherine agreed . . . but only after being advised that failure to do so would result in her body ending at the neck.

Peter spent hours wandering among the jars of specimens, all of which were pickled in alcohol, and his provincial governors were offered lucrative rewards for sending in suitable exhibits. Appropriately, the caretaker of the museum was a dwarf who had only two fingers on each hand and two toes on each foot and who knew that when he died he would be stuffed and put on display in the gallery.

By definition, Peter was one of life's enthusiasts. He had an inquisitive mind and loved to master new skills, and whenever he was shown around a factory, he would try his hand at whatever was being made. During his first foreign tour the German princesses he met concluded from his conversation that he was a master-craftsman in fourteen different trades.

After his death, it was found that almost every place in which he had lived for any length of time was full of model boats, chairs, crockery, and snuff-boxes that he had made. Shipbuilding was a particular passion, and no affairs of state could detain him if there was the chance of working on the wharves. On a visit to London, the man who founded the Russian navy once worked incognito in the shipyards at Deptford to pick up tips.

Unwilling to acknowledge his limitations, Peter overstretched himself sometimes. He loved toying with explosives, sometimes to the cost of those in close vicinity. As a boy he played war games with a real cannon, until in one unfortunate incident he managed to kill 24 people.

He first became interested in dentistry on a trip to Holland and was taught the basics by a travelling dentist whom he met in the market at Amsterdam. From then on he performed extractions at every opportunity, regardless of whether or not the patients were willing – for Peter's sheer strength and size ensured that they were kept in a vice-like grip throughout their ordeal. Any courtiers who complained of toothache were immediately subjected to the tsar's new-found expertise and if none was forthcoming, he would carry out on-the-spot inspections on passers-by, pulling any tooth that looked diseased to his untrained eye. Unfortunately, he was so enthusiastic that occasionally he removed not only the bad tooth but also a section of the gum.

Peter also fancied himself as a surgeon and anatomist. When the widow of his half-brother Theodore died, Peter personally opened up her corpse to see if it was true that she really was still a virgin at 49. He was immensely proud of his work in removing 20lb of water from the dropsical wife of a Russian merchant and was mightily aggrieved when she had the effrontery to die shortly after the operation. To clear his good name, he immediately ordered an autopsy, which naturally absolved him of any blame.

For in spite of his eccentricities, Peter was not a man to cross. He was incredibly strong – he could twist silver coins with his fingers – and possessed a temper to match. Scarred by atrocities he had witnessed in his youth, he developed a serious nervous disorder, which manifested itself sometimes in a twitch or, during moments of particular stress, in alarming facial convulsions. His fierce countenance was intimidating at the best of times, but when seized by a black mood, he could be as cruel as any man in history. He would fly into sudden rages at his courtiers, thrashing them with a cudgel for no obvious reason. He derived considerable pleasure from personally decapitating dissidents with an axe, and the road to the Kremlin was littered with headless corpses left to rot in the snow. The heads were placed on spikes and served as food for crows.

In 1687 – by which time he had been tsar for five years – the fifteen-year-old Peter suspected that a plot was being hatched to take his life. He was just about to set off on one of his trips to Western Europe and so, after having the ringleaders arrested and tortured, he decided to give any potential rebels something to think about in his absence. First he disinterred the remains of another leading dissident, Ivan Miloslavsky, who had been executed twelve years previously, and had the decomposed corpse dragged by pigs to the place of execution, where it was placed directly beneath the scaffold. Then he had the current ringleaders taken to the scaffold where they were dismembered and then beheaded so that their fresh blood dripped down on to Miloslavsky's rotting corpse. With the rebel heads arranged on spikes, the tsar ordered that the gruesome exhibition remain in place until his return from his travels. It was a chilling warning.

The sight of blood gave Peter a hearty appetite and since he liked to sit down for a meal every few hours, this was bad news for his enemies. He watched torture sessions with unbridled enthusiasm, roaring with pleasure and urging the torturer on to greater depravities. His table manners in general left something to be desired. He was not one to wait patiently while food was passed to him, opting instead to trample across the banquet table, treading on dishes and cutlery with his huge unwashed feet.

Neither did Peter show any mercy towards those close to him nor display any remorse for his actions. The day after he had

131

flayed his son and heir, Alexis, to death in 1718, there were widespread celebrations and a new ship was launched: business as usual. Alexis, a feckless youth who dismally failed to match up to his father's lofty expectations and who at one stage wanted to become a monk, was accused by Peter of being a traitor when in truth his only crime had been to befriend the tsar's critics. When Alexis was arrested, Peter supervised the torture and actually joined in. The flogging and racking continued long after a confession had been extracted, until the tsarevitch died from his injuries.

Infidelity was similarly punished. On learning that his ex-wife Eudoxia had taken a lover, Stephen Glebov, Peter ordered that Glebov be impaled and made to wear a fur skin so as to prolong his agony in the Russian winter. And when Peter discovered that his wife Catherine had been unfaithful, he had the head of her lover, his own chamberlain William Mons, chopped off and inserted in a large jar of alcohol. Peter then placed the jar with its gruesome contents on Catherine's bedside table to remind her of the error of her ways.

Ironically, Peter had countless mistresses, especially among Catherine's four hundred ladies-in-waiting. Among his lovers was Mary Hamilton, a Russian girl of Scottish descent, but her career at court came to an abrupt end when she was found guilty of infanticide and theft and sentenced to death. Peter made a point of attending the execution in person, kissing her tenderly and then watching as her head was chopped off. It is said that he then picked up the bloodied and severed head, kissed it on the lips and dropped the head in the mud before walking off.

Peter's most violent outbursts could usually be attributed to his fondness for alcohol, the vodka bottle being the unofficial emblem of Russia even in those days. Although he professed to be devout, Peter loved drunken revelry and founded a drinking society called the Most Drunken Synod of Fools and Jesters. He drew up its various rules with the same attention to detail that he applied to the nation's laws, the first commandment being 'to get drunk every day and never go to bed sober'.

Calculated to poke fun at the Russian Church, the synod boasted a college of twelve so-called 'cardinals', all tipplers and gluttons, headed by the patriarch, Peter's former tutor, an elderly dipsomaniac named Nikita Zotov. Although wrapped in ceremonial order, Peter's Synod was nothing more than an excuse for week-long drinking sessions. In his role as 'deacon', Peter would pour vodka down the throats of his friends with a funnel while Zotov, seated on a high chair, threw up joyously on the heads below. When Zotov (then in his eighties) was married to a young widow, Peter had the ceremony performed by a blind and deaf centenarian, and when the elderly ex-tutor eventually succumbed to the ravages of alcohol, the election to find his successor degenerated into a drunken orgy. There was no escape from the sessions, because Peter had sentries posted at the doors of the banquet hall to prevent the faint-hearted or the queasy from leaving and spoiling his fun. It was, by any standards, curious behaviour for a head of state.

Rather like England football supporters, Peter's cronies carried their wild drinking excesses into Europe. They trashed a Prussian palace and, lodging at the home of Sir John Evelyn in London, smashed paintings and furniture, used paintings as target practice for their guns and smeared vomit and excrement on the floors and walls. Sir John later presented the British government with a bill for £350 to cover the damage to his property. When the party moved on to Antwerp, Peter and a few friends consumed 269 bottles of wine in a day and a half. And on a visit to France in 1717, the host nation had to pay for women to undress the drunken tsar and clean him up after he had urinated in his pants following an official reception.

On his return from an earlier tour of Western European countries in 1698, Peter resolved to introduce their customs to Russia in a move to modernise his homeland. His first target was facial hair and on the day that he re-entered Moscow he produced a long razor and began cutting off the nobles' beards. He demanded that everyone at court be clean-shaven – any who objected were visited by the tsar's court jester armed with a cut-throat razor. Officials were empowered to shave on the spot any man who defied the law. Those who wanted to keep their beards on religious grounds were exempted on condition that they paid a tax of 100 roubles a year. Having done so, they were given a bronze medal to wear around their necks, bearing a picture of a beard and the words 'Tax Paid'. Peter later extended the ban to moustaches, although he surely overlooked a huge potential source of revenue by failing to include Russian women in the taxes on facial hair. Encouraged by the success of the beard tax, Peter went on to slap duty on births, marriages, funerals, horse collars, hats, beds, baths, beehives, firewood, drinking water and kitchen chimneys – everything, in fact, but the kitchen sink.

For a bear of a man who feared nobody, Peter had a surprising phobia about cockroaches and refused to enter a room until assured that it had been cleaned thoroughly and that no cockroaches were present. As his nervous disorder worsened and he began to suffer fits and blackouts, he developed a fresh fear – that of dying in his sleep. Consequently, in his later years he ensured that he never slept alone in case he suffered a sudden seizure. Years of heavy drinking had caused untold harm to his body, which his doctors tried to repair by advising him to drink spa waters. But old habits died hard and he always added alcohol to the water to improve the flavour. His premature death from cirrhosis of the liver was hardly a shock.

A NIGHT AT THE OPERA

PHILIP V, KING OF SPAIN (1683–1746)

Every night for the last ten years of his troubled life, Philip V of Spain commanded the Italian singer Farinelli to sing the same four Italian arias in his presence. By the time Philip died of a stroke in 1746, the dutiful Farinelli had thus performed for some 3,600 successive nights. A saner individual than the king might have tired of the repetition but by then Philip was described as 'disordered in the head' and consequently seemed to treat every concert as something new and different. Indeed, after each recital Philip excitedly tried to imitate Farinelli. It did not make for easy listening. As one observer recounted, the king 'throws himself into such freaks and howlings that all possible means are taken to prevent people from being witness to his follies'. Farinelli must have had grave doubts as to whether imitation really was the sincerest form of flattery.

A reign that ended so miserably had begun in glorious triumph. Despite being ill-prepared for the event, Philip V suddenly found himself appointed King of Spain in 1700 on the orders of his grandfather, Louis XIV of France. The decision was hotly contested by Archduke Charles of Austria and led to the thirteen-year-long War of the Spanish Succession. Philip's drive and determination in rallying the people to defend his crown earned him the nickname of '*animoso*', or 'the inspired', and was eventually rewarded in 1713 when the Treaty of Utrecht formally acknowledged him as Spain's monarch.

Yet even then such energy was out of character for Philip. He was a quiet, sombre man, lacking in confidence and fearful of those around him. He was also almost unique by royal standards in being utterly faithful, his strict conscience forbidding him to take a mistress. He was, however, highly sexed – a trait inherited from his grandfather, who was still making love twice a day at the age of seventy – so this put an enormous physical strain on Philip's wives.

Philip married his first wife, Marie Louise of Savoy, when she was just fourteen. She kept him waiting for two nights to teach him an early lesson but from then on he made up for lost time with a vengeance until the war brought about a prolonged instance of *coitus interruptus*. The enforced separation caused him enormous frustration. Every exploding cannon must have reminded him of what he was missing, yet never once did he consider the acquisition of a mistress. Instead, as soon as he was able to return to Spain he spent every available moment with the queen. Sadly, Philip's insatiable demands and the exertions of four pregnancies took their toll at a young age and Marie Louise died in 1714 at the age of 26. Even then, Philip had to be dragged from her deathbed as he tried to slip in one final sex session before she expired. He was too upset to attend the funeral and went hunting instead.

Given his needs and scruples, there was no chance of Philip remaining single for a night longer than was absolutely necessary, and seven months later, after a whirlwind trawl around the available princesses of Europe, he married Elizabeth Farnese, daughter of the Duke of Parma. A highly intelligent woman, Elizabeth quickly learned that the way to Philip's heart was through his genitals. By subjecting him to sexual blackmail, she was able to exercise complete control over him. Whenever she withheld her favours, Philip reacted angrily but he always backed down in the end and let her have her own way because she had something he simply could not do without. He became little more than her plaything.

She became, in effect, the real ruler of Spain, especially after 1717 when Philip was overcome by a deep depression that left him on the verge of insanity. The king said it felt as if he was being consumed by a fierce internal fire, as if the sun was sending a piercing ray to the very centre of his body. Convinced that he was about to die in mortal sin, he summoned his confessor to his bedside day and night, but his physicians could find nothing wrong and thought the king was simply suffering from hypochondriacal delusions. The French ambassador concluded that Philip's sexual appetite was at the root of the problem. 'The king,' he said, 'is visibly wasting away through excessive use he makes of the queen. He is utterly worn out.'

Certainly Philip had aged prematurely. After the Duke of Saint-Simon met him in 1722, he wrote:

He was very bent, shrunken, his chin poked far in advance of his chest; he planted his feet straight, touching one another, and though he moved quickly enough, his knees were more than a foot apart. His speech was so formal, his words so drawled, his expression so vacuous, that I was quite unnerved.

Then, in January 1724, Philip, fearing that he was no longer capable of ruling and that anyway death was lurking just around the corner, suddenly announced his abdication in favour of his son, Luis. 'I have resolved,' Philip declared, 'to retire from the heavy burden of governing this monarchy, in order to concentrate my mind on death during the time that remains to me and to pray for my salvation in that other and more permanent kingdom.' Bow-legged and stooped, he cut a pitiful figure and underlined his desire to opt out of court life by taking to dressing as a humble Franciscan friar. But seven months later, the seventeen-year-old Luis died from smallpox and instead of passing the crown to Luis's younger brother Ferdinand, Philip, encouraged by the domineering Elizabeth, resumed as king. It was a most unexpected turn of events.

Even on his return, Philip was still principally a figurehead. It was Elizabeth who concentrated on the business of government, particularly relating to Spain's foreign policy, while Philip adopted an increasingly eccentric lifestyle, in which he practically reversed night and day. At eight o'clock in the morning – the time when most people were preparing for work – he would go to bed, rising at midday for a light meal. At one o'clock he dressed and attended Mass before receiving visitors. He would spend the early evening gazing out of the window, playing with his clocks or being read a story, until it was time for a musical or theatrical entertainment. At around two o'clock in the morning he would call in his ministers to discuss any outstanding affairs of state and then at five o'clock he would have supper. Three hours later it was time for bed. This bizarre timetable imposed an added burden on his court.

Philip suffered further attacks of manic depression, during which he lost weight, developed insomnia and started biting himself. He thought he was unable to walk because his feet were of different sizes and he refused to have his hair cut or his beard shaved. Alternating alarmingly between the passive and the excitable, he sometimes lashed out violently at his doctors and even at the queen, who was subjected to verbal abuse and beatings that left her covered in bruises. To Elizabeth's horror, Philip again contemplated stepping down from the throne, but she tore up his abdication letter, insisting that it was illegal without her consent. From then on, she kept pen and paper out of his reach.

For a while Philip appeared to regain his sanity, at one point allowing himself to be shaved for the first time in eight months, but in 1732 he sank into another depression and refused to leave his bed even for meals or to be washed. For nineteen months he wore the same clothes, believing that if he changed them or washed, he would die. He refused to see ministers or sign documents, bit chunks out of his own arms and for days on end lay motionless in his own excrement. Eventually Ferdinand, a son by his first marriage, encouraged him to be shaved and to have his linen changed, but Elizabeth, anxious to retain total control over her ailing husband, brought an end to the interference and persuaded Philip to issue an order forbidding Ferdinand and his wife from appearing in public or receiving foreign diplomats. The songs of Farinelli provided the only light relief in those dark years up until his death.

Elizabeth was powerless to prevent Ferdinand succeeding him as king, but he, too, was prone to bouts of depression and fears of impending death. He tried to commit suicide, but then veered in the opposite direction and refused to go to bed for days at a time in the belief that he would die if he lay down. He eventually died a thoroughly unremarkable death in 1759.

LAND OF THE GIANTS

FREDERICK WILLIAM I, KING OF PRUSSIA
(1688–1740)

While Peter the Great liked to surround himself with dwarfs, the Prussian monarch Frederick William I harboured loftier ambitions. For the military-minded Frederick William devoted much of his time and energy to the creation of an elite regiment of excessively tall grenadiers, which came to be known as the Potsdam Giant Guards. What started out as a mere passion soon developed into an obsession, the king recruiting these outsize human specimens with the same zeal that an art lover collects a Van Gogh. And when there was a shortage of volunteers to the ranks, he resorted to kidnap and was even prepared to go to war to secure a sought-after giant. He was truly a man possessed.

Height was the only criterion for the Potsdam Guards: all recruits had to be at least six feet tall. In fact, the majority were more than seven feet tall, with the most prized freaks being little short of nine feet from head to toe. To emphasise their stature, Frederick William made them wear tall, pointed, red headgear, which added another couple of feet to their dimensions. These men may have been the tallest soldiers in Europe but they were by no means the most accomplished, a number being mentally infirm.

The first recruits were volunteers from his own country – Germans lured by the promise of a uniform and regular meals – or foreigners sent to the king as a goodwill gesture. Whenever

Frederick William went on a state visit, he would drop heavy hints that the type of farewell gift he would appreciate more than any other would be a giant or two. Peter the Great, a like-minded soul, sent Frederick William fifty tall Russian men a year, while other European courts came to realise that the Prussian king's fixation could be used to their own advantage. Tall men became bargaining tools during negotiations and the British government were able to persuade Frederick William to sign a treaty heavily weighted in their favour simply by promising to deliver to him fifteen lofty Irishmen. It was a bribe that the Prussian king could not resist.

When new recruits were in short supply, Frederick William hired agents who would hang around Prussian bars on the lookout for tall men. Other agents would be despatched to the four corners of Europe, offering bonuses to parents who surrendered their tallest sons or to landowners who sent the king their tallest farm workers. As the king grew more desperate to acquire still bigger soldiers, he introduced a bounty system, which increased with the height of the captive, and instructed his agents to use any means necessary to obtain the right man. As a result of these incentives, kidnapping became widespread. In Rome, the king's agents broke into a monastery and snatched a tall monk as he knelt in prayer; a giraffe-like Austrian diplomat was seized in Hanover; and a lanky Dutch preacher was hauled off in mid-sermon along with four of his congregation. Not all of the kidnappings produced the desired results. A towering carpenter was tricked into lying down in a box, which was then bolted shut so that he could be shipped to Potsdam. Alas, the agent had omitted to drill air holes into the box, with the result that the carpenter was found dead on arrival. An irate Frederick William had the agent responsible imprisoned for life.

Initially, the rest of Europe looked upon the king's weird hobby with a sort of detached amusement until his agents began crossing territorial boundaries and even inducing tall men in foreign armies to desert. The Dutch were infuriated over the kidnapping of their preacher and threatened to declare war on Prussia over the incident. Frederick William considered taking up the challenge before deciding to back down and call a temporary halt to the abductions. Instead he resorted to blatant bribery, the princely sum of £6,000 buying him a 7ft-2in Irishman by the name of James Kirkland. The king also tried eugenics, forcing every tall male in Prussia to marry a tall woman in the hope of producing tall children, but, as Peter the Great had found, the science was unreliable. Besides, Frederick William grew impatient with waiting and went back to kidnapping. He eventually managed to acquire some 2,000 giants for his monstrous regiment.

He was intensely proud of his two units of the Potsdam Giant Guards and considered them far too precious to be risked in battle. Instead they were used for ceremonial duties, marching alongside the royal carriage and linking hands over the top of it. When he was ill or depressed, he would cheer himself up by arranging for a few hundred of them to march through his bedroom!

The king also liked to paint life-size portraits of his grenadiers from memory, and when one exceptionally tall Norwegian soldier died, Frederick William honoured his memory by having him sculpted in marble.

However, despite the high wages the Potsdam Giants were paid, the feeling of adoration between the king and his soldiers was not reciprocal. Living conditions for this collection of social misfits were poor and suicide and desertion were commonplace. Mutiny was a regular occurrence as the hapless grenadiers, usually held against their will and often in a foreign land, tried to burn down Potsdam in the hope of killing the king. Much as he cherished the men in captivity, Frederick William would not tolerate these outbreaks of rebellion and clamped down brutally on any show of dissent. Escapees were tracked down by his bounty hunters and punished by having their noses and ears sliced off before being thrown into jail.

In all walks of life, Frederick William was a firm believer in imposing military discipline, which is basically a euphemism for the fact that he was an unpleasant, sadistic bully. A short, fat man who would have failed every audition for his Potsdam Giants, he possessed mad, bulging eyes that gave him an air of menace, a trait that he tried to emphasise by the unusual practice of smearing bacon fat on his face. Whether or not it made him more intimidating is unclear, but he was irresistible to dogs.

His favourite prop was his rattan stick with which he would thrash everyone within reach, including innocent passers-by. Not surprisingly, the streets of Berlin emptied at news of the king's approach. The royal household fared no better. At mealtimes he threw plates and cutlery at his servants in wild fits of rage, but nobody suffered as much as his son Frederick.

The king was determined that his love of all things military should rub off on his son and by the age of five the poor boy had been made to learn by heart all 54 movements of the Prussian drill code. Within a year he had been given his own company of young cadets to drill and by the time he was seven he had been presented with a miniature arsenal. But Frederick had no interest in such matters, preferring to read books and listen to music – an attitude that enraged his father. For the king detested anything remotely artistic: an object was of no use to him unless it was capable of inflicting serious injury. On acceding to the throne in 1713, one of his first moves was to tear down all the palace curtains and throw out the elegant furniture and carpets. Later, during a state visit to Poland, he smashed an entire Meissen dinner service on a whim. So he was truly horrified to learn of his son's cultural inclinations and did not hesitate to demonstrate his disapproval in his own understated way. If he found the boy studying Latin, he had him publicly flogged and when young Frederick was caught hiding in bushes reading a book instead of hunting deer, the king thrashed him with the dreaded rattan cane and made him kiss his boots. A girl who accompanied Frederick on the piano while he played the flute was arrested and whipped through the streets of Potsdam by the public executioner for corrupting the prince. Intent on moulding his son in his own image, Frederick William also had the boy beaten for such failures as being thrown from a bolting horse and wearing gloves in bitterly cold weather.

When the children were young, the king would punish them for some petty misdemeanour by starving them or spitting in their food, but his moods grew blacker still with age as he began to suffer from gout, migraines and, most seriously, porphyria, a condition that he had inherited from his mother. He suffered his first attack at the age of nineteen, prompting bouts of depression and rage, but it was from forty onwards that he was at his most irascible. Plagued by insomnia, he would spend entire nights wandering aimlessly through the palace while by day he would sit silently, weeping for hours on end. His temper became uncontrollable. He took pot shots at his servants with a pair of pistols loaded with salt, crippling one valet and taking out the eye of another. Such was the terror in which he was held that one servant, hearing that he had been summoned to the king's private quarters, dropped dead with fright. At an official reception the king was on the point of kicking the visiting British ambassador but then thought better of it. And on the army parade ground he delivered so fearsome a thrashing to one of his majors that the man shot himself in the head.

But as ever Prince Frederick bore the brunt of his fury. Whenever they met, the king would grab his son by the throat, hurl him to the ground and force him into the familiar ritual of kissing his boots. Then he would taunt him by saying: 'If my father had treated me like this, I would have put an end to my life long ago. But you have no courage.' The distinctly uneasy relationship between father and son came to a head in 1730, when they were invited to attend a military parade in Saxony on the invitation of the King of Poland. Suddenly, in full public view, Frederick William grabbed the prince, kicked and beat him, dragged him along the ground by the hair and sent him bleeding and dishevelled to make an official appearance. The prince could take no more and tried to flee to England, accompanied by a friend, Hans von Katte, but the pair were captured. Then, on the king's orders, Frederick was woken one morning and held at the window of his cell while von Katte was beheaded in the courtyard below for desertion. Forced to watch

144

the execution, the prince fainted just before the sabre sliced off his friend's head, but the body was left there for hours lest he forget. The king also seriously considered executing Frederick before eventually relenting.

Meanwhile, Frederick William's health was on the slide. He had a nervous breakdown in 1727 and two years later suffered an attack that left him completely lame in both arms and both legs, as a result of which he temporarily had to be pushed around the palace in a wheelchair. In later years his face turned bluish-red, he had difficulty breathing, his speech was slurred and his legs were hideously swollen. He became so depressed that on one occasion the queen found him with a noose around his neck. Nevertheless, he invariably regained sufficient energy to be able to give his servants and doctors sound beatings. It was when the king had neither the inclination nor the strength to inflict corporal punishment that the court knew there was something seriously wrong.

His condition was not improved by imbibing copious amounts of beer with his friends. When drunk, Frederick William enjoyed playing coarse practical jokes, selecting a member of court, Jakob Gundling, as the regular fall guy. One of their favourite pranks was to throw Gundling from the castle walls into the moat below, a jape that left the victim relatively unscathed until they repeated it on a winter's day when the moat was frozen solid. The king and his chums roared with laughter as the unfortunate Gundling bounced across the ice. Another time they set him on fire. What larks! When Gundling died from excessive drinking, the king had him buried in a barrel. It was what he would have wanted.

During the king's final illness, Prince Frederick suggested summoning a leading doctor, but Frederick William, displaying his usual contempt for the medical profession, replied that his own physician was perfectly capable of killing him without assistance. On 31 May 1740, riddled with dropsy and gout, the king finally gave up the unequal struggle, to be succeeded by his son, who immediately disbanded the grotesque Potsdam Giants. And the artistic boy whom his bullying father never thought would amount to anything and who had been humiliated, abused and taunted at every opportunity went on to become Prussia's greatest ever ruler, Frederick the Great.

THE PRACTICAL JOKER

ANNA, EMPRESS OF RUSSIA (1693–1740)

The sudden death of young Peter II in 1730 plunged Russia into a succession crisis. With no remaining male heirs in the Romanov line, the families that made up the ruling elite opted for Anna Ivanovna, daughter of the feeble-minded Ivan V and niece of Peter the Great, simply because they thought she would be easy to manipulate. A condition of her accession was that she sign a document agreeing to major restrictions on her power as a monarch, but as soon as she took the throne she tore it up and ruled in her own autocratic and highly idiosyncratic fashion.

Anna was something of a rough diamond. In fact, she was about as feminine as Genghis Khan. Her voice and manners were uncouth and even her interests – horseback riding and shooting – were considered manly. She did marry once, at the age of seventeen, to Frederick William, the Duke of Courland, a nephew of the King of Prussia. The marriage and the ceremony were arranged by Peter the Great who, with his love of small-scale spectaculars, introduced two enormous pies, from which a pair of dwarfs – one male, one female – emerged through the crust to start dancing around the table. But the marriage lasted just two months before Anna's husband died from alcohol poisoning.

Although she never remarried, Anna had a string of lovers of both sexes, including the detested Count Ernst Biron, whose wife was forced to work at the palace while he shared the empress's bed. Anna's reign saw the introduction of ballet and opera to the Russian people as well as a new holiday destination

– Siberia. Tens of thousands of her subjects were exiled to the barren wasteland.

Anna was a decidedly quirky character. She kept loaded guns by the windows of her various palaces so that she could shoot passing birds; she once stunned the eminent poet, Tredyakovski, who had just given her a private reading of his latest ode, by suddenly punching him in the mouth; she decreed that only bright colours were to be worn in her presence; and when a lady-in-waiting, who had been commanded to sing to her all night, collapsed from exhaustion part-way through the rendering, the poor woman was sent to work in the laundry. In mitigation, the laundry room was a major cog in the imperial machine. Only the most skilled washerwomen were allowed to handle the empress's undies and even then they were sworn to confidence as to the precise nature of the garment. All stains were unmentionable. To break that confidence would be to earn a one-way ticket to Siberia. To ensure secrecy, the empress's dirty underwear was always kept under lock and key away from prying eyes and no unauthorised person was allowed in the laundry while her linen was being washed.

Anna's eccentricity was evident in the punishments she devised. For in addition to the traditional tortures and executions, she came up with a number of penalties that were akin to cruel practical jokes. When two leading Russian nobles, Nikita Volkonskii and Aleksei Apraskin, committed some trivial offence, the empress ordered that they should live as hens for a week. Accordingly, they were dressed in feathered costumes and placed in large straw-filled baskets, which were positioned in the corner of one of the palace reception rooms. The two men were then made to sit on the nest, which contained a dozen new-laid eggs, and cluck away for the amusement of the empress and her court. They were left in no doubt that failure to maintain the impersonation for the full seven days would result in death. After Prince Volkonskii had angered the empress on another occasion, he was humiliated by being appointed official keeper of her favourite dog, a post that necessitated feeding the hound with jugs of cream at certain hours. Meanwhile, his wife was placed in charge of the empress's white rabbit. To teach a lesson to a pair of obese noblewomen, Anna had them force-fed vast amounts of pastries until they nearly choked to death on their own vomit. These degradations were widely resented, but few dared to decline. When Prince Balakirev did refuse to play one of her strange games, he was led outside and whipped.

Her most elaborate practical joke was saved for the distinguished noble, Prince Michael Alexsyevitch Golitsyn, who had offended her by marrying an Italian Catholic. Having already stripped him of his title and treated him as the court buffoon, the empress hatched a new plan. With his wife now dead, he was ordered to take as his next bride a servant named Anna Buzheninova who, by common consent, was the ugliest woman in the whole of Russia. And in those days the competition was fierce. In a style reminiscent of her own wedding, the empress arranged a lavish procession featuring all manner of human freaks and carriages pulled by pigs, goats, camels, cows and dogs. The carriages contained St Petersburg's worst drunkards, hand-picked from the city's gutters. The less-than-happy couple arrived in a cage strapped to the back of an elephant and then had to listen to the reading of a specially composed poem entitled 'Greetings to the Bridal Pair of Fools'. Following the ceremony, bride and groom set off on their honeymoon, which the empress had insisted should take place on the banks of the frozen River Neva, an inhospitable place at the best of times but even less desirable in the middle of the winter of 1740. There, at a cost of some 30,000 roubles, she had constructed a splendid palace, made entirely of ice. After leading them inside the palace, the empress made sure that they undressed and lay on their ice bed for the night. Guards were posted on the door to prevent escape. Remarkably, the couple survived and emerged unscathed the next morning. They had obviously decided that the best way to combat the freezing conditions was to huddle together because nine months later the ugly wife presented the handsome prince with twin boys. And the day after the birth, the Empress Anna died, leaving the prince with the last laugh.

THE SEX MACHINE

CATHERINE THE GREAT, EMPRESS OF RUSSIA
(1729–96)

Catherine the Great is often credited with pioneering one of the key accessories of modern woman – the toy boy. Some of her lovers were barely past the embryo stage when they were plucked from the ranks to satisfy Catherine's lust and to appear at official engagements on her arm: a glamorous trophy for an ageing empress. Her last lover was forty years younger than her – a statistic that even the most predatory Hollywood actress could only dream of. According to legend she bedded nigh on 300 men, although the true figure was probably barely into double figures, the popular estimate being as low as twelve. But she did wear them out at an alarming rate and at her peak she changed men almost as frequently as other women change their hairstyle.

Yet Catherine was very much a late starter in life and did not lose her virginity until the age of 24. Even then it had nothing to do with her first and only husband, a feeble individual who was more interested in his toy soldiers than his young bride.

Curiously, this most celebrated of Russian empresses was not Russian at all: she was born in Poland. In 1744 she was brought to Russia at the invitation of the Empress Elizabeth with a view to marrying the Grand Duke Peter, heir to the Russian throne, and the following year they were duly wed in St Petersburg. Catherine was a confident girl with a forceful personality but, at sixteen, she knew nothing about sex. Neither did her young husband, which, because she found him physically repellent, probably came as a relief. By seventeen he had already lost much of his hair due to the after-effects of measles and smallpox. Observers have described him as ugly, thin, sulky, in no way athletic, and 'a young barbarian with the manners of an unlicked cub', so when he collapsed into bed drunk on their wedding night and made no attempt to arouse his bride, she was not exactly overcome with disappointment.

However, the Empress Elizabeth was keen for Catherine to provide Peter with an heir as soon as possible in order to stabilise the succession. So against her better judgement Catherine thought she ought to make an effort and inquired of her ladies-in-waiting as to precisely what she and her husband had to do in order to consummate the marriage. But they were none the wiser and when a despairing Catherine then asked her own mother for advice, she was rebuked for her indecent curiosity. For his part, Peter decided to consult his drinking partners about the facts of life but they explained it in such coarse terms that the poor boy was left petrified. His reticence in the bedroom may also have been attributable to a physical defect – an over-tight foreskin that prevented him from gaining an erection. When he mentioned the little problem to Catherine, she was apparently less than sympathetic.

As weeks turned into months and months turned into years, Catherine became increasingly frustrated. Peter's attempts at affection were clumsy and brief and she soon tired of his immaturity. She later wrote:

The Grand Duke never entered my room except for the purpose of pacing up and down it, talking to me of matters which, no doubt, interested him, but had no interest whatever for me. He used to do this for hours at a time, and several times a day. I had to pace the room with him until I sank from exhaustion. I had to listen to him attentively and reply to him, though he generally talked the most insufferable nonsense . . . When he left me, it was a delightful relief to turn even to the most tedious book.

Peter's boorish behaviour was proving an embarrassment. He would pull childish faces at people, empty his wine glass over the heads of footmen, and play vicious practical jokes on the courtiers. He also treated his hunting dogs with great cruelty, whipping them pitilessly and ignoring Catherine's pleas to desist. The fact that he kept these dogs in his bedroom was simply another barrier to a sex life with his wife, who complained in vain about the smell, the incessant barking and the fact that she was often sharing their bed with half a dozen spaniels. Indeed, the only games she and Peter played in bed were with his wooden toy soldiers. Peter took great pride in his collection of miniature military men and would line them up on the table next to the conjugal bed. He invited Catherine to take part in the parades and the various war games that he had devised and reluctantly she agreed, often being obliged to play well into the early hours. All the while Peter would mimic the sounds of cannon fire, occasionally prompting concerned courtiers to check on the strange noises that were emanating from the bedroom. 'Often I laughed,' wrote Catherine, 'but more often still I was exasperated and even made uncomfortable. The whole bed being covered and filled with dolls and toys, some of them quite heavy.' Peter took his toy soldiering extremely seriously. When a large rat ate two of his miniature infantrymen, Peter had the dead rodent hanged in public view after finding it guilty of breaking military law. Catherine burst out laughing, at which point Peter's face darkened ominously.

After seven loveless years of marriage, Catherine was given permission by the Empress Elizabeth, who feared with good reason that the union would remain childless, to take a lover, a guardsman by the name of Sergei Saltykov. With Catherine soon pregnant, it was imperative that Peter be led to believe that the child was his own and when husband and wife finally had sex for the first time (Peter having been persuaded to have a circumcision), she cleverly convinced him that he was taking her virginity.

Peter's new-found capability cut no ice with Catherine. Having sampled a real soldier, she had little interest in returning to a toy, and had a small alcove built behind her bed where she was able to entertain her lovers in secret. If anyone asked what was behind the curtain, she said it hid a commode. Determined to enjoy herself at last, she had no qualms about deceiving her loutish husband. 'My head is made of iron,' she wrote, explaining her strong will, 'and very resistant.'

Her on-off lover for thirteen years was another soldier, Gregory Orlov, a bear of a man said to be indefatigable in bed. She had three sons by him, the first two while her husband was still alive. She managed to conceal the second birth from Peter, who had not even realised she was pregnant, by instructing her valet to start a fire in the servants' quarters, knowing full well that the blaze would distract him. Sure enough, Peter went to watch the fire, allowing the baby to be smuggled away.

When the Empress Elizabeth died in 1761, Peter and Catherine ascended to the throne as Peter III and Catherine II. Peter's obsession with all things Prussian ensured that the Russian people soon hated him as much as his wife did, and in June 1762, having belatedly begun to suspect Catherine of infidelity, he was toppled by a rebellion. The following month Peter was murdered by the Orlov brothers and Catherine was crowned Russia's sole ruler.

With her husband dead, Catherine was able to bring her lovers out into the open. The secret alcove was scrapped as the empress brazenly flaunted her sexuality. She expected her young men to be on the job 24 hours a day, ever ready to cater for her sexual needs. Failure to satisfy her did not bear thinking about, as a result of which the pressure on her lovers to perform was so great that a few resorted to aphrodisiac cocktails in order to guarantee that they were always up to the task. For they knew that there would invariably be a replacement waiting in the wings to take their place and to move into the suite of rooms that came with the position. But even those who ultimately shrunk from the challenge received a generous financial settlement.

Aware of the dangers of catching syphilis, Catherine had her potential escorts carefully vetted beforehand. First they were subjected to a rigorous medical examination by the court physician and then they were introduced to the empress's associate, Countess Bruce, who interviewed them, briefed them as to the empress's sexual preferences and sometimes put them through a sort of 'road test' to ensure that they were worthy of a place in the imperial bed. Once Catherine had indicated her approval, the successful candidate would be taken to his suite where a gift was waiting – a box containing 100,000 roubles. That evening he would be presented to court on the empress's arm; then at ten o'clock they would retire together to her bedroom. As lovers came and went, the walls of the room next to Catherine's main bedroom became adorned with miniature portraits of the men she had seduced.

Gregory Orlov, who had been so instrumental in her climb to power, was handsomely rewarded until he fell from grace for sleeping with his thirteen-year-old cousin. Catherine had him pensioned off and the influential figure in her bedroom became Gregory Potemkin, a huge one-eyed Russian with a fiery temperament. So close were they that rumours persisted that they had secretly married. Like Orlov, Potemkin was highly sexed, an attribute that kept him in favour for a few years. And even when he relinquished the imperial bed to marry his cousin, he continued to find new young lovers for Catherine and indeed was well paid for acting as her pimp.

Throughout the late 1770s imperial favourites succeeded one another at breakneck speed. Satirists of the time ridiculed the empress's sexual appetite and images of her being tickled by young men, the scandal prompting the English ambassador Sir James Harris to write of Catherine:

Her court, which she had ruled with the greatest dignity and with the utmost decorum, has gradually become an arena of depravity and immorality. This fall into decadence has been so rapid that in the brief time that I have been in this country a profound revolution has occurred in the mores and conventional habits of the courtiers.'

A few days after Potemkin had been elevated to his new role of empress's consort, Peter Zavadovsky, a handsome 26-year-old Ukrainian, was moved into the favourites' suite. However, he lasted only a few months before being relieved of his duties in return for a pension of 50,000 roubles and an estate of 9,000 Ukrainian peasants. In spite of the generous settlement, Zavadovsky was mortified at being usurped by a dashing young hussar, Simon Zorich. But the latter made the mistake of falling out with Potemkin and was ousted after eleven months. His successor was another young hussar, Ivan Rimsky-Korsakov, whose mighty member prompted an open-mouthed Catherine to declare that he was 'a masterpiece of nature'. But he lasted barely a year after being caught exchanging admiring glances with Countess Bruce.

Then, in 1779, Catherine homed in on Alexander Lanskoy, a 23-year-old captain in the Cavalier Guard. She saw him as the man to support her in her old age but he died of a fever five years later. Stories circulated that he had died because she had exhausted him with her sexual demands; others claimed she had forced him to swallow poisonous aphrodisiacs, which had made his body swell up and burst. She mourned his loss for a year before renewing her one-woman corruption of the youth of Russia.

Catherine dreaded the onset of old age and did her utmost to delay it. She employed two dwarfs to look after her beauty products and was notoriously sensitive about her hair, having seen it fall out on more than one occasion through illness. When she discovered that she was suffering from dandruff, she imprisoned her hairdresser in an iron cage for three years to stop the news from spreading around the court.

The empress was almost as devoted to nature as she was to her hair. Gazing from her window one spring morning, she spotted the year's first primrose and, to deter anyone from picking it, posted a sentry to guard it day and night. The sentry and his descendants continued to patrol the lawn long after the death of both Catherine and the primrose, simply because nobody had countermanded the order. It was some fifty years before Count Bismarck finally uncovered the folly and decided that the manpower could be more gainfully employed elsewhere.

Despite the attention lavished on her appearance, the ravages of time steadily caught up with and overtook Catherine. Her long hair had turned almost completely white, her complexion was pasty, most of her teeth had fallen out, her figure had ballooned and her legs were swollen and ulcerated. Indeed, ramps had to be fitted in place of the palace stairs because her legs could no longer support her weight. This was hardly a tasty dish to set before a virile young man, but she did still have one thing going for her: she was the empress. So, on turning sixty she made a desperate gesture to recapture her youth. The youth's name was Platon Zubov, a twenty-year-old guardsman. She never could resist a man in uniform – it always looked so attractive on her bedroom floor.

Catherine may have lingered under the misapprehension that she was still beautiful, but she could not deny the vast age difference between herself and her new lover and even referred to him as 'the child'. When Zubov was with her, his pet monkey often accompanied him because Catherine liked to be seen with something or someone young and lively. From Zubov's point of view, the monkey was probably better looking than the empress. Catherine tried to convert Zubov into a statesman, but although he assumed most of Potemkin's official powers, he lacked the necessary tact and intelligence. His arrogance infuriated the imperial courtiers but Catherine defended him to the hilt, telling one official: 'I am doing a great service to the state by educating young men.'

As the years of hard drinking and late-night love-ins continued to take their toll on her features, Catherine realised that this would be her last chance of 'arm candy'. She was even prepared to overlook Zubov's blatant attempt to seduce sixteen-year-old Elisabeth Alekseevna, wife of the future Tsar Alexander I. Driven by ambition rather than affection, Zubov shared the empress's bed for seven years until, on 6 November 1796, Catherine died at the age of 67. Some accounts, keen to talk up her legendary libido, claimed that she had died while having sex with a horse, but the truth was less spectacular. She simply suffered a massive stroke while sitting on the toilet and fell off. It was an undignified way to go.

But the stories of Catherine the Great's tremendous sex drive live on. After playing her on stage, American actress Mae West – herself no slouch in the bedroom stakes – said: 'Catherine was a great empress. She also had 300 lovers. I did the best I could in a couple of hours.' The number of young male favourites, like the horse tale, was almost certainly apocryphal but really there is no need to exaggerate what was in every sense a remarkable love life.

THE QUEEN WHO DRESSED
AS A CHILD

MARIA I, QUEEN OF PORTUGAL (1734–1816)

That Maria I should be insane for the last 24 years of her life was hardly surprising: it was the awful consequence of centuries of inbreeding within Portugal's royal family, the House of Braganza.

Certainly a glance at her family tree might have convinced Maria that it was best to stay in the womb. Her maternal grandfather was Philip V of Spain, a manic depressive driven by two obsessions: sex and religion. Her paternal grandfather, Joao V of Portugal, was also highly sexed and religious; he neatly combined his two passions by choosing nuns as his mistresses. Joao was also prone to bouts of dark melancholy and in the last years of his reign left the business of government to leading churchmen. Following Joao's death in 1750, the crown passed to Maria's father, Joseph I, but he was more interested in playing cards and hunting, leaving the country to be run by the unpopular Marquis of Pombal. In 1755 Lisbon was devastated by an earthquake and a tidal wave that left 30,000 people dead and instilled such a sense of fear into King Joseph that for months he refused to enter any of his palaces, preferring instead to live in a tent. Three years later he survived an assassination attempt, but the incident scarred him emotionally as well as physically and he distanced himself still more from matters of state. In fact, if he had withdrawn any further he would have been in Spain.

The Braganzas had learned nothing from their disastrous policy of marrying in-house and in 1760, the 25-year-old Maria was married to her 42-year-old uncle Pedro. Despite the age difference, the pair lived relatively happily and Maria gave birth to seven children, only three of whom survived infancy. On the orders of the king, the eldest boy, Joseph, was married to Maria's sister, his aunt Benedita, who was fourteen years his senior. Mercifully, this particular incestuous marriage proved barren.

In 1777 King Joseph died and Maria became queen with her husband/uncle serving as her consort. One of her first acts was to dismiss the hated Pombal but as she tried to rectify the mistakes that had been made during her father's reign, her conscience told her that by doing so, she was somehow sullying his name and reputation. The feeling of disloyalty nagged away at her until, one day in 1780, she scratched out her signature and exclaimed that she was 'condemned to hell'. She was carried off to her apartments in a state of delirium.

When Pedro died in 1786, Maria's mind was plunged into fresh turmoil. She grieved over her loss for months but no sooner had she started to show signs of recovery than she was struck by another mortal blow. For in 1788 her eldest son, Joseph, died of smallpox. Maria's guilt at not having had him vaccinated against the disease began to overwhelm her. Fate was not finished yet, though. Two months later her only surviving daughter, Mariana, also died of the disease and at around the same time the epidemic claimed the lives of both her confessor and chief minister.

This series of tragedies tipped Maria over the edge. Her grief was uncontrollable and she took to wearing children's clothes – perhaps in memory of her lost offspring. She lay awake at night, persecuted by guilt, and if she did drift into sleep she suffered recurring nightmares, convincing herself that she had been damned for all eternity. The so-called 'pink palace', a miniature Versailles built for her by Pedro, became her prison and by 1790 she had sunk into a state of permanent depression, punctuated by indecorous conversation quite unbecoming of a queen.

Her ministers decided that she was mad and invited her only surviving son, John, to take the reins of government. Meanwhile they summoned the controversial Dr Francis Willis, who had recently treated King George III of England for similar symptoms, to take a look at the queen. His methods brought about a short-term improvement but by the time he returned to England in 1793, she was worse than ever. Nevertheless, Willis pocketed a consultancy fee of £10,000.

Maria's religious mania was spiralling out of control. She would run along the palace corridors repeatedly wailing, 'Ai Jesus!' The traveller and diarist William Beckford arrived in Portugal when she was in full cry. He wrote: 'The most agonising shrieks – shrieks such as I hardly conceived possible – inflicted on me a sensation of horror such as I had never felt before. The Queen, herself, whose apartment was only two doors off from the chambers where we were sitting, uttered those dreadful sounds. "Ai Jesus, Ai Jesus!" did she exclaim again and again in the utterances of agony.'

In 1799 John was officially named Prince Regent but when Napoleon invaded Portugal in 1807 the royal family fled to Brazil, taking their valuables and art treasures with them. Maria's enforced exile enabled her madness to be kept secret from her subjects but a change of air had no beneficial effect on her illness. When the royal ship landed in Bahia following a turbulent 52-day crossing, the queen became terrified of the natives dancing around her chair to obtain a close view of European royalty. A friendly Brazilian welcome was interpreted by Maria as a sign that she was in hell with devils pursuing her. Before long, she was confined to a convent where she died in 1816 to be succeeded by her son John as Joao VI, although he did not return to his homeland for another six years.

THE RICE-BOX KING

SADO, KING OF KOREA (1735–62)

With no heir to the throne, King Yongjo of Korea explored every possible avenue to find a successor. Since his queen was childless, he devoted his considerable energies to impregnating his favourite concubine, Lady Sonhui, and in 1735, following a series of daughters, she finally gave birth to a boy, Prince Sado. The news heralded wholesale rejoicing yet Sado would prove to be such a psychopath that his mother ended up begging his father to kill him in order to protect the future of the country.

Owing to the fact that he had been born to a court lady rather than the queen, there was some opposition from within the court to little Sado being given the title Crown Prince, but the king's argument won the day. Sado grew up with little parental guidance and even less parental affection. The king was an impatient man who appeared constantly irritated by his son and frequently scolded him in the presence of others. Lady Sonhui was only marginally less intimidating, with the result that the boy lived in fear of the pair of them and was often too afraid to speak in case he incurred their anger.

When he was just nine, Sado was ordered by his parents to marry eight-year-old Lady Hong, the daughter of a noted scholar, but less than eighteen months after the wedding, the prince fell victim to a mystery illness, which led to him behaving slightly strangely. Six years later a measles epidemic claimed the life of his favourite sister, Hwayop. Sado also caught the disease and although he quickly recovered, he began

161

suffering from frequent delusions and nightmares during which he said he could see an apparition of the god of thunder. He became terrified of the sky and of the characters for 'thunder' and 'thunderclap', and whenever a powerful thunderstorm occurred, he feared that the king would hold him responsible.

King Yongjo had a problem with words, too. Whenever he heard any that he considered ominous – such as 'death' – he used to wash his ears immediately. It seems that speaking to his son was an even greater ordeal, for at the end of any conversation with Sado, the king would rinse out his mouth, wash his ears and change into a clean robe. He also developed a system whereby he used one door for pleasant duties and a different one for unpleasant tasks, such as presiding over a torture. Indeed, he came to be so uneasy about supervising punishments that he often asked Sado to deputise for him, but the prince's performance always left a lot to be desired in Yongjo's eyes.

Relations between father and son were further strained when Sado made one of the court ladies pregnant. Dreading his father's reaction, Sado tried to procure an abortion but the birth went ahead and sure enough the king flew into a fierce rage, conveniently forgetting that he himself had recently made another of his concubines pregnant. The fallout caused Sado's mental state to deteriorate and he began stammering. When the king called on him unexpectedly in the summer of 1756, he found his son confused and incoherent and wrongly assumed that he was drunk. After receiving yet another dressing-down, Sado took out his anger and frustration on his servants.

With each passing year, Sado became increasingly violent, raping court ladies and killing eunuchs and maids. He proudly displayed the impaled head of one murdered eunuch to the women of the court, explaining: 'It relieves my pent-up anger to kill people or animals when I am feeling depressed or on edge.'

Sado then took up with a seamstress, Ping-ae, and housed her in an expensive suite of apartments. When the king expressed his anger, a distressed Sado threw himself down a well, but the well was full of ice and he was rescued. Shortly after Ping-ae had given birth to a son, Sado fatally injured her during one of his violent fits.

In the meantime Sado had become obsessed with clothes and before he went out anywhere, his servants had to prepare as many as thirty silk outfits from which he would make his final choice. To help him make his decision, he would sometimes burn several outfits as an offering to a spirit figure. If his valet made even the slightest error while helping him dress, Sado would become extremely agitated and feel unable to wear that particular outfit. He was a living nightmare.

In the spring of 1761 the king, in one of his more amenable moods, allowed Sado to accompany him on a visit to a royal tomb but when it started raining heavily on the way, Yongjo blamed the prince for the downpour and sent him back. For his part, Sado blamed the incident on a wrong choice of clothes. Some might say they almost deserved one another.

The following year the prince went on an unauthorised pleasure trip and on his return suffered an attack of malaria that laid him low for several months. Although alcohol had always been strictly prohibited at the Korean court, Sado began drinking heavily to counter his depression. He started seeing imaginary passers-by, he swore at his ageing mother, and organised late-night orgies. He also tried to have sex with his younger sister, Princess Hwawan. His acts of violence intensified, royal physicians, translators and court workmen being maimed or slain to satisfy his need to inflict suffering. Every day a batch of dead bodies was carried from the palace, each the victim of Sado's handiwork.

In May 1762 Lady Sonhui left in tears after visiting her son. The following month the king received a document from one of his ministers detailing the gross misconduct of the prince. Among the most serious charges was one of 'bringing a nun into the court and cohabiting with her'. The minister paid for his revelations with his life and Sado, suspecting that his brother-in-law was behind the treachery, announced his intention to kill him. Sado also stepped up his campaign of harassment against his sister, stalking her and trying to break into her apartments.

With charges hanging over him of raping palace women, murdering eunuchs and seducing a nun, Sado was in an invidious position. Everyone at court was so terrified of his unpredictable behaviour that Lady Sonhui, still disturbed by her previous visit, decided that it was time for drastic action and ordered the king to kill Sado in order to protect the kingdom. On 4 July, King Yongjo summoned his son, deprived him of his royal status, and ordered him to take the honourable way out by drinking poison. When Sado refused, the king had him shut up in a huge rice-box, where he was left to starve. Eight days later he was dead.

Having treated his son so heartlessly during his life, a remorseful Yongjo at least had the decency to restore him posthumously to royal status.

THE MADNESS OF KING GEORGE

GEORGE III, KING OF ENGLAND (1738–1820)

The popular image of 'Mad King George' is that of a deranged monarch shaking hands with the branches of an oak tree in the belief that it was the King of Prussia. Consequently he has all too frequently been portrayed as a barmy German – a blot on the otherwise glorious throne of England. Yet in truth George was the kindest and most compassionate of kings – a devoted husband who had the misfortune to sire a wastrel son and to suffer from a hereditary disease, porphyria, which periodically put him on a different planet from the rest of the world. Nor was he helped by the fact that he was being treated by a bunch of physicians and quacks who would have struggled to cure ham.

When the insecure George acceded to the throne in 1760, he followed the advice of the Earl of Bute on every matter, including that of finding a suitable wife. George had fallen in love with Sarah Lennox, daughter of the Duke of Richmond, but Bute poured scorn on the idea of such a marriage, forcing the new king to look elsewhere. In haste he settled on the German Princess Charlotte of Mecklenburg-Strelitz who was unflatteringly nicknamed 'monkey face' on account of her large mouth, flat nose and swarthy complexion. Although she may have been better suited to a zoo than a palace, George fulfilled his marital duties in the same conscientious manner as he fulfilled his kingship, and they bred fifteen children – nine sons and six daughters.

It has to be said that they were not the most charismatic of couples. She liked playing the clavichord and sewing; he liked collecting watches and model ships, studying the technique of agriculture, and early nights. Their court was reputed to be the dullest in Europe.

George was a firm but fair father who adored his children and was deeply distressed when both Alfred and Octavius died young in successive years. The death of Octavius at the age of four in 1783 hit him particularly hard, as the child had always been one of the king's favourites.

Apart from the occasional fever, George had always enjoyed excellent health and kept in shape by taking plenty of exercise and eating frugally. Then in June 1788 he suffered from a violent bilious attack. He recovered but two months later he complained of pains in his stomach and back that were making breathing difficult. His doctor, Sir George Baker, diagnosed it as a chill caused by wearing wet stockings.

Around the middle of October he began passing dark-coloured urine – a symptom of porphyria – and on the night of the 17th he was seized with another bilious fever and asked for opium to relieve the pain. His eyes were wild and his voice agitated and he complained that both his vision and hearing were impaired. He began long rambling monologues, once talking for sixteen hours non-stop until his voice was hoarse. He entered a fantasy world, believing London to have drowned. He stayed awake for some 72 hours and spent much of the time writing long letters to foreign rulers on imaginary subjects.

On 5 November the king became more confused and incoherent, while continuing to talk incessantly, and at dinner he lost control completely and lapsed into delirium. Witnessing this, the queen became hysterical and was greatly relieved when George was persuaded to let her sleep in a separate room that night. Dr Baker reported that the king was 'under an entire alienation of mind'. He surmised that the cause was gout, which had originally attacked his feet but 'had flown to his brain and lodged there', and a treatment was applied to his head in the hope of driving it down again. When Baker himself

166

was taken ill, Dr Richard Warren, physician to the Prince of Wales, visited the king but George loathed Warren and refused to allow him into the room to examine him. So Warren listened from behind the door and heard enough wild ravings to tell the Prince of Wales that the king was suffering a 'seizure upon the brain' and that, 'If he did live, there was little reason to hope his intellect would be restored.' Just in case the prince had failed to grasp the significance of what he was saying, Warren added helpfully: '*Rex noster insanit* – our king is mad.'

George was now more agitated than ever, producing staccato cries of 'What! What! What!' and foaming with rage. At other times he sank into deep melancholy. As his condition showed no sign of improving, his doctors searched for an alternative explanation. Some blamed the mineral waters of Cheltenham Spa, which he had been drinking shortly before the illness.

At the end of November, the king was moved from Windsor Castle to Kew because it had a private garden where he was not at risk of being seen by the public. New opinions were sought, among them those of Dr Francis Willis, a clergyman who had set up a madhouse in Lincolnshire and had been awarded a medical degree by the University of Oxford. Willis and his sons had the bedside manner of Attila the Hun. Believing that the king's condition could be controlled by intimidation, coercion and restraint, they put him in a straitjacket whenever he appeared remotely out of sorts. If he refused his food, started sweating in bed or became slightly restless, they would strap him into the restraining device with a band across his chest and his legs tied to a bedpost. He was often kept in the straitjacket for 24 hours at a time. Sometimes they used the jacket in conjunction with a special restraining chair, which George called his 'coronation chair', and when he began using obscene language, they had him gagged. They also prescribed that hot mustard plasters be placed on his legs, stomach and chest to 'draw out the evil in his body'. Although the king despised their brand of patient care – he was particularly horrified at being tied to the bed – he had little choice but to submit to their disciplinarian methods.

There was no sign of an instant improvement. George's flights of fancy became ever more alarming. He issued orders to people who were long since dead, tried to sexually assault a housemaid, and imagined that his pillow was his dead son Octavius. According to a royal equerry, the king 'got a pillow-case round his head, and the pillow in bed with him which he called Prince Octavius who he said was to be born this day'. George also fantasised that he was married to Lady Pembroke, a sombre lady-in-waiting to the queen. Meanwhile, he told the queen that he loved another, that she was mad and that he had decided not to admit her to his bed for another five years. When she did appear, he told her that she was an impostor!

Against the odds, George's condition slowly improved over the first months of 1789 and he appeared to have made a full recovery, but the symptoms returned in 1801. His physicians thought he might have caught a chill from sitting in a cold church, but whatever the cause, the Willises were in no doubt as to the cure: out came the straitjacket again. George accepted the treatment stoically.

Three years later the muscular pain, fever, swelling and nausea returned and within a few days George was unable to walk without a cane. This time Dr Samuel Foart Simmons – a specialist physician in a hospital for lunatics – was summoned, but his methods were no different to those of the Willises and soon the king found himself trussed up once more in a straitjacket. After this attack, Queen Charlotte decided against resuming sexual relations and from then on they lived more or less separate lives while continuing to appear together in public.

During his sane periods George was the finest – and certainly the most moral – of the Hanoverian monarchs, but the porphyria that poisoned his entire nervous system, including his brain, continued to lead to episodes of wildly eccentric behaviour. He became convinced that he could see Germany from his Windsor bedroom; he once agreed to have half of his face shaved but not the other half; and on another occasion had to be forcibly restrained from riding his horse into a Weymouth church. Other tales are most likely apocryphal, including the famous story that, while being driven by carriage through Windsor Great Park one day, he suddenly ordered his driver to stop, got out, walked over to an oak tree, shook hands with one of its branches and talked to it for some minutes under the impression that it was the King of Prussia. Contemporary accounts of his madness told how he thought beef grew like vegetables and tried to prove it by planting four pounds of meat in the kitchen garden at Windsor Castle. And on a trip to Cheltenham he was said to have been so deranged that he tried to race against a horse. He is also rumoured to have gone through a phase of deliberately ending every sentence with the word 'peacock'. Apparently a minister solved the problem by agreeing with the king that 'peacock' was indeed a fine word with which to finish a sentence and that in fact it was too good a word to be wasted on the ears of mere subjects. Instead the minister suggested that the word should be whispered, and so at the king's speech to parliament, George paused meaningfully at the end of each sentence but the word 'peacock' was inaudible to the masses.

So sensitive were his subjects to the king's predicament that all theatre productions of *King Lear* were banned in the United Kingdom between 1788 and George's death, as the story of Shakespeare's deranged monarch was considered to be a little too close to home.

In 1810, shortly after celebrations for his golden jubilee, George suffered another relapse. The attack also followed hot on the heels of the death of his youngest daughter, Amelia, from tuberculosis and indeed George declared: 'This one is occasioned by poor Amelia.' Once again he was confined to a straitjacket and when released he cut a pitiful figure, shuffling around in a tattered dressing-gown. His obsession with Lady Pembroke, who by then was 75, was renewed and he besieged the bemused woman with love letters. Complaining about his physician, Sir Henry Halford, George raged: 'They refuse to let me go to Lady Pembroke although everyone knows that I am married to her; but what is worst of all, is that the infamous scoundrel Halford was at the marriage, and now has the effrontery to deny it to my face.'

The following year it was decided that the king was no longer fit to rule and the Prince of Wales (the future George IV) was named regent. For the remaining nine years of his life, George III virtually lived in another world. He began to lose his memory and senile dementia set in. He became blind and deaf, rambling incessantly, and referring to himself in the third person as if he were dead. Princess Mary related one visit: 'I went down with the Queen and it was shocking to hear the poor, dear King run on so, and her unfortunate manner makes things worse.' From 1812, the unsympathetic Queen Charlotte left the duty of visiting her ailing husband to her children.

When Charlotte died six years later, George was not informed and straw was laid down on the Windsor courtyard so that the wheels of the hearse carriage would not disturb him. By now old and thin and increasingly deluded, he spent most of his days shambling restlessly from room to room buttoning and unbuttoning his waistcoat, but when he lost the use of his legs permanently, even that small pleasure was denied him. His other passion was cherry tart, until he reached the point where he began to decline food. Growing steadily weaker, he died on 29 January 1820.

While recent research suggests that arsenic in his powdered wigs may also have contributed to his malaise, nineteenth-century royal biographers blamed George's illness on his failure to take a mistress. At least Prince Charles has done his best to ensure that history will not repeat itself.

THE TOUGH GUY

CHRISTIAN VII, KING OF DENMARK (1749–1808)

To Christian VII's eternal regret, he was built more like Charles Aznavour than Charles Atlas. So short in stature that he might almost have been welcomed at the court of Peter the Great, Christian developed a complex about his frail physique and went to extreme lengths to prove his toughness. Even though he must have been aware that if he threw his weight around there was a very real danger of him floating away, he went on violent rampages through the streets of Copenhagen, terrorising those who stood in his path. Before he descended into full-blown madness, he became Europe's most unlikely bully.

Like many bullies, Christian endured a loveless upbringing. His mother died when he was just two and his father, Frederick V, had little time for him. His tutor, Ditlev Reventlow, believed in stern discipline and thrashed the young prince into submission, treating him as his 'doll'. After a particularly savage beating, Christian could be found on the floor foaming at the mouth. His next tutor, Elie-Salomon François Reverdil, was altogether more compassionate but could see that the boy was haunted by feelings of insecurity and inadequacy. In a prophetic statement, Reverdil described himself as 'a madman's keeper'.

Christian's life took a turn for the worse when his father married Juliana Maria of Brunswick-Wolfenbüttel. She bore Frederick a physically disabled son and resented Christian who, as the eldest, stood in the way of the boy's inheritance.

She was an overpowering, fiercely ambitious woman who drove her husband first to drink and ultimately to a complete nervous breakdown.

In the meantime Christian was determined to show his steel. Initially this manifested itself in childish pranks. He threw a bowl of sugar over the head of his prim grandmother and once stuck pins in the seat of her throne to see her jump. Another time he hurled a ban at a visiting Lutheran pastor. All of these antics were relatively innocuous but he then took to prowling Copenhagen by night, armed with a spiked club, which he had snatched during an earlier street brawl, and viciously attacking passers-by. The prince and his gang became feared throughout the city.

In 1766 the broken Frederick V died at the age of 42 and the equally fragile Christian succeeded him as king. Although he was almost seventeen, his behaviour was more befitting a naughty seven-year-old. He liked to play leapfrog over the backs of visiting dignitaries when they bowed to him or to slap diplomats around the face during an important discussion, without reason or warning. It was just a big game to him and for once not even his spiteful stepmother could tell him what to do.

Shortly after his accession, Christian married his fifteen-year-old cousin, Caroline Matilda, sister of George III. The girl was stepping into an emotional minefield. She had already been forced to leave behind all of her English ladies-in-waiting and therefore arrived in Denmark in a state of high anxiety. Any enthusiasm the young king might have had for his new bride evaporated almost overnight and he soon made his position abundantly clear, publicly remarking that it was 'unfashionable to love one's wife'. He was so disenchanted with her that he hung her portrait in the royal lavatory. Nor could she expect any support from the Dowager Queen Juliana, who feared that Caroline Matilda might provide Christian with an heir.

Such a prospect seemed slim, as Christian neglected his wife in favour of his twin pursuit of whores and young men. In the company of his young male favourite, Conrad Holcke, and his dubious mistress, known as 'Katrine with the boots', he returned to rampaging through Copenhagen, smashing up shops and brothels. Often he would return to the palace with black eyes and bruises. Encouraged no doubt by Katrine and her fancy footwear, he developed a taste for sado-masochism and built his own rack on which Holcke was required to stretch him, or flog him until his back bled or he fell unconscious. In a further demonstration of his machismo, the king liked to burn his flesh and rub salt into the wounds. He also became fascinated by executions, secretly attending dozens of public punishments in disguise and staging mock executions of his own courtiers.

On a state visit to London in 1768 Christian and his companions vandalised their lodgings at St James's Palace and went out at night disguised as sailors in the hope of picking up prostitutes. He even installed a stripper at St James's. The writer Horace Walpole described the Danish king as an 'insipid boy' yet in spite of Christian's obvious character defects, the trip was viewed as a success.

Back home, Christian had managed to spend long enough with his wife for her to give birth to a son, Frederick, but he remained more interested in his mistress and elevated her to the rank of baroness until mounting public disquiet forced him to end the relationship. For by now his outrageous behaviour and appalling treatment of his young wife had angered the Danish people.

Christian now began to fall increasingly under the spell of his physician, Johann Struensee, who, as the king's mental state steadily worsened, became an all-too-frequent visitor. Christian started to suffer wild hallucinations: sometimes he thought he was the King of Sardinia or that his wife was really his mother. He began insisting that he was not the rightful King of Denmark, that he was illegitimate, even though Struensee continually reassured him. With his moods fluctuating from manic laughter to dark depression and his speech often incomprehensible, he experienced violent fantasies, once waking in a state of high excitement after dreaming that he had killed six people in a single night. And he grew increasingly angry should anyone attempt to persuade him that these feats were all in his imagination. By turns violent and fearful, he would attack his entourage and then ask Struensee to check under his bed for assassins.

All the while he remained obsessed with building up his own physique. Reasoning that a real man could endure pain, he would bang his head repeatedly against the palace walls until it bled. Another time he put burning strips of firewood on his skin. He indulged in further acts of vandalism with his friends, smashing the windows of his own palace and breaking furniture in the staterooms. One of his favourite pastimes was wrestling with his black page, Moranti. In the course of these fights, Christian would often beg Moranti to bite and scratch him in order to increase the pain. During one romp he nearly threw both the page and his dog from the palace balcony to the courtyard below.

However, Christian overreached himself when, at the royal dinner table, he threatened Count Enevold Brandt, a government minister, with a sound thrashing. To the king's surprise, Brandt did not back down and later that evening challenged him to a duel. Christian managed to get the stakes lowered to a fistfight but was left battered, bruised and begging for mercy, as Brandt pulled no punches. The self-styled tough guy still had a long way to go.

Gripped by depression, Christian contemplated suicide but was afraid of the scandal it would create. And what advice did supposedly the finest physician in the land offer for relieving the king of his torment? Struensee's prescription was that Christian should take cold baths.

In view of his limited medical expertise, it was perhaps as well that Struensee turned to politics. Under royal patronage, he rose rapidly to the post of Minister of the Privy Council, making him arguably the most powerful man in Denmark, but his carefully calculated rise to the top had included one major blunder – he had been having an affair with the queen. Lonely, young and all but abandoned by her inconsiderate husband, Caroline Matilda had befriended Struensee following a severe attack of colic and ended up falling hopelessly in love with him. Relishing the affection, she boasted openly of the affair to her chambermaids and spent entire evenings at court balls dancing with him. Her second child, Louisa, was born in 1771, and the baby was said to bear a marked likeness to Struensee. Throughout the resultant whispering campaign, the king appeared wholly indifferent.

However, Struensee's enemies, including Christian's stepmother, were not as apathetic. Struensee's policy was to keep the king out of the public spotlight on account of his delicate mental condition, but most Danes had no idea that their monarch was a schizophrenic madman and thought that he was being hidden away against his will. Rumours spread that Struensee was plotting to engineer the death of the king so that he could marry the queen and seize power, and this state of mistrust allowed those who were jealous of Struensee's influence at court to make their move. In January 1772 a group of conspirators, led by the scheming Juliana, the king's half-brother, and politician Ove-Høegh-Guldberg, organised a coup. While the queen and Struensee were dancing at a masked ball, the gang of three broke into Christian's bedroom and scared him out of what passed for his mind. He was coerced into signing orders for the arrest and imprisonment of Struensee, Brandt and the queen, although he had no idea what he was doing. Chained to the wall of his cell, Struensee was tortured into confessing to his affair with the queen and sentenced to a particularly gruesome death. First his right hand was chopped off, then his body was quartered and broken on the wheel, and finally he was beheaded. From her vantage point Juliana watched the barbarity with great pleasure. Her only regret, she said, was that she did not see Caroline Matilda's corpse thrown into the death-cart as well. Brandt was also executed but the twenty-year-old queen, having confessed all in the vain hope of saving her lover, escaped with life imprisonment and the annulment of her marriage on the grounds of infidelity. Under pressure from George III, she was soon released and sought exile in Hanover, but her respite was brief and she died shortly before her 24th birthday.

175

With Struensee out of the way, the three conspirators took over the day-to-day running of the country until 1784, when Crown Prince Frederick asked the king to sign a document establishing a regency. Once again the bewildered Christian signed it without hesitation, thereby effectively ceasing to rule although he continued as king in name only until his death. In the interim, he was wheeled out semi-coherent by his stepmother for state occasions. Otherwise he remained behind closed doors, from where he could sometimes be seen pulling faces at passers-by. He was seemingly unaware of his queen's imprisonment, exile or death. He was never actually placed under confinement but servants were instructed *not* to obey his orders. During the Napoleonic Wars he was moved to Rendsborg in Schleswig and is said to have died from shock at seeing Spanish troops entering the city in 1808.

THE VULGAR BOATMAN

FERDINAND IV, KING OF NAPLES (1751–1825)

The man known at various times as Ferdinand IV of Naples, Ferdinand III of Sicily and Ferdinand I of the Two Sicilies certainly had no shortage of royal titles. Alas, he did not possess the commensurate social skills, generally preferring to practise coarse behaviour than statesmanship. To be honest, he was more interested in passing wind than passing laws.

At court festivities he would indulge in juvenile horseplay, slapping ladies' buttocks, kicking gentlemen's bottoms, and shouting obscenities and vulgar jokes at the top of his high-pitched voice. When rude noises emanated from orifices at either end of his body, he excused himself by maintaining that it was necessary for his health. He was the king who never grew up.

The third son of Carlos VII of Naples, Ferdinand was born in that city and when his father ascended the Spanish throne in 1759 as Carlos III, Ferdinand, in accordance with treaties that forbade the union of the two crowns, succeeded him as King of Naples under a regency presided over by the Tuscan Bernardo Tanucci. The latter, keen to retain his grip on government, deliberately neglected the young king's education with the result that Ferdinand was almost illiterate. Instead, Tanucci promoted Ferdinand's love of pleasure and his devotion to outdoor sports such as shooting and fishing in the hope that he would refrain from involving himself in matters of state. Ferdinand needed little encouragement to pursue base amusements. Ignorant and ill-bred, he made his friends among the lower echelons of the palace hierarchy – gamekeepers and beaters – and delighted in the company of the *lazzaroni*, the most degraded class of the Neapolitan people, whose dialect and habits he affected. On his return from fishing expeditions, the king himself would auction his catch at the fish market, haggling over the prices like a commoner. He would then give the proceeds to the poor, which greatly endeared him to his subjects.

Ferdinand's minority ended in 1767 and the following year he married Maria Carolina, daughter of the Empress Maria Theresa of Austria and a sister of Marie Antoinette. Asked how he liked his bride, Ferdinand replied with characteristic bluntness: 'Sweats like a pig.'

Maria Carolina was considerably more refined and energetic than her idle husband. Beautiful, clever, proud and ambitious, she soon clashed with Tanucci, the resultant power struggle ending inevitably in his dismissal. Thereafter she became the true ruler of Naples while Ferdinand continued to neglect his royal duties in favour of trivial pursuits. For hours on end, he would force his courtiers to encircle him and amuse him with their conversation, knowing full well that he was incapable of contributing to the witty repartee.

Ferdinand was now gaunt and gangling, the owner of a huge nose that earned him the nickname of '*Nasone*'. His brother-in-law, the Emperor Joseph III, offered the following testimonial: 'Although an ugly prince, he is not absolutely repulsive. He is clean except for his hands: and at least he does not stink.' But he was a coward and while he liked venturing out in boats, he would scream hysterically if the sea were rough. He also had an aversion to crowds, not necessarily the most desirable attribute in a monarch.

In spite of – or perhaps because of – Ferdinand's unwillingness to participate in government, the first three decades of his reign saw an increase in his popularity. Then the beheading of her sister by the revolutionaries of France understandably unnerved Maria Carolina, who roused her husband from his slumbers and urged him to halt Napoleon's advance into Italy. Ferdinand made a token gesture but when the French army closed in on Naples, he fled to his second kingdom of Sicily. With the *lazzaroni* reaffirming their support for the king, the French were soon driven out but the queen, who still twitched at the mere mention of the word 'revolutionary', demanded that an example be made of those who had supported the invaders and presided over the hanging of 99 rebels. Her only regret was her inability to make it a nice round number.

Although restored to power, Ferdinand chose to remain in Sicily where the woodcock shooting was excellent. He also lost interest in the queen when her looks began to fade and by the time of her death in 1814 they were living apart. Two months later Ferdinand married his mistress, Donna Luca Migliaccio, morganatically. In the meantime Naples had become a Napoleonic satellite kingdom with Joseph Bonaparte, the emperor's brother, on the throne, Ferdinand having all but abdicated, partly through military pressure and partly through indifference. Naples was simply too much trouble for him, whereas in Sicily the living was easy. Yet following the fall of Napoleon, Ferdinand stirred himself once more and returned to Naples in triumph, merging Sicily and Naples to form the throne of Two Sicilies.

Described in his later years as 'the very picture of a respectable farmer' (the only time he had ever been described as anything approaching respectable), Ferdinand survived another revolt in 1820, but still refused to allow politics and rebellions to interfere with his leisurely lifestyle. The day before his death in 1825 he was out shooting. The lower classes of Neapolitan life may have been sorry to see him go but the ladies at court were mightily relieved.

THE LAW-MAKER

PAUL I, TSAR OF RUSSIA (1754–1801)

In his mercifully brief reign, Tsar Paul showed himself to be a stickler for red tape and officialdom, introducing so many petty laws and regulations that the printing presses of St Petersburg had to work through the night, every night. He sought to control the way Russian people dressed, how they wore their hair, what music they listened to, even how they threw a party. Hardly a day passed without a fresh proclamation, leading his own son to remark: 'My father has declared war on common sense with the firm resolve of never concluding a truce.'

Paul was the illegitimate son of Catherine the Great and her first lover, Sergei Saltykov, although, along with the rest of Russia, he had been led to believe that his father was Tsar Peter III, the man who loved playing with toy soldiers in bed. A bald little man with the disproportionately large head and snub nose associated with sufferers of congenital syphilis, he grew up bitterly resenting his mother for reigning so long. He was 42 when he finally became tsar in November 1796, and one of his first acts was to avenge Peter's memory. To this end, he decided to have Peter restored to his rightful place on the throne . . . even though he had been dead for 34 years. For Paul this was but a minor inconvenience and so Peter's rotting body was exhumed, dressed in one of the late tsar's favourite military uniforms, robed in ermine, and taken to the throne room at the Winter Palace. With the imperial crown perched on its skull, the corpse was then seated on the throne and court officials were ordered to acknowledge the 'true tsar', who had been so cruelly usurped by his wife. Satisfied that his 'father' had been suitably recognised (although given his condition this was a spiritual rather than physical observation), Paul arranged a joint funeral in which the bodies of Peter and Catherine were laid next to each other so that their remains could mingle. It was almost as near to intimacy as they ever managed while alive.

Paul was determined to enjoy the respect that he felt Peter had been denied and reintroduced an old custom whereby any citizen encountering a member of the imperial family was immediately obliged to stop his horse or coach, alight, and prostrate himself on the ground, even in deep snow or a sea of mud. To ensure that this ritual humiliation was performed correctly, Paul helpfully produced a series of accompanying rules. He even demanded respect from his four-legged subjects. When his horse stumbled while transporting the tsar through St Petersburg, Paul instantly dismounted and sentenced the animal to fifty lashes, dutifully counting each one.

Despite the fact that he was not Peter III's real son, Paul inherited his fixation with the Prussian military, but instead of playing under the sheets he fulfilled his fantasies on the parade ground. To the discomfort of the Russian troops, he issued orders that the entire army be forced to wear the Prussian uniform of his hero, Frederick the Great, including the antiquated gaiters and powdered pigtails. Each individual item was covered by precise regulations, right down to the necessary measurement between the end of the gauntlet and the elbow of the sleeve. With Paul, image was everything. He made the soldiers wear straitjackets beneath their uniforms so that they would stand stiff and upright, and to achieve the perfect goose-step without any bending of the legs, he strapped steel plates to their knees. The hairpiece was of immense importance to this most particular of rulers and he insisted that the soldiers wear thick, heavy wigs with iron rods inserted to guarantee that the hairpiece sat straight on the head. On the eve of a parade the troops would toil until dawn, covering their wigs with grease and chalk, knowing full well that a hair out of place could mean arrest, a thrashing, or even deportation. Indeed, soldiers were known to have been banished to Siberia for committing the unpardonable sin of marching out of step. So wary did the men become of the tsar's attention to detail and demand for perfection that as a precaution they used to say a final farewell to their wives and families before going on parade.

Perhaps they would have been more understanding of the tsar's uniform edicts if there had been any method to his madness. Instead, the soldiers were required to wear uniforms so tight that breathing became difficult and fighting virtually impossible. A ball and chain around the ankle could scarcely have brought about a greater reduction in mobility. Over-looking practicalities in favour of dress design, Paul had created a show army that was barely more useful than a bunch of chocolate soldiers. It was like letting Vivienne Westwood loose on the SAS. To underline Paul's lack of military appreciation, he once ordered an entire regiment to undertake a 2,500-mile march, which took two years to complete and resulted in the deaths of hundreds of horses.

The tsar was not content with telling only the military how to dress: he imposed similar rules on ordinary Russian citizens. He banned pantaloons, round hats, low collars, tailcoats, trousers, boots, shoes with laces, and waistcoats – all garments that were associated with the French Revolution and were therefore, in his mind, symbols of political upheaval. In their place, Paul said the only permissible dress code was tricorne hats, stiffened high collars, tight tunics, breeches, gaiters, and square-toed shoes. Although people protested that the new outfits offered hopelessly inadequate protection against a typical Russian winter, Paul was hellbent on enforcing the law. Armed police patrolled the streets of St Petersburg in search of the improperly attired, any transgressors being liable to arrest. The police were also given the power to seize and destroy any offending garment on the spot. For good measure, Paul also stipulated that all of his subjects had to powder their hair and brush it well away from the forehead.

As Paul himself liked to be at work at six o'clock in the morning, he ordered all government ministries to start the day's business at that early hour. It provided him with more time to introduce some daft new laws. He seemed particularly worried that social occasions were not being organised properly and so he brought in a series of laws governing the staging of such events, which stipulated precisely how to conduct a wedding, funeral, concert, dance or party. Should anyone wish to throw a party, it was first necessary to inform the local police, who would then send a uniformed officer to attend and be on the lookout for any violation of the official rules of conduct. This must have made every party in Russia really go with a swing.

Paul was in full flow now. He banned all cab drivers in St Petersburg after one of them had been found carrying a gun and imposed a nine o'clock curfew in the capital. The city that had flourished under Catherine was now a ghost town. As he became ever more crazed – suffering increasingly from what he termed his 'black butterflies' – and ever more sensitive about his appearance, he issued another proclamation banning from the Russian language the words for 'baldy' and 'snub nose'. One soldier who unwisely referred to the tsar's lack of hair was executed.

Eager to control his subjects' thoughts at every turn, Paul banned the import of all foreign books and music for fear that they would harm national morality. For the same reason he deleted from the Russian dictionary the words 'citizen', 'club', 'revolution' and 'society'. After banning all foreign literature, he then decided that Russian books were equally dangerous and shut down all but two of the nation's printing works . . . a particularly bizarre action, as it jeopardised the publication of all the new laws and proclamations he was introducing.

After just over four years of Paul's barmy bureaucracy, his enemies, led by the head of state police, Count Pahlen, and Catherine the Great's last lover, Count Zubov, decided to put an end to the edicts. On the night of 11 March 1801 a gang of drunken conspirators broke into the royal residence and found the tsar hiding behind a screen in his chamber. They invited him to sign an abdication form and when he resisted they strangled him in an alcohol-induced frenzy. The official announcement was that the tsar had died of 'an attack of apoplexy'. His loss was not greatly mourned. As one official put it the following morning: 'Terror has taken flight and joy reigns supreme in the capital.'

THE PRINCESS OF SCANDAL

CAROLINE OF BRUNSWICK (1768–1821)

Women were a source of constant misery to King George IV of England. The woman he loved, he couldn't marry; and the woman he married, he couldn't love. For even by royal standards, his union to Caroline of Brunswick was an acrimonious affair, littered with accusations, recriminations, plot and counterplot, and outright hostility. They were a perfect match only in the respect that they probably deserved each other since he was a selfish, philandering spendthrift, and she was common, loud and vulgar.

George was the son of 'Mad King George', and one can only speculate as to the extent that having such a wastrel for a son contributed to the monarch's state of mind. Raised in a stifling environment, the young Prince of Wales was headstrong with his tutors and disrespectful to the king. One tutor remarked prophetically: 'He will either be the most polished gentleman or the most accomplished blackguard in Europe. Possibly both.' For George was not without wit or intelligence and this, allied to the fact that he happened to be heir to the throne, meant that he had no shortage of female admirers. Once freed from the shackles of his strict education, George wasted no time in tasting the fruits of his position. His excesses – financial and carnal – became the talk of London society. A new entry into that exclusive circle was Mrs Maria Fitzherbert, recently widowed following the death of her second husband. Mrs Fitzherbert was said to be neither witty nor outstandingly beautiful, but she did have 'exceedingly full breasts', which in George's eyes (as they often were) counted for a great deal. George was soon smitten with the woman six years his senior, even though both knew from the outset that the relationship was doomed. For under the Royal Marriages Act of 1772 the Prince of Wales was forbidden to marry without his father's consent. Clearly this would not be forthcoming in the case of a twice-married commoner who, worse still, was also a Catholic, as it was illegal for anyone married to a Catholic to inherit the throne.

But George would not be denied his true love. He drank himself into several stupors and, after a clumsy faked suicide attempt, persuaded Mrs Fitzherbert to get engaged. On 15 December 1785 the pair secretly married at her London house in an illegal ceremony conducted by an Anglican clergyman, recently released from prison, in return for the promise of a bishopric when George became king. A friend kept watch on the door for snoopers.

Unable to live openly with his bride, George became increasingly frustrated; and the more frustrated he became, the more he started to spend. By the summer of 1786 he was nearly £300,000 in the red and over the next decade his love of the high life saw his debts rise to a point where parental pressure was brought on him to sort out his finances. The obvious solution was for him to marry into money and he reluctantly agreed to find a suitable bride, which meant a German girl to appease his Hanoverian father. Still in love with Mrs Fitzherbert, the Prince of Wales showed little appetite for the task, deciding that just about any German princess would do, and muttering, 'One damned German frau is as good as another.' It is said that he plucked the name of his first cousin, Princess Caroline of Brunswick, out of thin air, or that he chose her in a fit of pique to get back at his father. Given the stories that began to filter back from Germany about her wayward behaviour, it would seem that the latter was the more likely explanation.

Caroline Amelia Elizabeth of Brunswick-Wolfenbüttel experienced a similarly restricted upbringing. At thirteen she had a governess who would not allow her to go to the window and she was rarely permitted to venture downstairs from her room when there was company. Her resentment at being shut away surfaced in an explosive incident when she was sixteen. After being forbidden to attend a ball, she flounced off to bed announcing that she was pregnant. She made such a fuss that her parents sent for a midwife, whereupon Caroline jumped up, shouting: 'Now will you forbid me to go to a ball again?'

Caroline lacked and never acquired the social graces needed for London high society. By her twenties she had a reputation as something of a flirt and was notorious for her unbridled conversation in public company. It was rumoured that she had once had an affair with 'a man of low birth' and that she was indiscreet to the point of reckless. When requested to do so, Arthur Paget, the British envoy in Berlin, deemed it unwise to describe her character on paper but expressed the opinion that the proposed marriage was far more likely 'to ensure the misery of the Prince of Wales, than promote his happiness'. Another English diplomat considered her to be 'exceedingly loose', while George III's wife, Queen Charlotte, put about the rumour that Caroline's governess used to follow her around during dances to prevent the princess from 'making an exhibition of herself by indecent conversations with men'. Writing to her brother, Queen Charlotte concluded: 'There, dear brother, is a woman I do not recommend at all.'

Furthermore, Lord Malmesbury, who had been sent to Germany to make the formal marriage request to Caroline, harboured grave reservations. He was particularly concerned about her lack of personal hygiene, observing that she never washed and that her underclothes were invariably dirty and rarely changed. He also thought her to be headstrong and lacking in diplomacy but, as a sole redeeming feature, essentially good-natured. However, because he had been sent purely to acquire Caroline's acquiescence and not to report back on her traits, Malmesbury kept his misgivings to himself.

One English historian had no such qualms and later wrote of Caroline: 'She swore like an ostler and smelt like a farmyard.'

The prince remained indifferent to this gossip – his interest in marrying her was solely financial – and the marriage treaty was duly signed on 3 December 1794 . . . before the couple had even met.

The opportunity for that did not arise until the following spring, just a few days before the wedding. Caroline had barely set foot on English soil for an hour before she displayed her talent for ill-chosen words. While awaiting the prince, she was met by the inmates of Greenwich Hospital and remarked of the crippled patients: 'What, is every Englishman without an arm or a leg?' She made Prince Philip look like a Foreign Office diplomat.

When George finally put in an appearance after keeping her waiting for over an hour, he was clearly less than impressed. Although she was short and dumpy, she was described as having a pleasing face, but after a cursory embrace, he swiftly retreated to a far corner of the room and, suddenly announcing that he didn't feel well, demanded a glass of brandy. Caroline was equally disappointed, declaring privately that George was fat and not as handsome as in his portrait.

At dinner that evening, Caroline showed her true colours, foolishly hinting at the relationship between George and his latest mistress, Lady Jersey. Lord Malmesbury's diary recalled the episode. He wrote: 'I was far from satisfied with the Princess's behaviour; it was flippant, rattling, affected raillery and wit, and throwing out coarse vulgar hints about Lady [Jersey], who was present . . . The Prince was evidently disgusted; and this unfortunate dinner fixed his dislike, which, when left to herself, the Princess had not the talent to remove; but, by still observing the same giddy manners and attempts at cleverness and coarse sarcasm, increased till it became positive hatred.' Another guest, Lord Holland, later commented that Caroline was 'utterly destitute of all female delicacy'. The omens were not good.

Three days later – on 8 April – the party assembled for the wedding in the Chapel Royal at St James's Palace in London. The bride's dress was so heavy that it nearly caused her to fall over. In a bid to forget, the groom had been drinking heavily beforehand, and when he lurched into the chapel, he had to be supported by aides to prevent him collapsing in an undignified heap. The only colour in his cheeks was caused by alcohol; otherwise, in the words of one eye-witness, he 'looked like death'. Lord Melbourne remarked that 'the Prince was like man doing a thing in desperation; it was like MacHeath going to execution.'

Throughout the ceremony, George could barely bring himself to look at his bride until, in the middle of a prayer, he suddenly stood up, as if about to leave. The Archbishop of Canterbury, John Moore, who was conducting the service, paused for a moment, unsure of what to do, but the matter was resolved when the king stepped forward and firmly pushed the prince down again. Then, when the archbishop reached the part of the service where he asked whether or not there was any impediment to lawful matrimony, the prince began to cry!

The ceremony over, the prince hardly spoke. He continued to ignore his new bride all evening, preferring the company of drink. He finally staggered to her bedroom but, as Caroline recalled, he 'passed the greatest part of his bridal night under the grate, where he fell, and where I left him'. He at least sobered up sufficiently to climb out of the fireplace and into bed with her in the morning and consummate the marriage, but it was more out of duty than desire. For Caroline, that was as good as it got.

Their honeymoon was spent in a rented house filled with George's disreputable friends, who, according to Caroline, 'were constantly drunk and filthy, sleeping and snoring in bouts on the sofas'. George had also brought along his mistress, Lady Jersey. No wonder Caroline said the place 'resembled a bad brothel much more than a palace'.

The newlyweds stopped sleeping together after, at maximum, three weeks of marriage, but that was long enough for them to produce a daughter, Princess Charlotte, who was born in January 1796. Two days after the birth, George drew up a new will in which he left all his personal property to 'my

Maria Fitzherbert, my wife, the wife of my heart and soul'. To 'her who is call'd the Princess of Wales', he left the princely sum of one shilling. Furthermore, he specified that Caroline should play no part in raising Charlotte.

With George continuing to flaunt Lady Jersey in her face, Caroline responded by entertaining various male friends, news of whom quickly circulated around court circles. In May he demanded a formal separation, but the king poured scorn on the idea. In utter despair at his predicament, the Prince of Wales pleaded with his mother, who detested Caroline, to use her powers of persuasion on the king. In letters, George described his wife as a 'fiend', 'treacherous' and 'mischievous', and labelled her 'The vilest wretch this world was ever cursed with.' But the king remained unmoved and ordered that Lady Jersey be removed from the princess's service in the hope that this might bring about a reconciliation. Caroline was prepared to give the marriage another try, but when she learned that George was still seeing Lady Jersey it was the last straw. Indiscreet at the best of times, Caroline now talked openly of her husband's failings, making it known how drunk and inadequate he had been on their wedding night. George became a national laughing stock. Even his own brother, the Duke of Clarence, had little sympathy for him, commenting: 'My brother has behaved very foolishly. To be sure he has married a very foolish, disagreeable person, but he should not have treated her as he has done, but have made the best of a bad bargain, as my father has done.'

Appalled at being the object of public ridicule, George announced that he would rather see toads and vipers crawling over his food than even so much as sit at the same table as Caroline. She fought back by declaring that she would no longer obey her husband, and soon they inevitably went their separate ways, never to live under the same roof again. In her new home at Blackheath, Caroline consoled herself by entertaining young men. She also liked to sit on the floor and gossip with her entourage – conduct hardly becoming of a princess – and to flirt, eat raw onions and drink ale. In

Caroline's mind at least, eating raw onions and flirting were appropriate bedfellows.

One visitor to Blackheath described Caroline as having a 'coarse mind without any degree of moral taste', while Lord Holland thought that, 'If not mad, she was a very worthless woman.' Hearing reports of her scandalous behaviour, George convinced himself that she was insane, and once more sought comfort in the ample bosom of Mrs Fitzherbert.

The flow of scurrilous stories emanating from Blackheath increased dramatically in 1805 following a strange spat between Caroline and her erstwhile friend and neighbour, Lady Douglas. The latter accused Caroline of sending anonymous letters to her and of making obscene drawings alleging that Lady Douglas was having an affair with Rear-Admiral Sir Sydney Smith. Defending her reputation, Lady Douglas countered by claiming that it was the Princess of Wales who had enjoyed an affair with Sir Sydney and that she also had a secret son by him three years previously. Supporters of this theory pointed to the fact that Caroline had adopted a little boy. Was he her illegitimate son? George was certainly eager to uncover anything that might help him obtain a divorce and prompted a government commission to investigate the allegations. Whilst the testimony did little for Caroline's already shredded reputation, the commissioners could find no evidence of a pregnancy.

Frustrated at his inability to secure the divorce he craved, George encouraged newspapers to publish sordid stories about Caroline's sex life. Tired of coming under constant scrutiny, Caroline decided to leave England in 1814 and spent the next few years travelling through Europe in company with her daughter's ex-lover, Captain Hesse, and a young doctor, Henry Holland. As usual, she made no concession to taste, running up huge debts, wearing see-through dresses that were totally inappropriate for a princess (especially a fat one), reportedly having affairs with her servants, and generally giving her husband's spies plenty of ammunition. Meanwhile, the death of Princess Charlotte in childbirth left George without an heir.

As his father's health deteriorated, George prepared for the moment when he would become king. Determined that Caroline should never be able to assume the title of queen, he hatched a new plan to blacken her name. In 1818 two lawyers and an army officer were despatched to Milan, where Caroline was now living, to make official inquiries into her conduct. The Milan Commission, as it was called, subsequently concluded that she had indeed probably been guilty of adultery although there were too many likely candidates for any one name to be put forward. This was music to George's ears, and the government was forced to agree that she should not be crowned queen. In the light of these revelations, George demanded a divorce, but Caroline was unwilling to surrender her claim without a fight.

Upon the death of his father in 1820, George became king. Appealing to her basest instincts, he and the government offered Caroline an annuity of £50,000 on condition that she relinquished her title of queen and remained abroad. Instead she immediately set off for England, announcing her intentions in a letter that, to George's horror, she signed 'Caroline Queen of England'. As far as George was concerned, she was a nasty smell that would not go away.

The English people had long felt that Caroline had received a raw deal from the marriage and now they had the opportunity to demonstrate their support. Mobs roamed the streets of London shouting 'Long live the queen' and attacking those who refused to join in. But George had no intention of veering from his course of action and on 5 July a Bill of Pains and Penalties was introduced into the House of Lords. It accused Caroline of adultery, and sought to deprive her of her title and to dissolve her marriage. The debate over the bill lasted more than three months and was, in effect, the public trial of Queen Caroline.

Caroline attended the proceedings almost every day, though she sometimes grew so bored that she went into the next room and played backgammon. Much of the evidence centred on her relationship with an Italian manservant, Bartolomeo Pergami, who, while travelling with her, had allegedly shared her tent . . .

and her bathtub. Witnesses were brought forward to testify that they had seen her with her hand on the Italian stallion's genitals and dancing naked before an open window. However, public opinion remained with Caroline. As one observer, Lady Cowper, wrote: 'The Queen has a strange luck in her favour; the worse she behaves, the more it rebounds to her credit . . . She is a coarse low-minded woman, I have no doubt, but it is hard on her to have such disgusted details invented about her, and they really must have done in so many instances . . . She says it is true she did commit adultery once, but it was with the husband of Mrs Fitzherbert [the king]. She is a droll woman.'

In the end the bill was defeated. The king would not get his divorce, but nor would Caroline get her crown.

His coronation was set for 19 July 1821 at Westminster Abbey. Caroline, who was not invited, decided to go anyway, only to be turned away at the door. When the French Emperor Napoleon died that year, news was brought to George that his greatest enemy was dead. According to popular legend, he replied: 'Is she?'

A month after the coronation Caroline *was* dead, but even in death, she was a thorn in his side, her funeral sparking riots among the populace, who still held her in great esteem. After all, she did have the common touch – it was just that it was too common for royal circles. Given her continued public support, George was mightily relieved to learn that her will indicated a desire to be buried in her native Brunswick. For once, he was more than happy to agree to her wishes.

THE KING AND THE SHOWGIRL

LUDWIG I, KING OF BAVARIA (1786–1868)

For 21 years Ludwig I was a cherished, if eccentric, ruler of Bavaria. He was very much a man of the people and shunned the use of a coach, even on state occasions, preferring to stroll along the streets of Munich, playfully knocking off the hats of passers-by. He had an eye for art and beautiful women but even a succession of mistresses did nothing to dent his popularity. Then, at the age of sixty, when he was definitely old enough to know better, an exotic Spanish dancer calling herself Lola Montez high-stepped into his life. He was bowled over by her brashness, swept off his feet by her Latin passion, but the enthusiasm for Lola was not shared by his subjects, who turned against their monarch almost overnight. What he hoped would be the road to true love turned into a cul-de-sac to abdication.

Ludwig's fall from grace was all the more unexpected because throughout his reign he had studiously avoided becoming embroiled in politics, the army, or any other controversial areas, choosing instead to establish himself as a leading patron of the arts. His love of art at the expense of military matters stemmed from his childhood. As a small boy he was partially deafened by a cannon blast, which explains not only his distaste for armoury but also why he derived particular pleasure from the visual arts such as architecture and painting. He was said to be a morose, unsociable child, due in so small part to the atrocities of the French Revolution, the effects of which reverberated around Europe. A devastating blow was the death of Marie Antoinette, his godmother. In 1810 Ludwig married Princess Theresa of Saxe-Hildburghausen, an event that was marked by the first-ever Oktoberfest, a celebration that proved so popular that it continues to this day.

The art of drinking vast quantities of Bavarian beer was not exactly the sort of cultural image Ludwig had in mind for Munich. Having discovered the joy of Roman architecture on a trip to Italy, he resolved, after becoming king in 1725, to create a wonderful visual spectacle for his capital city. Indeed, he was prepared to live a comparatively frugal existence in order to pay for widened streets and classical buildings. He built art museums, attracted major German artists to Munich and actively supported the university, appointing respected scientists, philosophers and historians to key posts there. He also saw himself as something of a poet in the style of Byron. However, he did not care for competition and had the poet Heinrich Heine banished for writing superior verse.

Ludwig's appreciation of artistic beauty extended to pretty girls. He built up a private collection of paintings of the most beautiful women in his realm. With status immaterial, these included the daughters of the court butcher and the town crier. When meeting veiled ladies on the streets of Munich, the king used to lift their veils to examine the face beneath. On finding one less-than-picturesque countenance, he quickly replaced the veil with the words: 'Madame, you are right.'

His wife presented him with nine children but he eventually became bored with her and, combining his two great loves in life – the arts and women – he took a series of beautiful actresses as his mistresses. But by the time he reached sixty, he had not had a mistress for some years. It seemed that he was slowing down, ready to see out the remainder of his reign with dignity and restraint. Then along came Lola with her shining black curls, blue eyes and welcoming bosom. But as the king would learn to his cost, there was more to Lola than met the eye.

For a start, her name was not Lola Montez, it was Eliza Gilbert; and she was born nowhere near Madrid, but in Limerick, Ireland. However, these facts did not emerge until a

London court case of 1858 so, as far as Ludwig was concerned, she was a *bona fide* Spanish dancer. In fairness she did have Spanish blood – on her mother's side – but her father was Irish. The woman born Marie Dolores Eliza Rosanna Gilbert took to calling herself 'Lola', a diminutive of 'Dolores'. She was educated in Scotland, England and finally Paris, where she was caught flirting indecorously with her music-teacher. At fifteen she was due to be married to a wealthy old judge – a union arranged by her stepfather – but, sensing her despair at the prospect, one of her many admirers, Captain Thomas James, suggested she marry him instead. The very next day they fled to Dublin and were wed at Meath.

To the discomfort of her husband, Lola continued to attract men like moths to a flame. He tried to remove her from the path of temptation by taking her to the peace and quiet of the country, but there she found her vivacious spirit stifled. Later she joined him in campaigns in India and Afghanistan, to the obvious pleasure of his fellow officers. On the journey back to London in 1842, her association with a certain Captain Lennox resulted in divorce from Thomas James.

She now decided to reinvent herself as Lola Montez, glamorous Spanish dancer, making her debut at Her Majesty's Theatre, London, on 10 June 1843. The manager had billed her as an intoxicating beauty from the Spanish heartland and, although her dancing owed more to energy than rhythm, her striking looks appeared to have won over the packed house until a leading young socialite recognised her and angrily shouted out for all to hear: 'Why, it's Betty James!'

In the wake of the humiliation, London would not accept her as Lola Montez and she was forced to try her luck abroad, appearing as a beautiful virago and making a name for herself by boxing the ears of anyone who offended her, and on one occasion horsewhipping a policeman who was guarding the King of Prussia. She attempted to resurrect her dancing career in Paris and when that failed, and with no discernible talent on which to fall back, she resorted to becoming little more than a coarse exhibitionist in Dresden and Warsaw, mouthing obscenities at spectators and flinging her garters in their faces. When she went further still by removing her skirts and undergarments, her manager quickly cancelled her contract.

She had numerous lovers, among them the composer Franz Liszt and a young French journalist, Alexandre Dujarier. The latter was killed in a duel over her but left her 20,000 francs and some securities, which meant that she no longer had to sing in the streets as she had in Warsaw.

So in 1846, at the age of 27, she headed to Munich for a planned engagement at the Court Theatre, only to be refused permission to perform there by the theatre director, who had heard accounts of her being hissed off stage in Paris. Angry at the snub, she went over his head and appealed directly to the king. Once accredited with masculine good looks, Ludwig was now ruddy-faced and weather-beaten, which, coupled with his parsimonious ways, gave him more the air of a German farmer than the head of a royal house. Nevertheless, he retained his eye for beauty and was intrigued to hear that a Spanish dancer was about to call on him and make a personal plea. While a royal aide put Lola's case at some length, the dancer herself waited outside the king's chamber, growing increasingly irritated by the delay. Eventually her patience snapped, as did her bodice during a struggle with a guard attempting to prevent her from storming into the king's room. However, she broke free from the guard's clutches, slammed the king's door behind her and locked it. Astounded to see this dishevelled vision of loveliness suddenly appear before him, Ludwig was even more taken aback when she boldly asked him to investigate what remained unexposed inside her torn dress (some claim she ripped the dress deliberately in order to stage a dramatic entrance). Wishing some privacy for such a delicate operation, the king immediately dismissed his aide. The outcome of that meeting was that Lola was granted her theatrical engagement and was also invited to entertain the king in full Spanish costume at a special royal performance.

Ludwig was captivated, seeing in Lola's swarthy features an artistic perfection worthy of inclusion in his portrait gallery. 'I am bewitched,' he told friends. He sent Lola a daily poem, to be read when she woke up, and they spent hours together behind closed doors, a situation that inevitably sparked rumours although she subsequently denied that their relationship was anything more than platonic. For the most part, he read to her and she played the piano or sang, his appreciation of her performance enhanced immeasurably by his deafness.

Living up to the adage that there's no fool like an old fool, the formerly thrifty monarch had a grand palace built for his new best friend and lavished expensive gifts upon her. He also provided her with a generous pension. Naturally, Lola was in no hurry to move on.

However, Ludwig's Jesuit advisers quickly came to resent her hold over him. The Jesuits had been forced out of most European countries but, under a tolerant king, had been allowed to prosper in Bavaria, where they occupied the key government posts. Now they could see their power ebbing away – and all because of a common dancer. The Jesuits saw Lola as anti-Catholic and accused her of being a British agent sent to destroy them. Until Lola arrived on the scene with her liberal views, Ludwig had never thought of opposing the concept that the church had the right to political power and that he had to carry out its policies. Indeed, he had never thought much about politics at all, which made him putty in her manipulative hands.

Acting on her advice, he sacked his prime minister, Carl Abel, informing the deposed official that he would do whatever Lola suggested. The Jesuits were enraged and tried to turn Ludwig against the woman who was becoming known throughout Bavaria as 'the king's whore'. But Ludwig would not listen. He worshipped the ground on which Lola danced (badly).

It was not only the Jesuits who disapproved of Lola. The king's previous mistresses had always been kept discreetly in the background and maintained on a low budget, but Lola's expensive tastes and love of the limelight made her a different proposition altogether. Her fiery temperament did nothing to win over the burghers of Munich. She was discourteous to the queen, she swore readily, threatened to hit anyone whom she disliked, and was accompanied everywhere by a large menacing bulldog. She could have been Bill Sykes in drag.

The dog was at the centre of two incidents that sealed her unpopularity. First she set the animal on a prominent Jesuit, university professor von Lassaulx, and then she brutally whipped a nervous tradesman who had tried to fend off the dog. Still licking his wounds, von Lassaulx proceeded to protest to the king about the dismissal of Prime Minister Abel, whereupon Ludwig, rattled by anyone who dared to question Lola's judgement, promptly sacked the professor too. Hearing this news, a mob of hostile students gathered outside Lola's palace. Brazen as ever, she strode out on to the balcony sipping champagne. She raised her glass in a toast to the crowd, who replied by hurling a volley of bricks through her windows. The tension was calmed temporarily by Ludwig's arrival but when he left several hours later he still required a military escort to protect him from the people who, until recently, had always held him in great affection.

Derogatory songs about Lola began doing the rounds and handbills circulated depicting the king as a helpless plaything in the arms of a whip-cracking senorita. Word spread about disgusting orgies taking place in her boudoir, while some said she was a witch who had cast the king under her spell and that her demands – physical and financial – were killing him. Even Ludwig's half-sister, the Austrian Archduchess Sophie, labelled Lola a gold digger, but he was unmoved and continued to describe the dancer as 'the star of my life'. However, her political meddling ensured that her star would soon be on the wane.

Never one to shy away from a fight, Lola thought she could win the students round but her decision to establish a university corps – a guard devoted to her service and funded by Bavarian taxpayers – had the opposite effect. Only twenty out of the 1,000 students at the university joined the corps, known as the Alemannia, but the sight of their uniforms and red caps led to further unrest, during which one of the few students who dared to wear her colours was beaten to a pulp. The creation of this corps solely for the worship of Lola Montez was the last straw for the Jesuits, who now demanded that all good church members drive her out of Bavaria. On a journey to Bamberg she was pelted with stones, to which she responded by reaching into her bag, pulling out a pistol and daring her persecutors to continue the attack.

She began behaving regally, refusing to stand for the king when he entered the royal box at the theatre and demanding to be made a countess – a gesture guaranteed to rile the aristocracy. To prove her eligibility, she produced a connection with the titled Montalvos family of Spain (to whom her mother was related) and the ever-compliant Ludwig duly made his flamboyant dancer the Countess of Landsfeld.

Meanwhile the student riots continued, turning Munich into a war zone. Lola inflamed the situation by threatening to close the university and once again had to be rescued by Ludwig. With the city in uproar, the demand of the populace – that Lola should be banished – was put before the king. 'I would rather lose my crown,' snapped Ludwig, not realising until he observed the faces of his courtiers that he had just mentioned the alternative course of action. Reluctantly he agreed to sign a decree that ended Lola's two-year stay in Bavaria. The mob yelled with joy and burned her house, poor Ludwig watching the tumult by the light of the leaping flames. Before leaving the city, Lola was smuggled into the king's palace wearing men's clothes so that they could bid each other a sad farewell and he wrote a final poem for her, entitled 'Lamentation'.

Ludwig may have hoped that by evicting Lola he could cling to power, but the whole sorry episode had damaged his reputation irretrievably and later that year – 1848 – he was forced to abdicate in favour of his son Maximilian. Yet he remained infatuated with her, sending tender letters and leaving what remained of her house exactly as she had left it.

Lola soon moved on to new conquests. In England she entered into a bigamous marriage with a young officer and within two weeks they had been forced to flee to Spain to evade the law. After her husband drowned, she married again and visited Australia, where she became involved in a fight with a strapping woman who clawed Lola's face until she fainted from the pain. In 1858, by which time Ludwig was 72, it is claimed that she finally took the former King of Bavaria as her fourth husband. They are said to have honeymooned in Italy, only to separate because Ludwig insisted on consummating the marriage. It was not just his age that she objected to; he had a venereal disease and when Lola contracted it, she began to lose her beauty. And her face was her fortune.

She set off for America with her new jewels and her magnificent wardrobe, though without her new husband, intending to resume her flagging theatrical career. But by then her true identity and colourful past had been revealed to the world and she drifted into poverty, dying in 1861 at the age of 43.

Ludwig's reaction to hearing that his Spanish Lola was really an Irish Lizzie has never been recorded. He died in Nice in 1868. A king who should have been revered for his patronage of the arts and for turning Munich into a city of culture is instead remembered as an old fool who lost his throne for the love of a bogus showgirl.

THE SELF-STYLED EMPEROR

NORTON I, EMPEROR OF THE UNITED STATES AND PROTECTOR OF MEXICO (1819–80)

The customary method of voicing disapproval at the state of the nation is via the ballot box or in a stiff letter to a newspaper. Joshua Abraham Norton, a bankrupt ex-businessman who lived in a fifty-cents-a-day boarding house in San Francisco, had a grander scheme. On the evening of 17 September 1859 Norton, sensing that his country was drifting into decline, called on the editor of the *San Francisco Bulletin* and left a document proclaiming himself Norton I, Emperor of the United States. Over the next 21 years he carried out his unofficial imperial duties with great gusto, levying taxes, issuing decrees and making such an impact that when he died, some 20,000 people filed past his coffin to pay their respects to America's first and last emperor.

Ironically, this esteemed patriot was not even born in the United States, but across the Atlantic in England. When his parents emigrated to South Africa, he settled around Algoa Bay, near the Cape of Good Hope, and displayed considerable business acumen. With $40,000 to his name, he moved to San Francisco in 1849 and set himself up in the real estate and import brokerage business. Acting shrewdly, he saw his savings grow to $250,000 in just four years.

Unfortunately, his downfall came just as rapidly as his success. Envisaging a huge rice demand from the large number of Chinese immigrants in San Francisco, Norton bought up as much rice as he could in an attempt to corner the local market. As he anticipated the price of rice soared, but before he could take advantage of the situation that he had craftily created, two Japanese ships unexpectedly arrived in the harbour laden with rice. His vast holdings became virtually worthless. Joshua Norton was ruined.

For a few years he disappeared from view, spectacularly resurfacing with his note to the editor of the *Bulletin*, which read: 'At the peremptory request of a large majority of the citizens of these United States, I, Joshua Norton, formerly of Algoa Bay, Cape of Good Hope, and now for the past nine years and ten months of San Francisco, California, declare and proclaim myself Emperor of these U.S., and in virtue of the authority thereby in me vested, do hereby order and direct the representatives of the different States of the Union to assemble in the Musical Hall of this city on the 1st day of February next, then and there to make such alterations in the existing laws of the Union as may ameliorate the evils under which the country is labouring, and thereby cause confidence to exist, both at home and abroad, in our stability and integrity.'

Only the Great Train Robbers managed a longer sentence.

Norton's proclamation was published the following day on the front page beneath the headline: 'AN EMPEROR AMONG US?'

The meeting at the music hall never did take place, but that did not prevent Norton assuming the trappings of power, and rather than treating their self-styled monarch as a deluded megalomaniac, the people of San Francisco adopted him as a loveable eccentric, saluting or bowing to him as they passed him. He could regularly be seen walking the streets of the city dressed in a baggy, faded blue, military-type uniform, complete with gilt epaulets and shiny brass buttons. He habitually wore a tall black beaver hat with a bright green plume and a pair of outsize boots slit at the sides to accommodate his corns. Beside him clanked a heavy sabre, purchased from a local blacksmith, and he carried either an umbrella or a walking stick as his sceptre. Although his uniform appeared somewhat the worse

203

for wear, the bearded, stocky figure looked the part as he strutted around his domain, and when the ceremonial attire did eventually fall to pieces, the city, amid great fanfare, presented him with another. The emperor had his new clothes.

For the city did more than just tolerate him, they actually afforded him the royal treatment he commanded. He was able to eat free in some of San Francisco's finest restaurants, which, as his fame spread, actually began to vie for his patronage. In return he allowed them to put up signs reading: 'By Appointment to His Emperor, Joshua Norton I.' He had a standing ticket – together with his two dogs, Bummer and Lazarus – for any play or concert in the city's theatres; he was given a bicycle by the city as his means of royal transport; and he was even allowed to review the police to check that they carried out their duties, a special chair being reserved for him at each precinct. He was also accorded the honour of marching at the head of the annual police parade and of reviewing the cadets at the University of California.

And all the while he lived at a boarding house on Commercial Street; in an 1870 census he was listed as 'Emperor, living at 624 Commercial St.' He refused to pay his rent on a weekly basis, choosing instead to settle day by day.

In an enterprising move, he proceeded to print his own money, printed free by a local firm and bearing Norton's portrait. While saner men who had tried to break the currency monopoly had always been arrested, Norton managed to get away with it, presumably because he was not perceived as a threat. And when an overzealous police officer, Armand Barbier, did arrest Norton for vagrancy, the incident prompted outrage. It was pointed out that because the emperor had $4.75 in his pocket and lived in a lodging house, he was not technically a vagrant, but Barbier then declared that Norton was of unsound mind and arrested him as a danger to himself and others. This caused public uproar and several scathing newspaper editorials attacked the heavy-handed officer. Norton was held in custody pending examination by the Commissioner of Lunacy but the city police chief made sure that the hearing was never held and ordered the emperor to be released with an apology. From then on, all police officers saluted Norton I when he passed them on the street.

He was also allowed to levy his own taxes, which he collected personally, although he was careful not to outstay his welcome by overburdening the people. Since his needs were modest, his periodic demands on his subjects for financial assistance were kept to a minimum: small shopkeepers were charged twenty-five cents, bigger businesses three dollars. Few had the heart to refuse him.

The two mongrel dogs that accompanied him everywhere became almost as popular as the emperor himself, not least because they kept the rat population in check. When a new dogcatcher mistakenly took Lazarus into custody, an angry mob gathered to demand the animal's release. City officials defused the protest by announcing that both dogs were to have free run of San Francisco. Lazarus's death beneath the wheels of a fire-truck in 1863 was marked by a public funeral and when Bummer died two years later, Mark Twain, who worked next door to Norton's boarding house, composed an epitaph in memory of the noble hound.

Norton added 'Protector of Mexico' to his title because, he claimed, Mexico had 'beseeched him to rule over her'. However, he soon tired of the additional responsibility, explaining that it was 'impossible to protect such an unsettled nation'.

Others might have viewed him as a joke, but Norton took his imperial duties extremely seriously. On his daily patrol, as well as checking that the police were keeping the crime rate under control, he would ensure that all sidewalks were unobstructed and that all necessary street repairs were progressing satisfactorily. He also inspected any buildings under construction, any drains that caught his eye, and generally saw to it that all of the city's ordinances were enforced.

Much of his time was taken up by paperwork, principally taking the form of a series of proclamations, which he felt compelled to issue in order to remind people of his authority. Most of these were nonsensical but one or two demonstrated remarkable foresight. For while he stated that anyone who shortened the city's name to 'Frisco' was guilty of a high misdemeanour, punishable by a fine of 25 dollars. He was also the first person to propose the building of a suspension bridge across San Francisco Bay. His idea was greeted with ridicule but 65 years later, in 1937, the Golden Gate Bridge was constructed on the exact site he suggested. Today a plaque honours the emperor's sound judgement: 'Pause traveller, and be grateful to Norton I . . . whose prophetic wisdom conceived and decreed the bridging of San Francisco Bay.'

He also issued a decree that San Franciscans advance money to local inventor Frederick Marriott for his 'aerial machine' experiments . . . 34 years before the Wright brothers' maiden flight.

The emperor was not content with restricting himself to local issues and sought to exert his influence on the national and even international stage. At the outbreak of the American Civil War, he tried to mediate by sending letters to President Lincoln and Jefferson Davis, President of the Confederacy, demanding that they attend talks with him in San Francisco. Neither replied. He proposed the formation of a League of Nations that would help prevent war and also suggested that an international Bible seminar should be held to help establish a world religion. In 1869 he famously ordered the dissolution and abolition of the Democratic and Republican parties because he thought they were corrupt and causing divisions within the United States. The sentence for violating the decree, he ordered, was between five and ten years' imprisonment. It is not known whether anyone ever attempted to impose the imperial edict.

Norton's policy stance was generally constant, although his position on the rising issue of women's rights seemed to fluctuate alarmingly. Having signed a petition to the California Constitutional Convention calling for an amendment 'that no citizens of the State shall be disenfranchised on account of sex', he stood on stage at a women's rights movement lecture and promptly told all the women in the audience to go home and mind their children. On that occasion he might have needed his sabre.

On 8 January 1880 Norton died suddenly of apoplexy while making his daily rounds. In his pocket was found a two-and-a-half-dollar gold piece, three dollars in silver, an 1828 French franc, and a few of his own bonds. When curious reporters searched his tiny apartment, they discovered that his worldly possessions consisted of his collection of walking sticks, his sabre, some news clippings, his correspondence with Abraham Lincoln and Queen Victoria, plus 1,098,235 shares in a worthless gold mine.

Newspapers wrote glowing tributes. 'San Francisco without Emperor Norton will be like a throne without a king,' ran one obituary. Flags hung at half mast, businesses closed out of respect and the funeral and burial arrangements – all paid for by wealthy citizens – were the most elaborate that San Francisco had ever seen. The funeral cortege was two miles long and thousands turned up to give him the type of send-off that a real emperor would have received.

The eccentric emperor's fame might have been expected to end with his death, but 54 years later, when his body was moved to a new site, 60,000 people attended the ceremony, which featured full military honours. And as recently as 1980, the centenary of his death was commemorated by special events throughout the city. America has not forgotten its only monarch – no matter how crazy he was.

Some might say that the country maintains the fine tradition of worshipping loony leaders. But these days they are called presidents.

THE PIGEON FANCIER

KHANDE RAO GAEKWAD, MAHARAJAH OF BARODA (1828–70)

As one of the richest men in the world, Khande Rao, Maharajah of the Indian state of Baroda, owned such fabulous diamonds as the 128-carat Star of the South. Yet for all the precious pearls, emeralds and diamonds at his disposal, he derived more pleasure from his collection of pigeons.

Being the man he was, it was no ordinary collection of pigeons; at 60,000 strong, it was the biggest in the world. He took enormous pride in his flock and was said to be on first-name terms with every bird. He even staged a sumptuous wedding for his finest cock and hen, the two birds being married with due solemnity by his most trusted priest. Following the ceremony there was a celebratory wedding breakfast, illuminated by a fantastic firework display. It is not clear whether the breakfast menu stretched beyond seed. Sadly, the maharajah's hopes of breeding the perfect pigeon were dashed when the palace cat ate the groom before the union could be consummated.

To console himself, Khande Rao turned to another part of his aviary and arranged a battle between 500 nightingales.

He became maharajah in 1856 and in that capacity he was the object of undiluted adoration. Fawning courtiers stood around his bed waiting for him to wake up each morning and whenever he yawned they would automatically snap their fingers to deter flies from venturing into the royal gullet. Yawns or sneezes were greeted enthusiastically by comments such as 'Excellent, Your Highness.' Even if he passed wind or burped, his aides would applaud politely. They were certainly easily pleased. However, any courtier that happened to sneeze was suspended immediately and everything was shut down for the day lest the maharajah caught a chill.

Khande Rao was prone to sudden flights of fancy, which, given his status, were inevitably granted. He paid £15,500 for a bust of Queen Victoria and had salute cannons and elephant chains cast in silver and gold. With money no object, he decided that he wanted to donate a luxurious pearl carpet to the shrine of the Prophet Mohammed in Medina, Arabia. His advisers were none too keen on a Hindu sovereign (Baroda was a Hindu state) making a grand gesture at an Islamic shrine, but the maharajah refused to back down and insisted on the carpet being prepared. However, when he died, his advisers had their way and the carpet remained in Baroda as a state treasure.

On another impulse he decided that he needed a guru – a wise sage to offer the wisdom that his ministers lacked. After much searching, he finally found a grizzled old man sitting on a dunghill by the side of the road. Although there are grounds for debating whether sitting on a dunghill is necessarily an indication of perspicacity, Khande Rao was convinced and had the old man brought back to the palace, where everyone waited eagerly for streams of knowledge to flow from his sacred lips. Unfortunately, the chosen one preferred to keep any nuggets to himself. Seemingly incapable of communication, he simply stared blankly into the distance. In despair, the maharajah's men tried firing a starting pistol next to his ear in the hope of producing some form of reaction, but even that failed to stir him into life. Eventually the maharajah had to admit defeat and acknowledge that his sage was more of a cabbage.

THE BIRD-BRAINED SULTAN

ABDUL AZIZ, SULTAN OF TURKEY (1830–76)

Just as Khande Rao of Baroda was a pigeon fancier, so another wildly extravagant ruler, Abdul Aziz, had a thing about chickens. Some potentates liked to relax with a good book; others enjoyed watching tortures and executions; Abdul Aziz preferred chasing chickens around his palace.

Although the chase may have looked a Keystone Cops affair, the rules governing the pursuit were set in stone. After the birds had been released at a given signal, the sultan would stalk them through the palace corridors until he caught one. He would then reward the captured hen by hanging the Ottoman Empire's leading award for gallantry around its neck. Should a hen that had been honoured in such a way ever appear at any subsequent chase without its medal, the servant responsible for the oversight was dismissed on the spot without the right of appeal.

The sultan's infatuation with chickens even extended to his diet. He was known to eat a dozen fried eggs at a sitting, which partly explained why he weighed seventeen stone.

Abdul Aziz became sultan in 1861. A talented painter and composer, he enjoyed the finer things in life and although his dress was relatively basic, his extravagances became the talk of Turkey. No sooner had he attained the throne in succession to his brother than he gave notice of his intentions by ordering an eight-foot bed and increasing the sultan's harem to 900. There was just a possibility that the two demands could have been linked. He clearly liked to be surrounded by people, for his staff included 5,000 house servants, 400 grooms, 400 musicians, and 200 men to look after the creatures in his private zoo. Each house servant had his own area of expertise. One man's sole duty was to replace the royal backgammon board after use; another was responsible for cutting the sultan's fingernails.

Quite apart from the 400 musicians on the payroll, while on a trip to Britain Abdul Aziz further demonstrated his love of music by ordering dozens of grand pianos, which he planned to strap to the backs of his servants so that he could hear music wherever he went. These purchases helped to push his annual expenditure beyond the £2,000,000 mark, his personal civil list alone accounting for fifteen per cent of Turkey's yearly outlay. He built a number of grand palaces, including the Beylerbeyi Palace, a fantasy in white marble with magnolia-filled gardens standing on the Asian shore of the Bosphorus. Used as the sultan's summer residence and hunting lodge, it was also offered to the most distinguished of visiting foreign dignitaries. Other items were less justifiable. As part of his plan to expand the Ottoman navy, he bought a quantity of iron ships, but they were left to rust in port because nobody knew how to operate them. Similarly, he purchased – at great expense – a fleet of shiny new locomotives, seemingly oblivious to the fact that Turkey had no rails on which to run them.

Further money was frittered away on diversions, such as the nocturnal war games that he liked to arrange. Purely for the sultan's amusement, dozens of his troops would be marched down to the palace cellars at night and forced to engage in mortal combat while he looked on approvingly. Not only was it a waste of money, it was also a waste of men.

As the first Ottoman ruler to travel to Europe, Abdul Aziz saw himself as an international statesman, yet his approach to history was strangely insular. For example, he ordered that all of the country's schoolbooks should be rewritten to exclude any mention of Turkish defeats as well as Christianity and the French Revolution. Turkish failings were not his only phobia. He had a morbid fear of fire and would never go to bed until assured that his room had been emptied of all wooden objects.

He also had a phobia about black ink and would only sign and read papers that had been copied out in red.

His ideas became increasingly eccentric. On discovering that one of his bureaucrats was also named Aziz, he passed a law making it illegal for any government official to share his second name. Thus all those called Aziz (one of the most common names in Turkey) were obliged to change their name just to keep the sultan happy.

An ally of Britain during the Crimean War, Abdul Aziz fell foul of many foreign nations when he was caught indiscriminately massacring Christians. Yet it was primarily unrest brought about by his excessive personal expenditure that led to his overthrow in 1876. Two weeks after the coup he was found dead in the palace to which he had been confined. His slashed wrists prompted an official verdict of suicide, but rumours spread that he had been murdered . . . by one of the few people who weren't on his payroll.

A BROKEN WOMAN

CHARLOTTE, EMPRESS OF MEXICO (1840–1927)

If she had remained in her native Belgium, Charlotte would probably have lived a calm and contented existence, warranting little more than a footnote in nineteenth-century world history. Instead, she chose to pursue her dream of ruling Mexico in conjunction with her husband Maximilian. But the dream turned sour, depriving Maximilian of his life and Charlotte of her sanity and turning her into a tragic, haunted figure for the last sixty years of her life.

The only daughter of Leopold I (the first King of Belgium) and his second wife Louise d'Orléans, Charlotte was named after her father's much-lamented first wife, Crown Princess Charlotte, the sole issue of the ill-fated marriage between the future George IV and Caroline of Brunswick. An intelligent, well-read girl with a fondness for Bach, she overcame the loss of her mother when she was just ten and continued to behave with the dignity expected of one in her position. In the summer of 1856 her natural charm and beauty (she had a slim figure, delicate features, long black hair and mesmerising dark brown eyes) caught the attention of the 24-year-old Habsburg Archduke Maximilian, younger brother of the Austrian Emperor Franz Joseph. Maximilian was tall, handsome, witty and energetic, and the sixteen-year-old Charlotte was instantly smitten.

Although Leopold preferred Pedro V of Portugal as a prospective son-in-law, he allowed his daughter to make her own choice and, seduced by Maximilian's tales of exotic travel and drawings of the medieval-style Miramar Castle, which he was having built near Trieste in Italy, she agreed to become his bride. They married on 27 July 1857 in Brussels and travelled on to Italy because Maximilian had been appointed Viceroy of Lombardy and Venice.

To the outside world the newlyweds appeared blissfully happy, but Maximilian had no intention of forsaking his bachelor ways and set off on lengthy jaunts to foreign fleshpots soberly disguised as state visits. In Maximilian's vocabulary the phrase 'diplomatic negotiations' was a euphemism for riotous parties and trips to brothels. When he went to Brazil on supposedly official business in 1859, rumours of his misbehaviour in Rio preceded his return. Still Charlotte gave him the benefit of the doubt . . . until he infected her with a sexually transmitted disease. Thereafter intercourse was off the menu and they slept in separate rooms.

While her husband was out partying, Charlotte was left behind at Miramar Castle. Although this offered her the chance to read, paint, swim and sail, she became frustrated at not being able to make a more positive contribution to world affairs. Understandably, she felt that her qualities were not being utilised to the maximum.

That opportunity arose in 1863 when Napoleon III of France invited Maximilian to become Emperor of Mexico. The previous year, enticed by the prospect of collecting thirty per cent of the proceeds, France had agreed to intervene in the recovery of 79,000,000 francs owed to a Swiss banker by the Mexican government. Master debt collector Napoleon persuaded Britain and Spain to join him in sending forces to occupy positions around the Mexican coast until the country's new liberal leader, Benito Juarez, paid up. In return for this aid, the French promised not to seek territorial rights or to interfere in the government of Mexico. However, the deposed Mexican conservatives convinced Napoleon that what the Mexican people really wanted more than anything else was a foreign ruler. Unlikely as the idea sounded it appealed to Napoleon, who promptly put forward Maximilian's name.

Maximilian expressed grave initial misgivings, but Charlotte was eager to establish European rule in Mexico after her father had rejected the Mexican throne in his youth. Besides, it would give her something meaningful to do. She pushed her husband into accepting and after Napoleon had promised continuing support, Maximilian was talked into signing the agreement. Hearing the news, Charlotte's French grandmother screamed: 'They will be killed!'

Franz Josef was equally unhappy with the arrangement and told Maximilian that if he accepted the Mexican crown, he would have to surrender his rights to the Austrian throne. With Maximilian wavering, Charlotte tried to negotiate with Franz Josef, but when the latter stood his ground she convinced her husband to relinquish his claim to the Austrian monarchy. With some reluctance, he agreed. She was so excited that she changed her name to Carlota, the Mexican equivalent of Charlotte.

The couple arrived in Mexico in May 1864 to a welcome that was on the cool side of lukewarm. Faced with the unwelcome prospect of living in the derelict Palacio National, they opted instead for the Chapultepec Palace, a neo-Gothic fantasy perched on a hilltop on the edge of the city. It proved only marginally more comfortable and on their first night Charlotte was kept awake by lice. Although Napoleon had sent 20,000 troops to quell Mexican resistance, Maximilian soon realised that the French government had been misled by the conservatives. The people did not want a foreign ruler at all. Furthermore, Maximilian's liberal views on religion cost him the support of the Pope.

With the emperor and empress continuing to sleep apart, Maximilian invited numerous other women to his bed, including a seventeen-year-old Mexican girl who gave birth to a son. Since Charlotte's sex ban meant there was little chance of him fathering a legitimate heir, he adopted two grandsons of a former Mexican emperor. However, the boys' mother quickly backtracked and told anyone who would listen that Maximilian had stolen her sons from her.

In 1866, under pressure from the United States, Napoleon reneged on his earlier promise and withdrew his troops from Mexico. He also informed Maximilian that he would not be providing further financial aid. Maximilian had been abandoned. Still reeling from news of her father's death, Charlotte sank into depression. Maximilian considered abdication, but she begged him to think again. With the country becoming increasingly dangerous, it was decided that Charlotte should travel to Europe and try to reason with Napoleon.

She was in a highly emotional state on her arrival in France, her rather fragile temperament not helped by Napoleon's intransigence. She blamed him for her predicament and at their final meeting became hysterical. When a servant produced a silver pitcher with a cooling drink, she pulled away sharply screaming that the drink was poisoned and that they were trying to get rid of her too. In letters home to Maximilian she wrote that Napoleon represented 'the evil on earth' and that he was 'possessed by the devil'. Maximilian did not need to read to the end to realise that he would not be receiving any more troops.

Travelling south to Trieste, Charlotte once again began behaving irrationally. She told her lady-in-waiting that a farmer in a field was an undercover assassin and ordered the coachman to increase speed. To avoid being recognised, she covered her face with a handkerchief for the rest of the journey. At Miramar Castle a courier arrived from Mexico with a desperate plea from Maximilian to ask the Pope for help. So Charlotte headed for Rome and was warmly greeted wherever she stopped. She chatted openly to people, appearing perfectly sane, but inside her stomach was churning with terror, for she had convinced herself that she would be poisoned if she set foot inside the holy city. She suspected everyone, even her own staff. When she finally met the Pope, she threw herself to the floor before him and begged him to let her stay the night at the Vatican as it was the only place where she could escape the threat of being poisoned. The puzzled pontiff had a bed prepared in the library. Officially it was the only time a woman has ever spent a night in the Vatican.

The next day, the mother superior of a nearby convent persuaded Charlotte to visit a local orphanage. With her handkerchief over her face, the masked empress travelled by coach to the convent, where she delivered a delightful speech. But her demons were lurking in the wings and took centre stage on a tour of the grounds. Hungry for food (which she was afraid to eat in case it was poisoned), she suddenly snatched a piece of meat from a hot pan in the kitchen. She burned her hand so badly that she fainted from the pain and had to be rushed to her hotel. She now refused to eat or drink anything that could have been tampered with. When thirsty, she took the Pope's glass and filled it with water at a public fountain; for dinner she insisted on a live chicken being tied to the legs of her table and then slaughtered and prepared in her presence. Nothing was left to chance.

Advised of Charlotte's condition, her brother Philip, Duke of Flanders, arrived to escort her back to Miramar, where her physicians attributed her spells of insanity to the effect of poison administered in Mexico, for it was said that while in Mexico she had eaten fruit laced with the poisonous juice of the milk tree. No visitors were permitted to Miramar, and because of her lengthy isolation it was later rumoured that she had given birth to an illegitimate child, having allegedly been pregnant on her departure from Mexico. According to some sources the child grew up to be the French Second World War General Maxime Weygand. The general himself never confirmed or denied the story. However, the diaries of the Miramar doctor revealed that Charlotte never missed a period and, besides, no matter how disappointing her marriage, she was surely too proud and haughty to have yielded to an affair.

In 1867 Maximilian, soldiering on alone, was captured by Juarez's rebels and executed. The news of his death brought about a further deterioration in Charlotte's condition and she was taken back to Belgium to live with her family. Initially the comfort of familiar surroundings appeared to have the desired effect, but then she was overcome by fits of frenzy and had to be kept in confinement, first in Castle Tervuren and then at the

Château de Bouchout, near Meise. Her moments of lucidity became increasingly rare. She talked incoherently and emotionally, sometimes veering between laughter and tears in the same sentence. At other times she would go completely berserk, smashing furniture, ripping up books, slashing paintings and breaking vases, although, even in these darkest spells, she always avoided damaging any items that reminded her of Maximilian. During the First World War the Kaiser ordered that the Château de Bouchout was not to be attacked because Charlotte was the sister-in-law of his ally, the Austrian emperor.

She remained in Bouchout, shut off from the outside world, right up until her death from pneumonia in January 1927 at the age of 86. Even in her final days some say that she still believed herself to be the Empress of Mexico.

THE PRINCE OF PARANOIA

ABDUL HAMID II, SULTAN OF TURKEY
(1842–1918)

Given that no fewer than seventeen of the thirty-four previous sultans of Turkey had met a violent death, it was perhaps not surprising that Abdul Hamid II lived in constant fear of assassination. Consequently, his paranoia reached such epic proportions that his own shadow might have been accused of following him.

Much of his insecurity stemmed from a sense of guilt. Following the overthrow of the spendthrift Abdul Aziz in 1876, Abdul Hamid's mad elder brother, Murad V, became sultan. Even by Ottoman standards, Murad was patently unsuitable for holding high office. A schizophrenic alcoholic, he was incapable of carrying out the most basic of tasks and after just three months, Abdul Hamid encouraged doctors to declare that his brother was incurably insane. Murad was then quietly locked away but even in confinement he continued to pose a threat to the stability of Abdul Hamid, who convinced himself that the British intended to kidnap Murad and to restore him as sultan. Clinging to an ancient Eastern belief that a representation of a man weakened his life force, Abdul Hamid had his personal wax-modeller (a key member of his entourage) make hundreds of models of Murad. If the modeller failed on any occasion to mould a good likeness from a single cast, Abdul Hamid regarded this as a bad omen and refused to make any decisions for the remainder of the day.

The new sultan recognised the importance of having a stout fortress for a home and, dissatisfied with the existing royal palace of Dolmabache, he set about building his own high-security complex at nearby Yildiz. For a man of such intense suspicion, it was an uncharacteristically reckless move to build his palace on the site of an old burial ground for criminals. Perhaps it was his soothsayer's day off.

Every stage of the planning of the new palace was drawn up amid fanatical secrecy. In the dead of night the sultan would order a horse to be saddled and, accompanied by a solitary trusted servant, he would ride off and reconnoitre possible sites. Eventually he settled on an area of Constantinople parkland, which, situated as it was on the banks of the Bosphorus, afforded excellent views of any potential invaders. A dozen architects were hand-picked to submit their designs for the various sections of the palace; for security purposes each architect was kept ignorant of his fellows' work. Similarly the builders, who were chosen for their loyalty to the sultan rather than their expertise, were all kept separate – for example, those working on the harem were never allowed to meet those constructing the private zoo. At Yildiz, if the right hand knew what the left hand was doing, it was liable to be cut off.

The finished article boasted nearly one hundred buildings and the labyrinth allowed Abdul Hamid to move his living quarters from one area to another on an irregular basis so as to confuse any would-be assassins. False facades were fitted to the front of the palace, and both the front and the approach from the sea were heavily guarded. Telescopes were trained permanently on the Bosphorus, the sultan himself often looking through them for added reassurance. The furniture in the sultan's rooms was deliberately arranged so that visitors could only enter in single file, which Abdul Hamid considered less threatening. Many rooms had mirrors so that he could see behind him and were connected by a network of secret passages. Some rooms were even booby-trapped. Innocuous-looking cupboards were placed facing the door but at the touch of a switch next to the sultan's couch, their glass doors would spring open to reveal a pair of pistols, which would fire automatically. For added protection, he kept loaded guns in every room, including two revolvers that hung next to his bath. With so many firearms about and the sultan permanently jumpy, accidents were inevitable. Once a gardener made a sudden movement near Abdul Hamid, who promptly shot him in the head.

The sultan was not one for taking unnecessary risks. He refused to have a telephone installed at Yildiz in case somebody sent a lethal current down the line to him, and not only did he hire a food taster but also a clothes sampler whose job it was to try on the sultan's garments every day in case they had somehow been poisoned. As an added precaution, all of Abdul Hamid's new clothes were first fitted on his foster brother and Keeper of the Imperial Wardrobe, Izzet, who was of similar stature, so that no tailor need ever touch the sultan's person. And before the sultan wore a new coat, Izzet always warmed it with his own body. To make doubly sure that he was bullet-proof, Abdul Hamid used to wear chain mail beneath his tunic and a steel-lined fez on his head.

If he did leave the palace, he crouched down inside his specially built armoured carriage, with one of his young sons perched on his knee to act as a human shield.

When it came to food, Abdul Hamid was naturally fastidious. His food was prepared in kitchens that had bars on the windows and bolts on the doors to prevent anyone sneaking in and adding poison to his meals. His water well was patrolled and every cow that provided his milk was guarded round the clock by armed soldiers. If he was feeling particularly vulnerable, he would refuse to eat from cutlery (lest it had been coated with poison) and would feed instead from the cupped hand of a harem girl.

All of his documents had to be baked in an oven and disinfected before being handed to him and his bed was checked by an aide before he climbed into it. At night he would frequently wander between the various houses in the palace, listening at doors or boring spy-holes in the walls for future use.

Sometimes these meanderings took him to the living-quarters of kitchen maids and boot boys, who were startled to find the sultan suddenly in their presence.

Some 20,000 people were employed at Yildiz, each confined to his own area, often within a single building. But whilst the workers were unfamiliar with each other, Abdul Hamid knew every single one, right down to the humblest servant, through spending hours studying individual photographs of his staff. He trusted few people and regularly staged exercises to test their loyalty. To find out what the women of his harem really thought about him, he ordered a wax doll lookalike of himself, dressed in his clothes, to be placed in a dimly lit room, bent over a book. Hidden behind a screen, the real Abdul Hamid scanned the women's faces, noting how some quietly withdrew in order to avoid disturbing him while others giggled like schoolgirls behind his back. The following evening two of those who failed the examination were sewn up in leather sacks and tossed into the Bosphorus to drown.

Nor did he trust doctors and pharmacists. He kept hundreds of pills to treat every known ailment but rather than rely on the advice of a medic, who may have been plotting his downfall, he preferred to empty the contents of several boxes into a bag and then select one pill at random. Little did he know, but that was probably the way his physicians operated too.

He didn't even trust his own ministers and instead turned to a motley collection of advisers, including a slave, a Punch and Judy man, and a circus clown. In the circumstances some of his policies inevitably caused raised eyebrows, although he did resist the temptation to quell an Armenian uprising with a dozen custard pies, a vat of crazy foam and six large buckets of water. No prizes for guessing who suggested that one. His most valued confidant was Abdul Huda, a young beggar from Aleppo, who rose through the ranks by pandering to the sultan's endless superstitions. Huda's appreciation of his master's insecurities earned him a sumptuous residence and one of the top jobs in government, being entrusted with setting the official seal on sentences of exile and death.

Aware that his guards could be responsible for his salvation or his overthrow, Abdul Hamid deliberately chose his personal protection to be formed of two groups of men who hated each other – Albanians and Arabs. His theory was that they would never join forces against him, not only because of their mutual dislike but also because each group would be constantly watching the other.

With every fresh hint of unrest in the country, the network of passages at Yildiz was extended and wooden doors were replaced with steel ones. The assassination in 1898 of the Empress Elizabeth of Austria made Abdul Hamid more jittery than ever. She was stabbed to death in Geneva by an Italian anarchist who had apparently intended killing King Umberto of Italy but didn't have enough money for the train fare to Rome! Following her death, Yildiz underwent further fortification. The sultan tried to turn the whole place into even more of a maze, making navigation of the corridors almost impossible, and therefore, he hoped, deterring assassins. Several dozen pianos were installed as decorative barricades – even though the sultan was not in the least musical – old walls were heightened, and new ones built. He ordered a redesign of the layout so that from every corner of his favourite houses – even the bathrooms – he was able to see entrances and any approaching enemy. Remembering an old superstition that a parrot screeches at the sight of a stranger, he had birdcages hung outside the windows. It may not have helped him spot any potential killer but at least he knew who was a pretty boy.

The merest mention of the word 'rebellion' was sufficient to bring Abdul Hamid out in a rash. Indeed, he decided to outlaw such words as 'freedom', 'revolutionary', 'republic', 'assassin', 'dynamite' and 'bomb'. Unfortunately he tended to confuse 'dynamite' with 'dynamo', as a result of which he flatly refused to extend the local electricity grid beyond the walls of Yildiz. And when the Emperor and Empress of Germany visited Turkey in 1898, the chef who wrote the words 'Bombe Glacée' on the official menu was instantly sacked. Any book or newspaper that angered him was used as fuel to heat his bath, but his censorship was so slavishly obeyed that he must have had a number of cold dips. For example, when the King and Queen of Serbia were murdered in 1903, Turkish papers stated that they had died of indigestion, the sultan having banned the press from reporting any act of regicide.

Impossible though it may seem, Abdul Hamid became even more paranoid towards the end of his reign. Turks were forbidden to travel even to the next town without a passport and a bundle of documents. And they were often refused permission to travel abroad simply because the sultan was suspicious of anyone wealthy. Life for the people of Constantinople became unbearable. The process of moving house, stressful enough at any time, was complicated by the sultan's insistence that soldiers search all furniture carts just in case revolutionaries or stores of dynamite were hidden away in that old chest of drawers. And any talk of stuffing an ottoman was highly seditious.

Although the threat from brother Murad vanished with his death in 1904, Abdul Hamid never relaxed his guard for a second, gradually becoming more and more remote and often sending lookalikes to perform official functions. The only time he ventured beyond Yildiz in later years was for his weekly dash to a mosque that had been specially built for him just outside the palace gates. Realising what he was missing, he attempted to simulate Constantinople street life inside Yildiz by creating a mock-up of a real street café within the safety of the palace walls. There he would drink coffee at an establishment where all the waiters were his bodyguards. But by now he was so petrified of assassination that he even refused to see the actress Sarah Bernhardt when she visited Turkey simply because she mimicked death so well.

During his reign Abdul Hamid had overseen the slaughter of over a million Bulgarians and Armenians and when the bloodshed spilled over on to the streets of Constantinople, his subjects decided to depose him. In 1909 he was toppled and sent into exile at Salonika where he died nine years later – not from poison, strangulation, or any of the other terrible deaths that he had envisaged over the years, but from natural causes.

THE DREAM KING

LUDWIG II, KING OF BAVARIA (1845–86)

In view of his family history, it should come as no great surprise that Ludwig II proved to be one of the pottiest potentates in history. After all, his aunt, Princess Alexandra, was convinced that as a child she had swallowed a full-size grand piano – and nothing could ever shake her from that belief. She may have talked a lot of nonsense, but she made a lovely tune. And his grandfather, Ludwig I, had been forced to abdicate after rashly falling in love at the age of sixty with an exotic Spanish dancer called Lola Montez . . . even though she was in fact Irish and her real name was Eliza Gilbert. So for Maximilian II to name his son after such an eccentric old fool was definitely tempting fate.

The future Ludwig II was born on 25 August 1845 in the last years of his grandfather's ill-fated reign. When little Ludwig was two, his father Maximilian, as Wittelsbach family heir, acceded to the throne of Bavaria. Ludwig and his younger brother Otto were brought up strictly, with an emphasis on duty. In keeping with the times, their parents were distant, but Ludwig did enjoy the summer holidays spent at the Castle Hohenschwangau, which his father had restored in a romantic medieval style. The boy was captivated by the Alpine setting and used to feed the wild swans that lived around the lake.

Ludwig was a singular child. He once told his governess: 'I want to remain an eternal mystery to myself and others.' When he was thirteen she wrote to him describing a performance of Richard Wagner's opera *Lohengrin*, the tale of a heroic swan-knight. Since the walls of Hohenschwangau were covered in frescoes featuring Lohengrin, a curious Ludwig acquired a copy of the opera's libretto and read it avidly. From an early age Ludwig had immersed himself in dressing up and acting out short plays and now he discovered a fresh outlet for his artistic bent. He was soon reading every available book by Wagner and in 1861 gained permission from his parents to attend a Munich performance of *Lohengrin*. Enraptured by the composer's music and writings, Ludwig then acquired Wagner's recently published *Ring* cycle, the preface of which contained a remark about the miserable state of German theatre. In order for the work to be produced, wrote Wagner, a German prince would need to be found to provide the required funds. To Ludwig, this was a direct message from the master. He would be that prince.

In March 1864 Maximilian II died and the eighteen-year-old Ludwig became king. He loved military uniforms but hated warfare and had no interest in politics, preferring to live in his own fantasy world. Shortly after the accession, his minister of justice, Eduard von Bomhard, remarked of Ludwig: 'He was mentally gifted in the highest degree, but the contents of his mind were stored in a totally disordered fashion.' Ludwig was as confused about his own sexuality as he was about the mechanism of government, having developed both a romantic attachment to his aide, Prince Paul von Thurn and Taxis, and a close platonic friendship with his cousin, Princess Elisabeth.

One of his first acts was to order his ministers to track down the impoverished Wagner. On the run from his many creditors, the composer was located in Vienna and brought before the king, who promised to cure his financial problems at a stroke.

The day after their meeting the infatuated Ludwig reiterated his position in a letter to Wagner: 'I want to lift the medial burden of everyday life off your shoulders for ever. I want to enable you to enjoy the peace you so long for that you will be able to unfurl the mighty pinions of your genius unhindered and in the pure ether of your rapturous art! Unknowingly you were the sole source of my joy from my earliest boyhood, my friend who spoke to my heart as no other could, my best mentor and teacher.'

Naturally Wagner was overjoyed at the prospect of acquiring a royal benefactor but, even after that brief encounter, he expressed concerns for the king's future. 'He is unfortunately so beautiful and wise, soulful and lordly,' wrote Wagner, 'that I fear his life must fade away like a divine dream in this base world . . . if he remains alive it will be a great miracle!'

Ludwig and Wagner were an odd couple. Ludwig was young, charming, and homosexual; Wagner was around twice his age, temperamental, and a notorious womaniser. But the king, with his passion for the medieval legends featured in Wagner's operas, had set his heart on becoming the composer's patron. And Wagner had no intention of declining.

Ludwig threw money at Wagner with gay abandon, paying off his debts and funding his lavish lifestyle. He soon found that Wagner's creative juices did not flow cheaply, requiring a luxurious rent-free house in Munich and an annual salary which greatly exceeded that of Bavaria's senior government ministers. His generosity knowing no bounds, Ludwig also proposed the construction of a large festival theatre in Munich to stage Wagner's operas, but these plans were put on hold following widespread discontent among the king's advisers. Since Ludwig had no personal fortune, his patronage of Wagner had to be financed from the civil list, and ministers became anxious that the king's obsession was bleeding the Bavarian treasury dry.

Ludwig and Wagner continued to exchange affectionate letters, in which the king pined for his soulmate whenever Wagner was away, but there was no stemming the rising tide of public opinion. For just as members of the court resented Wagner's arrogance, influence, and drain on the state's money, so the public became increasingly restless at the king's neglect of his political responsibilities while in search of aesthetic pleasure, and at Wagner's illicit relationship with Cosima von Bülow, wife of conductor Hans von Bülow. In December 1865 Ludwig was informed by his chief minister that unless he severed his friendship with Wagner, he would have to surrender his crown. Unable to bear the thought of life without Wagner, Ludwig considered abdication but finally bowed to pressure and reluctantly asked the composer to leave Bavaria for at least six months. As Wagner headed for exile in Switzerland, Ludwig wrote that he longed for the day when his friend 'will return and inspire me with his dear proximity,' adding tenderly: 'My love for you will never die, and I beg you to retain for ever your friendship for me.'

Wagner, who later admitted that he was puzzled by Ludwig's adoration, was not totally abandoned. The king still financed many of Wagner's most extravagant works and the Munich opera house was built on a reduced scale at Bayreuth. And when Ludwig heard of the composer's death in 1883, he ordered every piano in his castles to be wreathed in black crepe.

Shortly after Wagner was forced to leave for Switzerland, Ludwig surprised nearly everyone by becoming engaged to Princess Sophie, younger sister of his friend, Princess Elisabeth. During the engagement he showed distinct signs of mental instability. Although he spent a fortune on the building of a lavish wedding coach, he asked his physician for a certificate declaring him unfit to marry and told his court secretary that he would rather drown himself than go through with the wedding. He kept postponing the nuptials until even Sophie took the hint and realised that all was not well. Eventually her father offered the king a way out, which he readily accepted. That night Ludwig wrote in his diary: 'Sophie is finished with. The gloomy picture vanishes. I longed for freedom, I thirsted for freedom, to wake from this horrible nightmare.' He immediately fled to his beloved Alps and hid there in his dreams. In November 1867 he wrote to Wagner from Hohenschwangau: 'I write these lines sitting in my cosy gothic bow-window, by the light of my lonely lamp, while outside the blizzard rages. It is so peaceful here, this silence is stimulating, whereas in the clamour of the world I feel absolutely miserable. Thank God I am alone at last. My mother is far away, as is my former bride, who would have made me unspeakably unhappy. Before me stands a bust of the one, true Friend whom I shall love until death. If only I had the opportunity to die for you.'

It was in the late 1860s that, like Philip V of Spain before him, Ludwig decided to reverse day and night, waking at 7 p.m. and dining in the early hours of the morning. He began by having an artificial moon and stars painted on the ceiling of his bedroom before progressing to epic nocturnal rides. Sometimes wearing a bowler hat, he would embark on winter drives through the mountains in a golden rococo sleigh, accompanied by coachmen and outriders who were forced to dress in the style of Louis XIV. Another of Ludwig's moonlight escapades involved riding on horseback round and round the Court Riding School for up to seven hours at a time. The object of the exercise was to simulate the distance of heroic journeys, such as that from Munich to Innsbruck, and the riding time was calculated accordingly. At the halfway stage, Ludwig would dismount, change horses and sit down for a picnic.

Louis XIV was another of Ludwig's heroes and he later built the palace at Linderhof as a tribute to the French monarch. He sought to emulate Louis as a patron of the arts, often imitating his dress, signature and mannerisms and talking to imaginary guests in French. He would even order places at the dinner table to be set for dead French kings. One observer described Ludwig's Louis XIV walk: 'This walk was a total mockery of nature. Taking great strides he threw his long legs out in front of him as if he wanted to hurl them away from him, then he brought the front foot down as though with each step he was trying to crush a scorpion.'

With Bavaria becoming embroiled in Prussian military expansion, the peace-loving Ludwig withdrew into his own little dream world and began devising schemes for a series of fairytale castles where he would be able to escape from the trials of everyday life. As these plans reached fruition, he spent virtually all of his time in his Alpine retreats, refusing to see his ministers and remaining in the capital for only the 21 nights per year required by the Bavarian constitution.

The first of these fantasy buildings, Neuschwanstein, was designed not by an architect, but by a Munich scene-painter, Christopher Jank. Ludwig saw it as a magical paradise that would bring the imaginary world of Wagner's operas to life. Perched high on a Bavarian crag, it became immortalised as the white castle in Walt Disney's *Sleeping Beauty*. 'The spot,' Ludwig told Wagner, 'is one of the most beautiful that one could ever find, sacred and out of reach, a worthy temple for the divine friend.' Ludwig did not stint on the cost – after all, the Bavarian treasury was paying for it. Among his grander ideas was to have a waterfall tumbling down one of the staircases – until even he realised that the scheme was impractical.

Although relentlessly enthusiastic, Ludwig was not always the easiest man to design for. When artists outlined their plans for the huge decorative murals at Neuschwanstein, the king would invariably find fault. The artists would then become exasperated, whereupon a hurt Ludwig would shun personal contact, with the result that they were no longer allowed to show him their paintings. Given the king's attention to detail, it is perhaps not surprising that although preparatory work at the site commenced in 1868, the castle remained unfinished at his death nearly twenty years later.

His next project was the villa at Linderhof, his homage to Louis XIV, where special features included a 'magic table' that descended through the floor to a lower-level pantry so that servants could prepare and set the different courses of Ludwig's dinner without disturbing his solitude. When feeling particularly regal, he sat on a throne shaped like a peacock and, continuing the theme, mechanical peacocks were dotted around the grounds. But pride of place went to a fabulous grotto, complete with cast-iron stalactites and an underground lake with an artificial ripple effect, live swans and where the colour of the water could be changed at the flick of a switch. The grotto's backdrop was copied from *Lohengrin*, and it was on the lake that Ludwig acted out his Wagnerian fantasies. Imagining himself to be Lohengrin, the king would don a suit of armour and be ferried across the lake in a small cockleshell boat pulled by a mechanical swan while being serenaded by specially hired musicians hidden in nearby bushes.

He also built Herrenchiemsee, modelled on the royal palace of Versailles, as another sign of his worship for Louis XIV. He even maintained a state bedroom there for the Sun King . . . despite the fact that Louis had been dead for more than 150 years. Over 16,000,000 marks were spent on building Herrenchiemsee, yet Ludwig stayed there for a total of just nine nights.

His spending was spiralling out of control and when he announced plans to renovate another residence, Falkenstein, with jewel-encrusted walls, his long-suffering ministers finally called time on his building programme. In despair, Ludwig thought about funding future projects by robbing banks in Frankfurt, Stuttgart, Paris and Berlin. However, the servants he instructed to hold up the Rothschild Bank in Frankfurt had no previous experience of armed robbery and, after travelling to the city and laying low for a plausible length of time, they reported back to the king that there had been a last-minute hitch. Accepting their explanation, Ludwig turned to his stable quartermaster and ordered him to recruit a gang of ruthless Italians to kidnap the Crown Prince of Prussia. When this plan also came to nothing, Ludwig decided that perhaps he was not cut out to be the 'Mr Big' of Bavarian crime.

So he came up with another brainwave: he would sell Bavaria and use the money to set up a new kingdom in another part of the world where he would be able to build as many castles as he liked. The Director of the Bavarian State Archives, Franz von Löher, toured the world in search of Ludwig's enchanted land – Tenerife, Brazil, the Crimea, even Afghanistan (which was rumoured to boast a similar alpine landscape to Bavaria) – but was unable to find a suitable alternative. So although Ludwig had offered Prussia and his uncle Prince Luitpold first refusal on Bavaria, the sale fell through.

If nothing else, Ludwig had always treated his servants with a degree of consideration, even though they often disregarded his more outrageous orders and simply humoured him. But in his later years he grew increasingly unpredictable and the slightest offence could warrant violent retribution. He would box their ears, kick them or empty washbasins over their heads. The punishment rarely fitted the crime. One servant was transported for life for failing to catch a bird that had escaped from the royal aviary; another was ordered to wear a dress and ride around the palace on a donkey for committing some minor misdemeanour.

Meanwhile, Ludwig imposed a list of rules and regulations that made the Magna Carta look like a pamphlet. It was forbidden to sneeze, cough or clear one's throat in the vicinity of the king, offenders facing a flogging or even execution. As he became obsessed with Chinese court etiquette, he demanded that his staff wear oriental dress and approach him on all fours. Any servant unexpectedly meeting the king in a corridor or anteroom had to bow as low as was humanly possible without ever looking at him in the face. For breaking this rule, one valet, Mayr, was forced to wear a black mask in Ludwig's presence for over a year. The king began hearing imaginary sounds and seeing imaginary objects. Once he told the aforementioned Mayr to put away a knife. When the poor valet protested that there was no knife in the room, Ludwig raged: 'But there should be one there. Where have you put it? Why have you put it away? Put it back immediately.' The upshot was that although the pay was not to be sneezed at (certainly not in the king's presence), many staff feigned illness rather than wait on Ludwig and were eventually reduced to communicating with him through locked doors by tapping out a prearranged code on the woodwork. The last straw must have been when he invited his favourite horse to dinner and allowed it to smash all the plates.

Ludwig continued to find new infatuations to pass the time – anything to prevent him living in the real world. The French connection resurfaced with a sudden admiration for Marie Antoinette, a statue of whom he had positioned on the terrace at Linderhof. Whenever he passed it, Ludwig would remove his hat and stroke the cheeks of the statue. In 1880 the king became attracted to a 22-year-old actor by the name of Josef Kainz, who was due to appear in a Munich play that Ludwig was producing about William Tell. Night after night a weary Kainz was required to recite passages to Ludwig who then decided that, in order to get the feel of the part, Kainz should make the same journey over the Alps that his character (Tell's comrade Melchtal) takes in the play. Kainz may well have thought that this was taking the concept of method acting a little too far, but the king was a difficult man to refuse and so together they set off on the arduous two-day climb. However, by the halfway stage Kainz was utterly exhausted and refused to go any further, at which a dismayed but not defeated Ludwig suggested that the actor instead recite Melchtal's speech from the top of the shorter Riiti Mountain. Accordingly, at two o'clock in the morning, Ludwig dragged the suffering thespian to the summit and ordered him to recite the passage, but Kainz had neither the energy nor the inclination and promptly fell asleep. This marked the end of their friendship.

By now Ludwig was a liability, an extravagance and an embarrassment. His refusal to fulfil the responsibilities of his position and his ridiculous expenditures were causing grave concerns among his ministers, while the writing of begging letters to European heads of state in another desperate attempt to finance his castle-building had reduced Bavaria to a laughing stock. In the middle of 1885 the Bavarian prime minister, Johann von Lutz, met Prince Luitpold to discuss how to deal with a monarch who had outstayed his welcome. Their solution was to have Ludwig declared insane.

The certification of Ludwig's insanity was provided in June 1886 by Dr Bernard von Gudden and three colleagues, based on a mass of evidence that was, of course, deliberately weighted against the king. Those who believed that Ludwig was merely eccentric – and that was impossible to deny – found that the doctors had no interest in hearing their testimony. Without ever examining the patient in person, the medics pronounced that Ludwig was mad, that his madness was incurable, and that for the rest of his life he would be incapable of exercising his duties.

On 10 June Prince Luitpold was named as permanent regent in place of the sick king, whose affairs would now be controlled by a special commission. Intending to take Ludwig into custody, von Gudden, his assistant and the members of the commission set off for Neuschwanstein with a straitjacket and a bottle of chloroform, but Ludwig had been forewarned and they arrived to find the castle doors bolted and guarded by local police officers who refused to allow them entry. They were then attacked by one of the king's most fervent supporters – an elderly lady with an umbrella. While the humiliated commissioners considered their next move, Ludwig had them arrested and wrote an open letter to his subjects asking them, in effect, to rise up in rebellion should he be seized by his enemies. Ludwig also contemplated suicide, but his aide refused to go and out buy the poison.

After being freed, the commissioners returned and this time found no sentry barring their way. Inside, Ludwig appeared tired and dazed and offered no resistance as they led him away to Castle Berg, the fortress that was to be his prison. The following day – 13 June – he awoke in the early hours ready to get up, only to find that his clothes had been removed. So he took to pacing his room in a nightshirt. In the course of the day von Gudden observed a marked improvement in the king's condition and gave permission for him to take an evening stroll around Starnberger Lake. Naturally Ludwig could not be left to his own devices, so von Gudden joined him. The two men set out at 6.10 p.m. When they had still not returned three hours later, a search party was sent out into the torrential rain to look for them. At around 10 p.m., someone spotted a dark object floating in the water: it was the king's jacket and overcoat. Thirty minutes later, Ludwig's body was found floating face down in shallow water, some twenty metres from the shore. Von Gudden's body was found shortly afterwards. There were marks on his face, possibly indicating signs of a struggle. The general assumption was that Ludwig had committed suicide and that the doctor had either drowned accidentally while trying to prevent it or else had been deliberately drowned by his prisoner.

And so the man described by the poet Paul Verlaine as the 'only true king of this century' met an untimely end at the age of forty before fully realising his dream of turning Bavaria into a giant theme park, a Deutschland Disney. The irony for the Bavarian people was that Ludwig was succeeded by his younger brother, Otto, about whom there was never any question of insanity. For nobody needed to examine Otto to see that he was following in the family tradition of being stark, raving mad.

235

BARKING MAD

OTTO I, KING OF BAVARIA (1848–1916)

Replacing the insane Ludwig II with his brother Otto was rather like getting rid of an Alsatian because it was too big for the house and buying a Great Dane instead. In fact, Otto was very found of dogs and, in his more lucid moments, took to barking like one.

The Bavarian ministers' masterstroke in deposing one mad king and replacing him with an even crazier model was brought home to them the day after Ludwig's death, when they informed Otto that he was now the ruler of Bavaria. Otto's reaction was more like that of someone who had been told that dinner was ready. He showed not a flicker of emotion regarding his brother's death and immediately changed the subject. The government could scarcely have expected anything different: Otto had been declared incurably insane eight years previously and had been kept in confinement throughout that period. These were hardly the ideal credentials for assuming the monarchy.

In his youth, Otto had been regarded merely as unusually excitable and was known in Munich as 'the Merry Otto'. Given the family history of mental illness – grandfather Ludwig and his Spanish dancer, batty Aunt Alexandra who thought she had swallowed a grand piano – many must have feared that Otto's jollity would eventually transform itself into instability. Sure enough, the seemingly carefree exterior was replaced by black moods, hypochondria and panic attacks.

236

In a rare public appearance he deputised for his brother, who cited a prior dental appointment, at the Versailles Conference to discuss the future of Europe following the Franco-Prussian War. Otto sat through this historic gathering with his shoulders hunched and a glazed expression on his face, the only sign of life being the occasional involuntary body spasm. While the most important people in world politics were carving up Europe, Otto was having trouble keeping awake. His bizarre behaviour did not go unnoticed. The Prussian Crown Prince, sitting next to him, later said he was alarmed at how distracted the Bavarian representative seemed.

Ludwig's recurring dream was that one day he would be able to hand over the reins of monarchy to Otto, but abdication was clearly out of the question following his brother's abject performance at Versailles. One of the king's mechanical peacocks would have made a greater impact at the European summit than the listless Otto. Ludwig acknowledged Otto's condition in a letter to his former governess, Baroness Leonrod, dated January 1871: 'It is really painful to see Otto in such a suffering state which seems to become worse and worse daily. In some respects he is more excitable and nervous than Aunt Alexandra, and that is saying a great deal. He often does not go to bed for forty-eight hours, and did not take off his boots for eight weeks, behaves like a madman, makes terrible faces, barks like a dog, and, at times, says the most indecorous things.'

For Ludwig to describe anyone else as a 'madman' might seem rich, but the letter suggests, that, at least in those early years, he was in touch with reality even if they weren't on speaking terms.

By the following year Otto had become so deranged that his doctors ordered him to be detained at Nymphenburg under mild restraint, for his own safety. On the occasions that he was let loose among an unsuspecting public, his behaviour shocked even his own family who, in view of the Wittelsbach genes, should have long been immune to any embarrassment. His hallucinations developed a religious theme and one day in 1875, wearing a shooting jacket and deerstalker, he burst into a crowded church during High Mass, broke through a line of soldiers and hurled himself face down at the altar. There, at the feet of a mystified archbishop, he loudly confessed to a long list of sexual misdemeanours involving pageboys before being led away. After this episode, it was decided that his confinement be made more permanent.

In 1878 Otto was declared incurably insane and, smiling inanely and clutching one of his favourite childhood toys, he was led away to Fürstenried Castle near Munich, where he would be kept for the remaining 38 years of his life. Although technically he became king following Ludwig's death, the country continued to be ruled by a regent, his uncle Prince Luitpold. Otto was, however, given a mock court that addressed him as 'your majesty', just to make him feel wanted.

Life at Fürstenried was one of simple pleasures for a simple king. He played with toys, grew fat from overeating and lack of exercise, and indulged in a daily ritual, which, somewhat belatedly, he hoped would keep him sane. Otto harboured a deep mistrust of physicians after they had declared his brother insane and came to the conclusion that the only way to preserve his own sanity was to shoot a peasant every morning. His motto became: 'A peasant a day keeps the doctor away.' So he started taking pot shots at the peasants working in the royal garden. Now, some may argue that it was not the wisest move to allow a person who had been declared incurably insane to have access to loaded firearms, and the point was not lost on the peasants' union, whose numbers remained intact solely by virtue of Otto's inability to shoot straight. Understandably they feared it was merely a matter of time before he struck lucky.

With Otto refusing to be swayed from this course of action, his family took matters into their own hands. Each morning, before Otto awoke, a servant would creep into the royal bedchamber and load the king's pistol with blank cartridges. Simultaneously a guard, disguised as a peasant, would station himself in the bushes beneath the king's bedroom window. On waking, Otto would instinctively reach for his gun and fire at the fake peasant, who dutifully pretended to be dead. The king thus spent the rest of the day safe in the belief that he had shot his daily peasant. This curious exercise was repeated every morning until 1913 when Otto was finally deposed in favour of his cousin, Ludwig III.

It is just possible that Otto's cure for insanity was a major medical breakthrough waiting to happen. For no sooner had he been deprived of the opportunity to shoot his morning peasant than his mental condition deteriorated to the extent where his screams could be heard from outside the castle. Without his ritual, he lasted just three more years before joining the rest of his family in that great padded cell in the sky.

THE TRAIN NOW STANDING

MADHAVRAO SCINDIA, MAHARAJAH OF GWALIOR (1886–1925)

Dinner at the sumptuous Jai Vilas Palace, official residence of the Maharajah of Gwalior, was certainly a novel experience. For the food and drink were not brought to the guests by impeccably trained servants but by a silver model train that ran on a 250ft-long loop of silver track laid out from the kitchens to the banqueting hall.

During banquets the electric engine would chug slowly out of the kitchen, pulling various trucks loaded with desserts, sweets, cigars, and decanters of port and brandy. When it reached the hall, it stopped at each place setting, allowing the diner to take what he wanted, before moving on. The model train was the maharajah's pride and joy and moved at a pace generally associated with Indian trains. However, it occasionally displayed the unreliability of its British counterparts and once in the 1920s threw gravy, roast beef and a green pea purée over Lady Reading, the Vicereine of India!

Madhavrao Scindia, the eighth maharajah of the Indian state of Gwalior, was a bluff, chauvinistic ruler who generally preferred tigers to women. He was a hard taskmaster and enjoyed watching his ministers act as beaters on a tiger-shoot or work at clearing the jungle in stifling heat – anything to prevent them getting above their station. Naturally, they needed more than a sick note from their mother to escape such extracurricular duties, so it must have been with a heavy heart that they

240

watched the maharajah load his rifle in preparation for a day's hunting, although it is not known exactly how many cabinet reshuffles were necessitated by the shoots. He clearly had little faith in his advisers' ability either to govern the state or protect him and he once dressed up as a rickshaw driver to see if the security at the palace was really watertight.

Whilst most women were treated by the maharajah with disdain bordering on contempt, an exception to the rule was his own mother, who was afforded full royal protocol even after her death. When she died, he arranged for the building of a life-size statue of her. Every day female attendants were instructed to bathe and dress the statue, hang jewellery on it and even dab splashes of perfume into those nooks and crannies where moss was starting to grow. Food was placed at the statue's feet punctually at mealtimes (although not by model train) and a band played it a medley of favourite tunes. No consideration was overlooked. For example, in oppressive heat a servant would wave a cooling fan on the statue's face. The monument may not have shown much by way of gratitude, but it kept the maharajah happy and this ritual continued right up until his own death, in Paris on 5 June 1925.

PRINCE OR PAUPER?

MIR OSMAN ALI KHAN, NIZAM OF
HYDERABAD (1886-1967)

For the first half of the twentieth century, Mir Osman Ali Khan, Nizam of Hyderabad, was the richest man in the world with an estimated £100 million in gold bullion and silver and another £400 million in jewels. Yet far from living in the lap of luxury like so many Eastern rulers, he was a renowned miser who dressed in shabby clothes, drove a battered old banger, and haggled over the price of everything. He was not a man who could ever be accused of squandering his wealth.

The seventh and last Nizam of Hyderabad came to power in 1911 as the ruler of 86,000 square miles of India – an area bigger than England and Scotland put together. Even before that, the heir apparent had demonstrated his frugal tendencies. A favourite pastime of Indian princes in those days was to throw a silver coin high into the air and pierce it with a pistol shot. Osman Ali Khan was trained in this trick but his father, Mir Mehbub Ali Khan, was surprised on one visit to the training ground to see the young prince scrambling around in search of the blasted pieces of silver coin. When the boy announced that he intended keeping them rather than letting them go to waste, his indulgent father would leave extra bags of silver coins for his son to take. However this generosity had no effect and the prince continued to pick up the scraps before leaving the training area. It was symbolic of the way he behaved for the rest of his life.

Shortly after his accession the 25-year-old Nizam visited Delhi on a state occasion. Crowds flocked to see the richest Muslim potentate in India, including the Ghantawala family who had been official sweetmeat suppliers to the Mughal emperors for centuries. Realising that it would be good for business to have such a wealthy individual visit their shop, they asked Osman Ali Khan whether he would like to inspect the store. When he agreed, a respectful crowd followed him to the shop. Amid tremendous fanfare, the firm presented him with a huge packet of confectionery as a gift and the Nizam was so impressed by the quality of the goods that he said he wanted to buy more. But his enthusiasm evaporated when they told him the price, and he began shouting angrily that he had no intention of paying such an exorbitant amount. The crowd that had gathered to see an opulent Mughal could hardly believe their eyes and ears, and melted away on discovering that he was nothing but a miserly bargain hunter.

This set the tone for his reign. Much of his wealth was hoarded away for posterity and whilst he made generous charitable donations to theological schools, universities, hospitals and temples, his meanness became legendary. Although he owned a Rolls-Royce with a cocktail bar in the back, he usually drove into town in his favourite battered old 1934 grey Model T Ford. He had four brocade jackets encrusted with diamonds, rubies and pearls, yet preferred to buy most of his suits from Burtons. His jacket was often stained and he used to keep his white suit on in the bath, steaming it to save on laundry bills. And even though he had an annual income in excess of £2 million in the 1930s, he wore the same dirty fez for thirty years. When an aide bravely suggested that the Nizam should have a new shawl, Osman Ali Khan replied: 'My budget is only eighteen rupees and a good one would cost twenty rupees.'

On a state visit to Hyderabad in the 1920s, Lord Irwin, the Viceroy of India, was alarmed to see the Nizam leaning on a walking stick that was cracked at one end and warned him to be careful. The Nizam listened patiently to his lordship's forebodings and when they next met took great delight in showing him the same old walking stick, still in everyday use but tied together with string to repair the cracks. A similar incident took place thirty years later. General Chowdhury, the Military Governor of Hyderabad, objected to the decrepit *sherwani* (an Indian jacket) in which the Nizam was planning to greet Pandit Nehru on the first Prime Minister of India's forthcoming visit to Hyderabad. The Nizam promised to remedy the matter and as they were awaiting Nehru's arrival at the airport, he showed the general the newly darned neck portion of the old *sherwani*.

Naturally enough, the Nizam expected those on his payroll to be equally careful with money and whereas most job applicants are asked questions about previous experience and qualifications, those seeking employment in the service of the Nizam had to undergo an aptitude test known as the 'blanket check' (not to be confused with 'blank cheque', a phrase that was an anathema to Osman Ali Khan). For this test, the Nizam would first, in his own inimitable manner, find the price of the cheapest blanket available in Hyderabad market and then send the interviewee to buy him a blanket from the same market. Whoever paid the lowest amount for the blanket landed the job.

In all he employed over 11,000 servants, which meant he must also have owned an awful lot of blankets. Thirty-eight men were given the chore of dusting the palace's ornate chandeliers while others did nothing except grind walnuts (it is not known whether the broken shells were reclaimed for some future use). British visitors to his court found just one cigarette, one biscuit and one plain cup of tea as hospitality during their audiences. Sometimes the Nizam borrowed cigarettes from his official visitors and conveniently forgot to return the full packet. When Sir Tej Bahadur Sapru, the Nizam's legal adviser, accepted the generous offer of a cigarette, the Nizam promptly took it back, clipped it in two with a clipper he kept in his pocket, and offered just one half back to his guest. On another occasion, a resident's wife who bumped into the Nizam at Hyderabad racecourse was pleasantly surprised when he offered her an ice cream. This uncharacteristic lapse was quickly rectified when he proceeded to send the ice cream back to the restaurant three times because he thought it contained too much ice cream and he was afraid he would have to pay for the extra helping.

Although he had a fondness for champagne – particularly if someone else was paying – his menu was usually much more basic, and he demanded that those in his harem also avoided expensive tastes. Once while inspecting the palace store room he was horrified to find that hundreds of tins of ghee (clarified butter) presented to him by a maharajah had gone rancid because the cook had not used them in time. Sleepless with anger at the loss and wastage, Osman Ali Khan came up with a solution of breathtaking thrift. Tradition stated that any noble receiving a gift from the Nizam should acknowledge it with a return offering (or *Nazar*), which varied from a silver rupee to a hundred gold coins according to the noble's wealth. Now the Nizam had the perfect gifts for his nobles – tins of rancid butter. The scheme not only rid him of the rotten food but also filled his personal treasury with the gold sovereigns given to him in return. When some recipients started to complain about the unfairness of the exchange rate, the British felt it necessary to ask him to stop the practice and in future simply touch the *Nazar* coin before returning it to its owner.

Nevertheless, for many years the *Nazar* was a compulsory swap at state functions and if any of his most prominent subjects happened to be absent from a royal gathering, the Nizam would send a carriage to call on them within a few days . . . laden, of course, with tins of inedible butter. Whoever coined the phrase 'fair exchange is no robbery' obviously had in mind the seventh Nizam of Hyderabad.

In the 1930s, when he was at his wealthiest, it suddenly struck him that his subjects might rebel and force him to flee his dominions without any money. Prudently planning for the future, he ordered six lorry loads full of gold bullion to be parked in the palace backyard, ready to be driven off to British India in the event of such an emergency. After his death thirty years later, all of the lorries were found, their tyre rubber perished, wheels sunk to the hubs, but with their treasures intact.

The one thing on which Osman Ali Khan did not stint was sex. Fortified no doubt by his opium addiction (he took around eleven grains a day), he had a monumental sex drive and had so many concubines that he was believed to be supporting as many as 14,000 dependants at any one time. Every Friday he would visit the family mosque, surrounded by fifty sycophantic courtiers all wearing the same beige suit and red fez as His Exalted Highness, but if he spotted a pretty girl en route she would immediately be whisked off to the palace harem regardless of any parental protests. He had three official wives yet his daughter was forced to remain a spinster because of a deep-seated superstition that if she married, the Nizam would die. He was not averse to using women as a bargaining tool; as a boy he once sold one of his father's women for thirty rupees. If he ever got a pair of shoes for his wife, it was almost certainly an exchange.

Following Indian independence he became more eccentric than ever, shambling around the back streets of Hyderabad in disguise with a muffler over his mouth. By now a little old man, he may not have looked or acted much like a millionaire but he still liked to remind people that he was in control. At special banquets – where the food ran to a second bowl of rice – he was always the only person allowed to speak. As part of a fresh economy drive in 1956 he again flexed his ageing muscles by disinheriting his eldest son, whom he considered a womanising wastrel, and made his grandson his heir instead.

Eventually he became a recluse, living in the company of a band of tramps and a white goat. One British observer described him as, 'A snuffly clerk too old to be sacked.' By the end of his reign he claimed to be broke and living on the equivalent of 7s 6d a week . . . despite the vast gold reserves sitting in those trucks. He was knitting his own socks, living on rice and lentils, smoking cheap cigarettes, and bargaining with stallholders over the price of a soft drink. The man who combined the wealth of J. Paul Getty with the demeanour of Albert Steptoe finally shuffled off the face of this earth on 24 February 1967.

THE THIEF OF CAIRO

FAROUK I, KING OF EGYPT (1920–65)

The contrast between the last Nizam of Hyderabad and the last King of Egypt could not have been greater. Chalk and cheese would not come close; chalk and a great white shark would not even do it justice. For every rupee that the Nizam saved by prudent housekeeping, Farouk squandered a thousand times that amount on fast cars, gambling and expensive restaurants – in fact, whatever it took to develop and maintain his international playboy lifestyle.

Whilst Farouk's extravagance was thoroughly reprehensible, it was no worse than that of many other royals; what set him apart was a thieving streak that made the Artful Dodger look like Mother Teresa.

It could not have been the need for money that inspired Farouk's love of picking pockets, and in any case the objects he took were often of modest value. So it must be assumed that he turned to crime for the sheer thrill of it: his walk on the wild side. Naturally he wanted to be the best and, accordingly, he had a notorious thief sprung from Tural prison to act as his mentor. Under this dubious expert tutelage, the king practised on a suit into which tiny bells had been sewn. As the slightest tinkling would betray his intentions, he discovered the knack of operating stealthily and without arousing suspicion. He was certainly a quick learner and at official receptions and parties abroad he was soon relieving dignitaries and their ladies of watches, wallets, cigarette lighters and powder compacts. He collected hundreds of items, his booty eventually filling an entire warehouse and earning him the less-than-complimentary nickname of 'The Thief of Cairo'.

With his kleptomania escalating, he started robbing ordinary people but took most pleasure in his big-name victims – among them Winston Churchill, whom he relieved of a valuable pocket watch. To Farouk it was just a game but the British did not see the funny side and demanded that the watch be returned. Reluctantly the King of Egypt surrendered his prize. But he claimed an even bigger scalp in 1944 when the body of the Shah of Persia passed in state through Egypt. In a shameless act, Farouk stole the ceremonial sword, belt and medals from the corpse. The fact that the theft took place in Egypt, allied to Farouk's reputation, made him the obvious suspect, prompting strained relations between the two countries, but Farouk steadfastly denied any involvement. However, after he had eventually been deposed, the items were found in one of his museums and returned to the Shah's family.

It appears that Farouk was perfectly willing to capitalise on others' misfortune. When German residents fled Cairo at the start of the Second World War, Farouk organised night-time looting parties to strip the unoccupied homes of their contents. His scruples also went AWOL when he devised a profitable scam called 'Farouk's Treasure Box' whereby a businessman, keen to gain the royal seal of approval, was advised that the king would appreciate the gift of a box of chocolates from a certain shop. Although the chocolates were relatively affordable, the box – a jewel-encrusted casket – certainly was not, retailing at a cool £650. However, the businessman would be so eager to win royal favour that he would invariably buy the box along with the chocolates and present them to Farouk. After devouring the chocolates with his customary haste, Farouk would then return the box to the shop in readiness for the next sucker while calmly transferring the £650 into his own account. In his eyes, the monarch was above all considerations of morality.

The Egyptian monarchy had been set up by the British in 1922, the first ruler to have the title of 'king' being Farouk's father, Fuad I. As a boy, Farouk was a mass of contradictions. He cried inconsolably when a hawk swooped to kill his pet rabbit yet on another occasion he grabbed a cat by the tail and killed it by smashing its head repeatedly into a wall. He was horribly spoilt yet he donated half of his monthly pocket money to buy books for impoverished children. Unfortunately, his charitable deeds were invariably overshadowed by tales of misbehaviour with the result that Egyptian parents would tell their children: 'Don't be like that wicked boy in the palace.'

In 1936 the sixteen-year-old Farouk succeeded his father as king, marking the occasion with a public radio address to the nation – the first time a king of Egypt had ever spoken directly to his people. But this promising start quickly became a distant memory as the youthful monarch began to exhibit all the signs of overindulgence. He already possessed a fleet of expensive cars – the total would eventually reach over a hundred – which he loved to drive dangerously at breakneck speeds. When the police had the temerity to stop him for speeding, he had all his cars painted red and made it illegal for any of his subjects to own a vehicle of that colour. In future he could speed along safe in the knowledge that the police would recognise his car and not stop it. As far as he was concerned, he was above the law – and if any other motorist dared to try and pass him, he used to shoot at their tyres! As the Mr Toad of Egypt, he caused numerous accidents yet bridled at any criticism levelled at his driving. When a newspaper editor wrote that Farouk's car was always followed by an ambulance, the king had him jailed. Farouk no more believed in free speech than in the Highway Code.

He did receive a nasty shock when he drove his red MG sports car into a tree outside Cairo and wrote the vehicle off. The loss of the car was immaterial – he could soon buy another one – but he was terrified that his mother, Queen Nazli, would find out about the accident. He decided that the only solution was to obtain an identical replacement – no easy task, since he had forbidden everyone from owning a red car. Luckily the Cairo police came to his rescue by remembering a British resident in Alexandria with a red MG. Farouk summoned the man and bought his car, leaving Nazli ignorant of the crash.

Even at its most considered, his behaviour was impulsive. No sooner had he become king than he suddenly decided that he no longer liked the train station near Montazah Palace in Alexandria and demanded that a new one be built. Since the royal train only stopped there twice a year (when it transported the royal family to and from their annual holiday) such an expense was hardly high on the list of government priorities. Farouk went ahead and had architects draw up grand plans but the three regents who were running the country until the king reached eighteen demurred at the £30,000 cost and said they would build their own station for £2,500. Farouk had no intention of accepting a cut-price version and that same day led a convoy of lorries to Montazah, demolished the old station and built a new one himself.

His mother's hopes that the crown would bring about a long-awaited maturity in Farouk proved in vain. He would throw pellets at visiting dignitaries during formal luncheons, emitting a cry of joy whenever he scored a direct hit; he owned a car horn, which, when sounded, mimicked the screaming howls of a dog being run over; and at a country reception on a hot day he once slipped a piece of ice down the bra of a curtsying guest to help her 'cool off'.

Such adolescent behaviour led the British high commissioner, Sir Miles Lampson, to describe Farouk in a 1937 report to the Foreign Office as 'uneducated, lazy, untruthful, capricious, irresponsible and vain, though with a quick superficial intelligence and charm of manner'.

Farouk saw no reason to change. He once appointed a man to the key role of Minister of Justice simply because he liked his moustache. After having a series of bad dreams in which he was chased by lions, Farouk went down to Cairo Zoo and shot both the lions. (The nightmares continued.) He obsessively collected all manner of items – stamps, beer-bottle tops, razor blades and matchboxes – only to grow tired of them just as easily.

He also collected pornography and a vast array of sex aids designed to fit every occasion and orifice. As a child he had been considered somewhat effeminate and the rumours surrounding his sexual orientation and prowess continued into adulthood. It was said that he was lacking virility to the point of being virtually impotent. He certainly enjoyed female company and was married twice, but he tended to neglect his wives sexually in favour of women who had been procured by his servants. Even then he suffered humiliation, one dancer storming out of his bedroom complaining about having wasted her time on a boy with no spunk, king or no king.

One appetite that was never in question was Farouk's love affair with food. Even as a child he had an alarming tendency to put on weight and was put on a diet which made him so hungry that he once ate the cat's dinner. Now free to eat as he pleased, he became a dedicated glutton. The Open University don't have as many courses as Farouk's breakfast. First he would be brought a tray of thirty boiled eggs from which he would eat as many as he wished before moving on to a selection from such delicacies as lobster, steak, chicken and quail. Yet even after devouring this sumptuous feast, he would be hungry again a few hours later. Inevitably his body ballooned, not helped by the fact that he developed such a taste for fizzy drinks that he consumed more than thirty bottles of orange pop a day.

He was equally compulsive about gambling, but found it easier to lose money than weight. A bad night at Deauville Casino in France once left him £25,000 worse off. For Farouk that was the luck of the draw – there was always plenty more cash where that came from. Once while playing poker he was called when holding three kings to a full house. 'I am the fourth king,' he insisted, a touch optimistically. Although he took risks with his country's money while at the casinos, he was not willing to compromise his personal safety. Fearing assassination, he always sat at the gambling tables with his hand covering a tiny silver pistol and with a second revolver in his breast pocket as back-up.

Occasionally Farouk would cast aside the trappings of monarchy, surprising friends by arriving at their villas incognito and unannounced. Once he dressed up as an Arab sheikh and wandered the streets of Cairo with two of his attendants, both similarly attired.

But these were isolated episodes and for the most part he lived the royal life to the full. For although he already had thousands of acres of land, dozens of palaces and his fleet of cars, Farouk never seemed satisfied with his wealth and would often travel to Europe on grand shopping sprees, running up massive bills that the people of Egypt were expected to pay. During a royal trip to Paris his barber was flown all the way from Italy just to give Farouk a shave one morning.

The Egyptians were remarkably tolerant of his excesses until being subjected to the hardships of the Second World War when, understandably, they expected their leader to make similar sacrifices. None was forthcoming. Instead, his crass decision to keep all the lights burning at the royal palace in Alexandria at a time when the rest of the city was blacked out due to Italian bombing infuriated the Egyptian people. Nor were his Italian servants interned. When questioned about this by Sir Miles Lampson, Farouk allegedly replied: 'I'll get rid of my Italians when you get rid of yours' – a reference to the high commissioner's Italian wife.

The king's popularity was eroded further when, in 1948, he divorced his first wife Farida, a move that lost him the respect of his country. He compounded the error three years later by marrying a sixteen-year-old girl, Narriman Sadek, and embarking on a typically extravagant honeymoon costing an estimated £1,000 a day. The happy couple started out on the island of Capri, where they booked all 150 rooms at the luxurious Caesar Augustus Hotel. Thirteen weeks later they were still honeymooning, this time in 32 rooms of the Carlton Hotel, Cannes.

Despised at home and abroad as an ineffectual playboy and a thief to boot, Farouk was skating on thin ice. A group of army officers, led by Colonel Gamal Abdel Nasser, still blamed him for the ignominious defeat in the Arab–Israeli war of 1948 amid rumours that some of the king's closest associates had profited by supplying the forces with defective weapons. These allegations of corruption coupled with Farouk's scandalous and grotesquely self-indulgent lifestyle cost him the loyalty of the army and in 1952 Nasser directed a coup aimed at toppling the king. Shortly after midnight on 23 July, while the court was enjoying a late champagne and caviar picnic at the summer palace in Alexandria, some 3,000 troops took control of Cairo. In desperation, Farouk appealed to the American ambassador for help, but the Americans had no confidence in him and anyway the CIA had been encouraging the plotters. As the rebels closed in on Alexandria, Farouk moved to a palace near the harbour, but the coup leaders instructed the captain of his yacht not to sail without their orders. Some of the leaders wanted Farouk murdered but instead on 26 July, with the Ras el-Tin Palace surrounded by hostile troops, he was told to abdicate and clear his desk. He complied, nearly in tears, and at six o'clock that evening he sailed for Naples with his wife and children, seen off by General Neguib, one of the driving forces behind the plot, to the strains of the Egyptian national anthem and an almost apologetic 21-gun salute. He was forced to leave behind a thousand suits and his collection of pornography, but he did manage to smuggle out a number of gold bars hidden in crates labelled 'whisky' and 'champagne'.

His baby son, Prince Ahmed Fuad, was proclaimed king and a regency council appointed. However, a year later Egypt became a republic with General Neguib as president until the forceful Nasser ousted him.

While the new regime raised urgently needed funds by auctioning off Farouk's vast collection of trinkets and stolen treasures, the exiled king returned to Capri before eventually settling in Monaco. He continued to enjoy the high life, as his increasingly bloated frame testified. He divorced Narriman in 1954 and thereafter, with his reputation to uphold, the balding gigolo dated a succession of pretty young things. Queen Nazli despaired of him. 'He was a monster,' she admitted, 'he was

253

destined never to finish anything in his life – not his schooling, not his marriages, not his reign – not even his pre-natal development.'

By the early sixties he weighed nearly 300lb and spent most of his time lazing around eating chocolates. On 17 March 1965, shortly after his 45th birthday, he took his latest girlfriend, a 22-year-old blonde by the name of Annamaria Gatti, to a Rome restaurant for a late-night supper. After consuming a dozen oysters, lobster thermidor, a treble portion of roast lamb, chips, beans, chestnut trifle and two oranges, he collapsed at the table and was pronounced dead.

Rarely has the manner of death been more appropriate to the life that preceded it.

FOOT-IN-MOUTH DISEASE

PHILIP, DUKE OF EDINBURGH (1921–)

Prince Philip has always been a somewhat contradictory character: the consort to the Queen with an eye for the ladies; the President of the World Wide Fund for Nature who shoots animals for fun; an ambassador for Britain who, at one time or another, has managed to insult virtually every nation bar the Swiss. And their time may yet come.

It was Anne, the Princess Royal, who once said that her father suffers from 'dentopedalogy', the unfortunate habit of opening his mouth and putting his foot in it. Over the past half-century anyone worth insulting has been on the receiving of a tirade from the Duke of Edinburgh. Canadians, housewives, the Chinese: they all come the same to Philip. His intemperate comments on a wide range of subjects have ensured a steady stream of critical newspaper headlines, swiftly followed by diplomatic gestures from Buckingham Palace or Westminster to try and smooth the troubled waters. Accompanying Philip on a royal tour is rather like being the man with the bucket who cleans up the arena after each round at the Horse of the Year Show.

Philip's uncompromising attitude to life probably stems from his childhood. At a tender age, along with the rest of the Greek royal family, he was forced to flee the country – an event that so traumatised his mother, Princess Alice of Battenberg, that she later suffered a nervous breakdown. In her dotage she lived in Buckingham Palace and dressed as a nun for no other reason than it meant she did not have to change her clothes and have her hair done!

Philip was educated at Gordonstoun public school in Scotland and was so impressed by its harsh regime that he sent all three of his sons there whether they liked it or not. And with Prince Charles, it was definitely a case of *not*. But then Philip has never exactly been a role model for parenthood, his distant approach to his offspring being blamed in part at least for their inability to sustain a marriage much beyond the reception. With typical bluntness, he once said of the horse-loving Princess Royal: 'If it doesn't eat hay, she is not interested.' She may have been amused by the remark, but with Anne it's invariably hard to tell.

Even before his marriage to Elizabeth, concerns were voiced about Philip's tendency to speak his mind. Some of his verbal blunders were the result of his wicked, but often misplaced, sense of humour; others were simply crass.

In 1961 he told British industry to 'get your finger out' in a speech that angered MPs who didn't want him interfering in such matters. On another occasion he called Britain and the British 'overcrowded, smelly, impolite and dishonest' and in 1966 he famously remarked, 'British women can't cook,' thereby alienating half the nation at a stroke.

In 1968 he unveiled his unique policy on birth control, suggesting that there should be a tax on babies. One MP called him a 'useless reactionary parasite' and even Philip conceded: 'As so often happens, I discover that it would have been better to have kept my trap shut.'

Failing to heed his own advice, the following year, while on a state visit to Paraguay, he told the country's dictator, General Alfredo Stroessner: 'It's a pleasant change to be in a country that isn't ruled by its people.'

When Dr Allende, Chile's future president, turned up in an ordinary lounge suit for a reception that the Queen was attending, Philip asked: 'Why are you dressed like that?' Dr Allende replied: 'We are poor; I could not afford a dinner suit so my party told me to wear a lounge suit.' To which Philip snapped: 'I suppose if they'd have said wear a bathing suit, you would have done that too!'

On a state visit to Canada, he barked at an official: 'We don't come here for our health, you know!'

He once upset the French by saying: 'Isn't it a pity Louis XVI was sent to the guillotine?' He has also called the Dutch 'po-faced' and the Hungarians 'pot-bellied'.

Chatting with British students during a state visit to the People's Republic of China in 1986, he described Peking as 'ghastly' and warned them: 'If you stay here much longer you'll go back with slitty eyes.' The remark caused outrage but Philip wasn't finished yet. At a function attended by a number of Chinese people, he told a joke: 'If it's got four legs and it's not a chair, if it's got two wings and it's not an aeroplane, if it swims and is not a submarine, what is it? Answer: a Cantonese dinner – they'll eat anything that moves!' For this latest diplomatic disaster, one British newspaper labelled him THE GREAT WALLY OF CHINA.

In the course of a discussion in 1988 on the paradox of hunting animals while supporting conservation, he said that it was no different to a butcher killing animals and selling the meat for money. He then took his argument a step further by claiming that it was the same as wives and prostitutes. 'I don't think doing it for money makes it any more moral. I don't think a prostitute is more moral than a wife, but they are doing the same thing.' Philip was inundated with mail from angry wives. His own wife kept her thoughts to herself.

In 1995 he asked a Scottish driving instructor: 'How do you keep the natives off the booze long enough to pass the test?'

In 1996, following the call for tougher gun laws in the wake of the Dunblane school massacre, Philip expressed the view that a gun was no more dangerous than a cricket bat in the hands of a madman. 'If a cricketer decided to go into a school,' he said, 'and batter a lot of people with a cricket bat, which he could do easily, are you going to ban cricket bats?' His views were greeted with a mixture of incredulity and fury.

He once asked his Italian hosts if they knew what the smallest book in the world was, and then told them it was the Book of Italian Heroes. He followed that with a crack about Italian tanks being the only ones with one forward and four reverse gears.

In 1998 he suggested that tribes in Papua New Guinea still practised cannibalism. After hearing about a student who had trekked through the mountains there, Philip asked him: 'So you managed not to get eaten then?'

On one occasion, greeting the President of Nigeria, who was dressed in traditional robes, Philip remarked: 'You look like you're ready for bed!'

Attending a festival to mark the opening of the Welsh Assembly in 1999, Philip succeeded in upsetting a group of deaf youngsters by joking that it was standing too close to the loud music playing at the celebration that had made them deaf. Members of the British Deaf Association were said to have been shocked and insulted by the tactless comment.

Also in 1999, while touring a factory near Edinburgh, he remarked that a fuse box 'looked as though it had been put in by an Indian'. Buckingham Palace was forced to issue an apology.

In 2002, on a tour of Australia, he surprised the founder of an Aboriginal cultural park by asking: 'Do you still throw spears at each other?' One Aboriginal activist said of HRH: 'The man has shown by that remark that he is just plain ignorant.'

In December 2002, at an Asian youth club in London, Philip said of one boy: 'He looks as if he's on drugs!' The boy's parents were distinctly unimpressed, as were many in the Asian community.

Although now well into his eighties, Philip has lost none of his touch, recently informing a hapless thirteen-year-old schoolboy that he was 'too fat' to become an astronaut. He has always been quick to blame the Press for his problems, claiming that they exaggerate or distort his words. On a Caribbean tour, when a patron of a hospital spoke of the trouble they had with mosquitoes, Philip sympathised. 'I know what you mean,' he said. 'You have mosquitoes, I have the Press.' This time, Philip was forced to apologise to the uncharacteristically oversensitive newshounds for the wisecrack.

As the archetypal grumpy old man (former BBC royal correspondent Jennie Bond says he has perfected the art of saying hello and goodbye in the same handshake), Philip acknowledges that he will probably be remembered as the Prince of Gaffes. 'I've become a caricature,' he admits. But at least he will be remembered, and that is perhaps more than can be said for certain members of his family.

PLATFORM FOR POWER

PRINCE ROY OF SEALAND (1922–)

Six miles off the coast of Suffolk, a stark rusting platform perched atop two concrete towers rises above the choppy grey waters of the North Sea. It blends in perfectly with its inhospitable surroundings. Unlikely to feature in any holiday brochure – except possibly one for the masochistic – it is therefore one of the few places in the world safe from a visit by Judith Chalmers. Welcome to the principality of Sealand.

The word 'principality' should not lead to any confusion between Sealand and Monaco. There are no casinos on Sealand, no extravagant yachts moored alongside and no Grand Prix. Indeed, there would barely be room for a Scalextric set. It is a millionaires' playground only if a millionaire's idea of luxury consists of nothing more than electricity, double-glazing, a television set and a force-ten gale. But Sealand does have one thing in common with Monaco: its own royal family.

Roy Bates had risen to the rank of major in the British Army before becoming a successful fisherman. Then in the summer of 1965, inspired by the success of the pirate radio station Radio Caroline, Bates decided to set up his own rival station: Radio Essex. A tour of the unoccupied forts in the Thames estuary led him to settle on Knock John Tower as his base and, after evicting Radio City staff who had occupied the tower in his absence, Radio Essex began broadcasting in November of that year. However, the following year Bates was convicted of violating British broadcasting law and the station was fined £100 for transmitting from within territorial waters. Radio Essex changed its name to BBMS (Britain's Better Music Station) but closed down on Christmas Day 1966 due to lack of funds. The ever-resourceful Bates then decided to shift his operations to nearby Roughs Tower, a North Sea fort that had been built in 1942 to accommodate up to 200 Royal Navy personnel, but which had lain deserted since the end of the Second World War. Fighting off the attention of rival claimants from Radio Caroline, Bates annexed the 430ft x 120ft gun tower and, although no radio station ever broadcast from the new location, he and his wife Joan – a former beauty queen – decided to stay.

The idea for their new lifestyle had been born one evening over a few pints in a mainland pub, where Bates had discussed the possibility of claiming the disused fort as his own. At the time, the United Kingdom claimed territorial waters of three miles from its coast, but Roughs Tower was just beyond that limit. Bates consulted lawyers. He recalled: 'They told me, "Yes, legally you can do it, but it's impossible." It was the worst thing you could say to me!' So in September 1967 he declared the fortress to be an independent state, named it Sealand, and proclaimed himself and his wife to be its sovereign rulers – Prince Roy and Princess Joan.

In 1968 the Royal Navy tried to remove the Bates family from the principality, only to be scared off by warning shots. Prince Roy was duly summoned to explain himself before a British court, but the government was forced to drop the case as the incident had taken place outside British territory. For the Sealand royal family it was a moment of triumph and, as Roy saw it, a vindication of his stance.

Seemingly untouchable, Prince Roy and Princess Joan asserted Sealand's independence under a red, white and black flag. They issued Sealand passports, stamps, coins – which bore the head of Princess Joan – notes (a Sealand dollar being equal to a US dollar) and even came up with a Sealand national anthem. They declared their little empire to be a tax-free country and claimed exemption from British income tax. The British government did not take kindly to these upstarts and proceeded to harass the prince and princess at every opportunity. Their tins of food were opened during customs inspections when they came ashore for provisions and they were subjected to various litigations, including one alleging non-payment of a TV licence. But each time the court ruled that Sealand was in international waters and therefore not part of the United Kingdom.

In 1978 Sealand came under threat from a different quarter. While the prince and princess were away, Dutch and German businessmen seized the territory by force and kidnapped the heir to the throne, Roy's son Michael. Following Michael's release in the Netherlands a few days later, Prince Roy enlisted outside aid and, in a daring helicopter assault, retook the fortress. He then incarcerated the invaders in Sealand's cells – the ones originally intended for downed Luftwaffe pilots – labelling them 'prisoners of war'. The governments of the Netherlands and Germany petitioned Britain for their release but the British government washed its hands of all responsibility, citing the 1968 court decision. Following lengthy and delicate diplomatic negotiations, Prince Roy freed his captives and was able to claim that Germany's decision to send a diplomat to Sealand in person constituted official recognition of his state. Germany has yet to confirm this interpretation.

Nine years on, Prince Roy's plans were dealt a blow when the United Kingdom extended its territorial waters from three to twelve miles, thus placing Sealand inside British territory. Although the British government still refuses to acknowledge Sealand's independence, to date there have been no fresh attempts to reclaim the fort. Meanwhile, forged Sealand passports have turned up in the most unlikely places. Prince Roy had only ever issued them to a few friends yet thousands of black-bound Sealand passports embossed with the Bates seal – two crowned sea creatures – began surfacing in Europe and Asia. The Spanish police suspect that they have been used by gun-running and money-laundering rings and one was found on the killer of fashion designer Gianni Versace. There is no suggestion that the Sealand royal family were in any way connected with these crimes but the resultant police attention served as an unwelcome and unexpected by-product of setting up an independent state.

The buccaneering Roy Bates, now well into his eighties, has decided to take life a little easier of late. In 1999 he and Princess Joan vacated Sealand and left the day-to-day running of the state to Michael, the Prince Regent. While the royal family relax in the tropical paradise that is Westcliff-on-Sea or travel abroad as simple Mr and Mrs Bates, Sealand has, with Prince Roy's blessing, become an offshore computer platform for clients who wish to keep e-mail, e-commerce or banking transactions safe from prying governments.

The Prince Regent has no intention of abandoning his inheritance. 'It's not a palace, but it's not too bad,' he says with commendable understatement, adding that he is contemplating setting up a casino there. But somehow despite these ambitious plans, you still feel there is little chance of a windswept North Sea platform the size of a football pitch ever being twinned with the more celebrated principality of Monaco. Should it ever happen it would be just one more chapter in the remarkable history of the world's smallest state: Sealand.

THE RIGHTFUL KING OF ENGLAND?

MICHAEL ABNEY-HASTINGS (1941–)

One way or another the House of Windsor have had a pretty rough time of it over the last decade – much of it, admittedly, of their own making. What with Charles and Diana, Charles and Camilla, and associated revelations from butlers, bodyguards, servants and probably the corgis, virtually every year has been an *annus horribilis*. But if they thought 2004 would herald a fresh beginning, they must have been dismayed to read stories at the start of January which claimed that Elizabeth II was ruling under false pretences and that the real King of England was a 62-year-old forklift truck driver from New South Wales.

The claims were made by genealogist Dr Michael Jones, an acknowledged expert on the Middle Ages, who said Elizabeth's claim to the throne is false because her distant ancestor, Edward IV, was illegitimate. From evidence contained in a document in the library of Rouen Cathedral, Dr Jones suggested that Edward, who reigned from 1461 to 1483, was conceived when his parents were 100 miles apart and that his real father was not Richard, Duke of York, but a French archer. At the time of the conception Richard was fighting the French at Pontoise, near Paris, while Edward's mother, Lady Cicely Neville, was at court in Rouen – a five-day horse ride away – where she was said to be spending much of her time in the company of a local archer. Indeed, it was strongly rumoured that they were having an affair, so much so that King Louis XI of France once said of

Edward, 'His name is not King Edward – everybody knows his name is Blaybourne' – the name of the archer. In time-honoured tradition, the English royal family of the period did their best to hush up the scandal, even going so far as to promote the idea that the conception had taken place in May 1410 in Yorkshire before Richard set sail for France, a timescale that would have required an eleven-month pregnancy.

Dr Jones contended that, in view of Edward's alleged illegitimacy, he ought to have been replaced as king by his younger brother, George, Duke of Clarence, and the crown should then have passed down the Plantagenet line. Following that natural line of succession, Dr Jones ended up with Michael Abney-Hastings, a former livestock manager living in Jerilderie, a small town 400 miles southwest of Sydney.

The man proclaimed by the historian as 'Michael I' was born in Sussex and educated at Ampleforth College in North Yorkshire. As a direct descendant of George, Duke of Clarence, the Hastings family seat was Ashby-de-la-Zouch Castle in Leicestershire. But with the castle in ruins, Michael had to seek alternative accommodation and, passing Australia House in London one day, he saw a sign promoting the 'Come to Australia Programme'. He signed up and at the age of seventeen set off on the month-long voyage to the other side of the world.

Working on ranches, he fell in love with the rural lifestyle and married a local girl, Noelene, who died in 2002. In the same year he became the fourteenth Earl of Loudoun following the death of his mother, but refrained from publicising it because Australians have an aversion to titles. Instead, he carried on working at a farm, enjoying his role as a life member at the local football club and sharing a few beers with friends at a nearby bar.

'Then I got a knock on the door and this TV crew from Britain walks in and says they want to make a film about me. They tell me that some historian in England reckons I should be the King of England, not the present queen. I always knew I had Plantagenet blood in me, but had no idea that I might be more than just a minor royal. I was astounded.'

He was so taken aback that he decided to investigate his family tree. 'What it meant,' he said, 'was that if Edward IV was illegitimate, then that whole line that followed him from Henry VIII down to Queen Victoria and Elizabeth II ought not to be there because English rule does not allow illegitimate children to occupy the throne. If the true lineage had been followed, it would be me on the throne and not Elizabeth.'

However, the unassuming heir, who has five children and five grandchildren, remains firmly down-to-earth and admits that it is 'very unlikely' that he would be going to Buckingham Palace to demand entry. 'I wouldn't want to be king of anything,' he says. 'Just look at the royals today – they stagger from one crisis to another. They are hounded all the time. I wouldn't want to live in that sort of goldfish bowl. No, I think my life here is most satisfactory. I have my children and grandchildren around me, and a man couldn't be happier about that.'

Following the revelations, he received calls from all over the world, including some urging him to take up his claim to the throne. But he said the only change to his life was that his family sang 'God Save the King' to him at Christmas dinner.

Despite the expert historical evidence, there is one obstacle preventing Michael Abney-Hastings from becoming King of England – he is a staunch republican. 'As much as I love England,' he confesses, 'I honestly feel in this day and age Australia should be standing on its own feet in everything, and that means we have to be a republic. In the last referendum we had on it, I actually voted to become a republic.'

Off with his head . . .

THE KING ON WELFARE

TOGBI KORSI FERDINAND GAKPETOR II OF GHANA (1957–)

Until 1995 Henk Otte was just another unemployed builder in Amsterdam. Existing on state benefits following a serious injury at work, the overweight, middle-aged man lived with his wife Patience and two young children in a cramped, top-floor flat in a tough, multiracial public housing project on the outskirts of the city. Then, on a family holiday to West Africa, the white-skinned Dutchman was suddenly named Togbi (or King) of a region of Ghana. To his utter amazement, the unassuming Otte, anonymous in his home country, was now revered by thousands in a distant land.

Like his parents, Henk Otte was born and raised in Amsterdam; he was Dutch through and through. In 1981 he met the Ghanaian-born Patience when she was visiting relatives in Amsterdam but, although they married the following year, he had no idea that her late grandfather was a tribal chief. Henk had always been fascinated by Ghana, having read about the geography and history of the area as a child, and on one occasion a Ghanaian fortune-teller had predicted that he would obtain a position of power. Patience took Henk to Africa for the first time in 1987. 'People liked me from day one,' he recalls. 'It was a big party for six weeks.' But twelve months later he fell from a platform at work in Holland, permanently damaging his back. Since then he has had to survive largely on disability benefit.

267

In 1995 the couple paid another visit to Patience's home village of Mepe, some 45 miles east of Ghana's capital, Accra. Apparently a tribal elder had a vision of a white man from abroad, a reincarnation of their former king, who would help rescue Mepe from its economic plight. The elder decided that Henk Otte embodied that vision. From then on villagers began staring at him, maintaining that his 'aura' reminded them of the late king. As word of his presence spread, people walked for miles just to look at him. One evening Mepe's leaders told him that he was the chosen one.

'They asked me how I would feel about becoming king,' says Otte. 'My two brothers were there and when I translated for them what had been said, they almost choked with laughter.' Although Otte thought the idea 'insane', he realised what a tremendous honour was being bestowed upon him and graciously accepted. He spent the night before his inauguration in a dark room full of animal heads. The following morning the elders dressed the portly Dutchman in ceremonial robes, said prayers, talked to their ancestors and spirits and poured alcoholic libations on the floor. Hundreds of members of the Ewe tribe flocked from surrounding villages to attend the day-long festivities. They ate, drank, played drums, sang songs and slaughtered a sheep. This was a coronation Ghana-style.

Two years later, Henk and his wife returned to Ghana. 'I was thinking I would just go to my little village, talk to my people, have an easy time and that would be it,' he said. Instead he was invited to attend an even grander ceremony at which he was made a chief with special responsibility for development of the sixty-odd villages that make up the Mepe district. He was now the leader of over 100,000 people. As a sign of his status, he was awarded two plots of land and the name of his wife's grandfather, Ferdinand Gakpetor. For her part, Patience was made a 'Queen Mother' and given the name Mamaa Awo Mepeyo Kpui II.

Since then Henk Otte has led a remarkable double life worthy of Clark Kent or Bruce Wayne. In the living room of his humble Amsterdam abode an ordinary TV set and sofa stand next to 'his and hers' thrones, where the Togbi and his queen receive visits from expatriate Ghanaians who invite them to funerals, birthdays and other community events. He is driven around the city by his personal chauffeur, whose small Japanese car prompted a Dutch TV station to label Henk 'The King in a Nissan Micra'. Attending an international football match in Amsterdam between Holland and Ghana as a guest of the Ghanaian community, Henk stunned the Dutch fans by entering the stadium in full regalia – multicoloured robes, golden jewellery and a golden crown. 'That was hard,' he admitted in an interview with *The Times*. 'I'm a Dutchman and that can never change, but I couldn't stand there dressed like a Ghanaian chief and shout for Holland. I was thinking, "Let it be a draw so everyone can go home happy."'

Inevitably Henk's story attracted its fair share of publicity, not least from a New York film-maker who described his documentary as 'Homer Simpson gets a kingdom!' The attention did not please everyone and a Ghanaian organisation in the United States tried to have Henk deposed on the grounds that he was ridiculing the people of Ghana. The protest went as high as the Ghanaian foreign minister but, after assurances that he had been misquoted on certain matters, Henk was allowed to retain his position. He certainly takes his role seriously and spends much of his time raising funds for Mepe. Since being made Togbi, he has taken medical equipment, school supplies, water pumps and toys to Ghana.

There is a downside to being a tribal leader. Henk can no longer crack jokes or eat and drink in public and his subjects can no longer shake his hand unless he is seated. 'I can't do silly things in the street any more,' he laments. 'I have to be serious.'

Henk Otte remains cheerfully bemused by the extraordinary twist to his previously mundane life. 'I'm just a normal, modest person,' he sighs. 'Every day I ask myself, "Why me?" I'll never know the answer.'

BIBLIOGRAPHY

Alexander, John T. *Catherine the Great: Life and Legend.* New York, Oxford University Press, 1989

Ashe, Geoffrey. *Kings and Queens of Early Britain.* London, Methuen, 2000

Barker, Nancy Nichols. *Brother to the Sun King: Philippe, Duke of Orléans.* Baltimore, John Hopkins University Press, 1989

Barrett, Anthony A. *Caligula: the Corruption of Power.* London, Routledge, 2001

Bos, JNW. *Mad Monarchs* website

Burke's Royal Families of the World. London, Burke's Peerage Ltd, 1977

Cronin, Vincent. *Catherine, Empress of all the Russians.* London, Collins Harvill, 1989

Dales, Douglas. *Dunstan: Saint and Statesman.* Cambridge, Lutterworth Press, 1988

Dunlop, Ian. *Louis XIV.* London, Chatto & Windus, 1999

Erickson, Carolly. *Great Catherine: The Fascinating Story of the Empress of Russia.* London, Simon & Schuster, 1994

Goodwin, Jason. *Lords of the Horizons: A History of the Ottoman Empire.* London, Chatto & Windus, 1998

Green, Vivian. *The Madness of Kings.* Stroud, Alan Sutton, 1993

Haywood, John. *Encyclopedia of the Viking Age.* London, Thames & Hudson, 2000

Holdredge, Helen. *Lola Montez.* London, Alvin Redman, 1957

James, Edward. *The Franks.* Oxford, Basil Blackwell, 1988

Kamen, Henry. *Philip of Spain.* New Haven, Yale University Press, 1997

McBride, Barrie St Clair. *Farouk of Egypt*. London, Robert Hale, 1967

McIntosh, Christopher. *Ludwig II of Bavaria: The Swan King*. London, IB Tauris, 1997

McLeave, Hugh. *The Last Pharaoh: The Ten Faces of Farouk*. London, Michael Joseph, 1969

Marshall, Rosalind K. *Scottish Queens*. East Lothian, Tuckwell Press, 2003

Michael, Prince of Greece. *Louis XIV: the Other Side of the Sun*. London, Orbis, 1983

Morrow, Ann. *Highness: The Maharajahs of India*. London, Grafton Books, 1986

Paludan, Ann. *Chronicle of the Chinese Emperors*. London, Thames & Hudson, 2001

Pratt, Keith and Rutt, Richard. *Korea: A Historical and Cultural Dictionary*. Richmond (Surrey), Curzon Press, 1999

Randall, David. *Royal Follies*. London, WH Allen, 1987

Röhl, John CG, Warren, Martin and Hunt, David. *Purple Secret – Genes, 'Madness' and the Royal Houses of Europe*. London, Bantam Press, 1998

Ross, Stewart. *Monarchs of Scotland*. Moffat, Lochar Publishing, 1990

Scarre, Chris. *Chronicle of the Roman Emperors*. London, Thames & Hudson, 1995

Shaw, Karl. *Royal Babylon*. London, Virgin, 1999

Smith, EA. *A Queen on Trial: The Affair of Queen Caroline*. Stroud, Alan Sutton, 1993

Stadiem, William. *Too Rich: The High Life and Tragic Death of King Farouk*. London, Robson Books, 1992

Warnes, David. *Chronicle of the Russian Tsars*. London, Thames & Hudson, 1999

Wheatcroft, Andrew. *The Ottomans*. London, Viking, 1993

Wheatcroft, Andrew. *The Habsburgs*. London, Viking, 1995

Whitlock, Ralph. *The Warrior Kings of Saxon England*. New York, Dorset Press, 1991

Williamson, David. *Kings and Queens of Britain*. Leicester, PRC, 1992

Wittlin, Alma. *Abdul Hamid: The Shadow of God*. London, John
Lane The Bodley Head, 1940